BIBLE

CODE

BOMBSHELL

COMPELLING SCIENTIFIC EVIDENCE THAT GOD AUTHORED THE BIBLE

R. EDWIN SHERMAN

WITH NATHAN JACOBI, PH.D., AND DAVE SWANEY

New Leaf Press

First printing: May 2005
Second printing: May 2006

ISBN-13: 978-0-89221-623-9
ISBN-10: 0-89221-623-9
Library of Congress Control Number: 2005925564

Cover design by Left Coast Design, Portland, OR

Printed in the United States of America

Please visit our website for other great titles:
www.newleafpress.net

For information regarding author interviews, please contact
the publicity department at (870) 438-5288.

All Scripture Is God-Breathed…
2 Timothy 3:16a

Contents

Part 1

Part 2
Special Topics

Part 3
Appendices

Foreword

Who Wrote the Bible?

Radio astronomers have scanned the heavens for decades for evidence of intelligent life elsewhere in the universe. They have been looking for non-random patterns of sound — music or speech rather than just plain noise. Thus far, they have failed to experience anything even close to what Jodie Foster did in the movie *Contact*.

But now there is convincing evidence that some kind of exceptionally non-random, extraterrestrial communication with earthlings occurred during the writing of the Hebrew Bible — not just in the import of its magnificent surface text, but also in the presence of improbably extensive codes embedded beneath that text. What is intriguing is that this should be true for a text that (through various translations) has sold over six billion copies worldwide, according to some estimates.

Who wrote the Bible? Was it a series of desert mystics who conjured up the concept of God to help them cope with life in a savage world? Or was it the result of a faithful recording of the words of God revealed to scribes and prophets over many centuries? Could it be a mixture of these?

For the last two centuries, if not longer, academics have launched a concerted assault on the Bible, seeking to cut it down to the realm of man-penned books. By and large, they have succeeded. Or so they thought.

In 1994, three Israeli scientists introduced Bible codes to the world with an academic paper that startled the mathematically savvy. The paper claimed that the names of the most famous Jewish rabbis and dates of their birth or death were encoded in the book of Genesis, much closer to one another than could be explained by chance. Had the book of Genesis been written by an author who knew the future before any of these rabbis had lived?

Ever since publication of that paper, Bible codes have been under visceral attack. We have witnessed a series of unprofessional displays by reputable scientists, who forcefully asserted half-truths to shoot down straw men of their devising. All claims of valid Bible codes, past or future, must be false, they boldly proclaimed, as if they had any clue as to what evidence might surface in the future. Their attempts to discredit Bible codes have had the savor of desperation about them. Why would that be?

Could it be for motivations similar to those that drove Herod to order the Christ child murdered in His manger? To those that forced prayer out of public schools? Whatever their reasons, code skeptics have been fairly successful in turning much of the public against the concept.

When I first began investigating claims about Bible codes five years ago, I was thoroughly skeptical about them. Nevertheless, the possibility of their potential validity so fascinated me I couldn't walk away from investigating them thoroughly. And the intellectual challenge of deriving the math to test published claims was irresistible to someone who loves solving problems.

For some protagonists in the fray over Bible codes, their own personal opposition to religion evidently motivates them to set aside objectivity and ethics in their efforts to discredit code proponents. My own religious beliefs did not cause me to favor or doubt the purported reality of Bible codes. I have been a Christian for over 30 years, during which time, I have also been a practicing mathematician who has enjoyed a very successful career. Serving as a managing principal with a leading international accounting and consulting firm, and as the president of my own thriving consulting practice, I have served some of the most familiar names in American business and government.

I have never needed codes as proof of my beliefs. These were forged 25 years before I had ever heard of Bible codes. So, from that perspective, whether codes are bunk or real has never made any difference to me.

I will confess that in the last few years I have been partially motivated by my reactions to thinly veiled efforts by non-religious scientists to cut down any efforts to present scientific evidence in support of faith. Let the truth be known, not suppressed. I can be passionate about that.

As our research team has explored the Hebrew Bible, we have been repeatedly blown away by the truly astonishing phenomena we have found within its letters. We have tried to maintain a scientific cool as we communicated these findings on our web site and in a monthly e-newsletter that we have been publishing since 1999.

We have been inundated with code finds, and have often wished for the funding to retain a couple of dozen qualified researchers to pursue the leads that we have found. A number of times in computing the probability that a given code cluster could be due to chance, we reached the point where our Microsoft Excel spreadsheets could go no further. The odds were too overwhelmingly small. The things we found could not be the product of chance. They had to have been placed there purposely. Furthermore, it would be impossible for human beings to have been the originators of it, even using all of the Cray super computers ever built linked together. There is only one intelligence capable of such a feat, and He is commonly referred to as God.

A few "free" spirits will argue that intensely advanced aliens wrote the Bible. If that were so, why would the literal text itself constantly focus on God's dealings in human affairs? There is an axiom in logic called Ockham's Razor. It states that when there are two competing hypotheses that could explain something, the simplest and most straightforward one should be chosen. The "God hypothesis" is the clear choice. When the advocates of alien authorship can come up with some objective way to differentiate alien from divine doings, then the question of authorship might be reopened. Until then, God wins. I, for one, think that if aliens wrote the Bible, codes would largely be bizarre. To the contrary, codes echo the content of the literal text, seemingly affirming it.

9

This book presents two "sub-bombshells" — the mega-clusters of Isaiah 53 and Ezekiel 37 — in support of the main thesis. Each is sufficient to devastate the efforts of code skeptics who have been advancing half-truths in the hope of quelling growing public interest in Bible codes.

When Michael Drosnin, the author of the bestseller *The Bible Code*, set forth his trivial answers, it was easy for skeptics to derive comparable examples from non-inspired texts. The skeptics are too smart to think they can derive examples from non-inspired texts that might even begin to compare with the mega-clusters from the Bible presented in this book. So they will likely pursue other tactics.

These skeptics will not welcome new evidence that supports the reality of Bible codes. Nor will they appreciate a book that exposes their half-truths for what they are.

There is a juggernaut of inertia set against new ideas that challenge the ruling paradigm. Science cannot validate any form of religion, or so the dogma of the paradigm dictates. Will a few brave academics risk their careers to support the validity of recent code claims? Will any scientific journal risk its reputation by publishing research papers supporting codes? In the meanwhile, this book has rolled off the press and our biblecodedigest.com website continues to receive growing waves of hits.

As much as we've discovered in five short years, we have the strong sense that we are only starting to skim the surface of what lies beneath the literal text. We are about the business of advancing human knowledge in this incredible field. We wish we could also say that about our antagonists.

To the general reader following the controversy, making sense of Bible codes is a bit like trying to jump waves in heavy surf fraught with rip tides — with a heavy duty blindfold and ear plugs. The skeptics made these knowledge blockers by trying to get us to believe a lie — that all code examples are comparable in the sense that they could easily be the product of chance. The half-truth is that some published examples are just as they say. The whole truth is that other examples are so impossible they have to be intentional. We have the tools to gauge the difference. We can remove the blindfold and use unimpeded hearing.

An analogy might help here. A naïve person might claim that Mr. So-And-So's winning the lottery was a miracle. The skeptic will rightly say that sooner or later, someone had to win, so there is no miracle. But, what if the same guy won the big pot five times in a row? Then, a threshold will have been crossed. The winner is either a crook hardwired to those drawing the winning numbers, or he is seriously telepathic. Coincidence is not an option.

In doing our research, we used mathematically effective tools that enabled us to focus our attention on those events that are highly non-random. In other words, such events could not have been sheer coincidences. We can reasonably determine what the chances are that something is coincidental or not. Then, we can focus our mental energies on trying to discern what such non-coincidences imply.

Some conservative Jews and Christians would say that it is folly to use the methods of science to probe into matters of faith. That would seem like a rather defensive attitude for someone of a particular faith to have. If a person truly has a strong faith, shouldn't he have the view that his beliefs will hold up under any kind of fair investigation? If someone believed that God wrote the Bible, shouldn't they also believe that God might have written it in ways that would only further support and not undermine this belief? What is needed is the courage to seek the truth, even if that search causes us to modify our original views.

Frequently I was impressed with the unflinching objectivity of our Hebrew expert, Nathan Jacobi, Ph.D., as we investigated the possibility of long codes about Christ in Isaiah 53.

When we first contacted Nathan about the possibility of working with us, we were astonished when he told us he would only be willing to participate if we would devote a significant part of our research to Jesus codes. He has always been eager to find out if Bible codes might provide some clues on the highly controversial question of who Jesus was.

After working with us for the past four years, Nathan remains an agnostic. He will admit that there is something real about the phenomenon of Bible codes, but he will also say that he doesn't know what the ultimate implications of the existence of real Bible codes are.

This book would not have been possible without Nathan's extensive participation. Without him our research would have been confined to one, and occasionally, two-word codes. Such codes are seldom improbable. Short "codes" are everywhere in abundance — even in the Jerusalem phone book.

We needed to search for the highly improbable — long codes consisting of multiple sentences — to be able to explore reasonably the possibility that some Bible codes might be real. Such sentences had to be in grammatically acceptable Hebrew, and a good portion of them needed to say intelligible, plausible things. A Hebrew expert, highly fluent in both biblical and contemporary Hebrew, was indispensable. Nathan more than fit the bill.

Dr. Jacobi is a Holocaust survivor. He was born in France in 1938 of Jewish parents. His parents left him with an anti-Nazi German family as they went into hiding when the Nazis invaded France. After the war ended, his parents returned and he moved with his family to Israel, where he was educated (1945–1969). Nathan received a thorough education in both biblical and contemporary Hebrew. He received a Ph.D. in physics from Weizman Institute of Science in Rehovot, Israel. He received an M.Sc. in physics and a B.Sc. in mathematics from Bar-Ilan University in Ramat-Gan, Israel.

Nathan is a retired college professor with more than 30 years of research, development and scientific computing in applied physics, aerospace and geophysics. He has taught atomic and molecular physics, quantum mechanics, college algebra, trigonometry and analysis, analytic geometry, and calculus — in Israel and the U.S.

In the past several years, Nathan has taught classes in introductory and intermediate Hebrew. He routinely converses with his wife, Rhea, in Hebrew. He reads the news daily, in Hebrew, from the Ha'aretz website. His two children live in Israel.

Chapter One

Much Ado About Nothing?

Staccato cricket chirps laced the brisk night air. Faint twinkles of light dotted the open sky above the outdoor theater where a rampantly staged play was fast lurching to a close. Peter glimpsed the hands on his watch. *Eleven thirty! This silly production's been going on for nearly three hours. Didn't the author know that plays should have an ending — sooner rather than later?*

His mind flipped back to the course of the tumbling dialogue of the inexplicably merry actors:

Mystery Man A:
    Good morrow, Benedick. Why, what's the matter,
    That you have such a February face,
    So full of frost, of storm, and cloudiness?

Mystery Man B:
    I think he thinks upon the savage bull.
    Tush, fear not, man; we'll tip thy horns with gold,
    And all Europa shall rejoice at thee;
    As once Europa did at lusty Jove,
    When he would play the noble beast in love.

Mystery Man A:
    Bull Jove, sir, had an amiable low;
    And some such strange bull leapt your father's cow,

And got a calf in that same noble feat
Much like to you, for you have just his bleat.

Peter frowned, shaking his head. *February face? That's me. Frosted. Stormy. Cloudy-headed. Why did we pay $45 a ticket to see this? A three-hour medley of obscure words? Like birdbolt? And pleacht? And marl? Cozen'd? Misprising? Accordant? Good lord, what a puzzlement!*

Within seconds, the stage lights faded. Dozens around him sprang to their feet in applause. His eyes widened. He blinked further as the throngs continued their enthusiastic ritual of cheering and clapping. He put his arm around Linda, much in hope of drawing upon a sense of their mutual bewilderment.

"What a waste!" he muttered. "I hardly fathomed a thing. It's no wonder they called it *Much Ado About Nothing*. They got that title right!"

Linda nodded. "No kidding," she whispered, her eyes offering an empathetic glance.

"Why have this man's plays been so popular for so long?" he grumbled, totally befuddled.

"That's the great mystery of it, dear," she replied. "After all, they got us to go for it, didn't they?"

Peter sputtered. "Yeah, right. But that only works once. I get the feeling a lot of these people are the kind that keep coming back. That's what really mystifies me. There must be something other people know that I don't."

"Like Old English?" Linda offered, smiling.

Peter shrugged, grinning. "Sure would help. But that's still not enough to explain why this Shakespeare guy is thought to be so great. These plays of his are a fad that should have died out 400 years ago. Why do they linger . . . even thrive?" He opened the door of their Explorer for her to climb in.

As Peter cranked the key and the engine convulsed, she interjected, "Did you notice how crowded the concessions were during intermission?"

"Sure did. I wanted to get some ale and try one of those Old English dishes. You know, what did they call it?"

"Bangers and mash."

"That's it! Bangers and mash."

"Weird thing was, I had never heard of it before, but I wanted it really badly. Right in the middle of this scene. Isn't that bizarre?"

"That's funny. I had the same urge. It happened right as Benedick was philosophizing on how silly love is." Peter smiled with a broad tease gracing his face.

"You would remember that, wouldn't you?" She heaved a sigh of practiced frustration. "Peter, you're hopeless."

"That I am. But as I was saying, I had this strange urge, even though I wasn't at all thirsty, I had to have an ale. Of all things, ale! You know how I hate beer! Ale's even more disgusting. What came over me?"

Linda gasped, drawing back from cinching her seat belt. "You've got to be kidding. I got that same craving — at exactly the same time! I detest ale. Something very peculiar must have been going on. Booze vibes, maybe?"

"You know, the other day I read about how film makers will flash pictures of food or drink on the screen for only one or two frames every so often. Just long enough for those pictures to register in our brains — but not long enough for anyone to realize that those pictures were there. And then every one rushes out to buy a pop and a hot dog. What was that called?"

"You mean 'subliminal messages?' " Linda responded quickly, smiling at his acknowledgment of her brilliance.

"Yep. That's it."

"You know, I wonder if the reason Shakespeare has been around so long is that he somehow stuck subliminal messages in his plays so that people would buy more food and guzzle more during intermissions?"

"Yeah, right. That's pretty far out. I think booze vibes sounds more likely."

"I doubt it. You know, I think I'll check out the text for hidden messages."

"And how are you going to do that?" Peter looked characteristically skeptical.

"Well, remember that we both had the same urge for ale and bangers and mash at the same time? I'm going to type in Benedick's lines at that point into my computer and search for hidden messages."

"There must have been something brain warping in that ale. You had it two hours ago. It seems to affect you for a long time. I hope it hasn't done any permanent damage."

"For Pete's sake, Peter! Stop it. You're insufferable."

He nodded, admitting his stubbornness as they idled at the stoplight. "All right. I'm a sad case. No doubt about it. But how are you going to search for hidden messages with your computer?"

"Well, I guess I'll look for words hidden under the surface text. You know. Like suppose 'ale' is hidden there, but that it shows up by starting with 'a' and skipping five letters to come to an 'l' and another five letters to come to an 'e.' Maybe our brains can process information like that even when we're having a devil of a time understanding all that Old English in the plain text." Linda looked proud of her supposition.

"Devil is right. Sounds like you've thought of a way to find anything you start to look for." Peter's face curled up after another flash of doubtful insights.

"Perhaps. That's a good point. Maybe I'll have to do some math to figure out what the chances are that codes like that could happen by chance."

Peter tromped on the accelerator, initiating a cadence of rubber squeals on slick asphalt. "Sort of like that old joke about having a monkey dance his fingers on a keyboard long enough and, lo and behold, you'll wind up with . . . with . . . with another copy of *Much Ado*."

Linda guffawed. "Maybe you've got something there. Shakespeare was probably nothing more than a well-organized monkey."

"More efficient, though. I'd give him that much." A measured smugness spread over his cheeks.

"I guess before I horse around with a lot of formulas to figure out the chances, maybe I should first see if there are any hidden codes in Old Will's words?"

"I would, if I were you. No sense in making ever more ado about nothing than already has been."

The dimly lit den offered only a spare attraction — a glowing monitor that shimmered eerily. "You won't believe this, Peter. I've picked apart those lines where we both got that thirst for ale and that odd hunger for bangers and mash. Guess what I found?"

"More obscure language? Do 'fribbers' and 'gloop' sound appetizing?" Peter retorted.

"No, my love. I found the subliminal messages for ale and bangers right in Benedick's words. Come have a look."

"Give me a break, Linda. Have you been drinking more ale?"

"No. Here. Look at this. I've highlighted where 'ale' appears as a code."

I do much wonder th**A**t one man, seeing how much another man is a foo**L** when he dedicates his behaviours to lov**E**, will, after he hath laught at such shallow follies in others, become the argument of his own scorn by falling in love: and such a man is Claudio. (II, III, 7-12)

"So?"

"Well, the 'L' appears as the 37th letter after the 'A,' and the 'E' appears as the 37th letter after the 'L.'[1] These letters are equally spaced."

"Really spaced? Just like you and I?"

"Peter, stop it. See, you count the spaces."

He leaned down and began counting off the spaces between the "A" and the "L." "Should I count the spaces between the words?"

"No. Leave them out."

"All right. Since you insist. 1, 2, 3, 4, . . . 35, 36, 37. There are 37 spaces, just like you said."

"Okay. Now count the second set of spaces."

Peter's head bobbed minutely with each space he counted. "34, 35, 36, 37, again. I'll be a monkey's uncle. Hmmmm. Have you done the math?"

"Not yet, but I think I'd better. Look, I also found 'bangers' as a code, and 'mash' as a code. All within the first 100 letters of this one sentence of Benedick's words. That's got to be pretty improbable."

"I'm worried about you. How much time did you fritter away in looking for these supposed 'codes?' "

"Supposed? Now I know you've already made up your mind."

"And you haven't?"

17

"No, I haven't, but at least I'm willing to think there might be something real going on here. So, yes, I'm open."

"And how much time have you spent looking for these flukes?"

Linda guffawed. "About as much as you spent watching the 49ers lose to the Broncos. That's all. Once I wrote a simple program, these codes just fell out like that."

"So you did write a program. Can it find any code you ask it to?"

"Sure, if the code is really there."

Peter laughed. "Of course it will be there. I'll bet anything we ask it to find, it will find. I'm confident of that."

"Come on, Peter. Be reasonable."

"Hmmmm. Well, tell me, how does this program work?"

"All I do is open a text file, type in a word I'm looking for as a code, like 'ale,' and the computer searches the text for places where that word might occur as equally spaced letters. So, the program starts at the beginning of the text and finds the first time that the letter 'a' appears. Then, it finds the first time after that that an 'l' appears. It calculates how many letters apart the 'a' and the 'l' are and then goes out that many letters after the 'l' to see if there is an 'e' in that place. If there is, the program stops and shows me where in the text the code letters appear. If there isn't an 'e' there, it goes back and finds the second time an 'l' appears after the 'a.' Again it calculates how many spaces apart the 'a' and the 'l' are and moves out that many spaces beyond this second occurrence of the 'l' to look and see if there is an 'e' there. Once it finishes doing that for all the 'l's after the first 'a,' it moves on to the second 'a' in the text and does it all over again. With our 500 megahertz processor, it just takes a second to search out potential codes."

"Why did you decide to eliminate the spaces between the letters?"

"The program looks for codes both ways; both with and without spaces between words. When a text is entered, the program accepts it and creates another version with all of the spaces between words eliminated."

"Can I pick a word to search for?"

"Are you being open minded, or just your usual self?"

"Sort of open, but not so open that my brains might fall out."

Linda smirked. "You're a case, my love. Come on. Give me a word you're curious about. I'll type it in." Her lips pursed with curiosity.

"What about the word, 'fool?' " Peter said, smiling wryly.

"Is that a commentary about me? Did you think of that because that's a key word in Benedick's lines, or because it's pretty descriptive of the kind of people that go rooting around looking for esoteric stuff like 'bangers?' "

"What do you think?"

"Knowing you as I do, a bit of both."

"Quite perceptive."

"OK. Here we go . . . F . . . O . . . O . . . L."

The computer whipped back the letter positions where "fool" appeared as a code: 50, 85, 120, 155. "That's a skip of 35 letters," Peter noted. "Curiously enough, the code for 'fool' intersects exactly with the 'o' in the word 'love' as the 85th letter." His face bore the look of a self-justified man.

"So Shakespeare was a philosopher, too?" Linda queried.

"Perhaps. Or just a perceptive observer of life?"

"Suppose we arranged the letters in Benedick's lines as a crossword where the letter position increases by 35 as you go down from one line to the next."

"What would that do?"

"You'd get something that looked like this:"

e	r	t	h	a	t	o	n
i	s	a	f	o	o	l	w
t	o	l	o	v	e	w	i
a	l	l	o	w	f	o	l
y	f	a	l	l	i	n	g
a	m	a	n	i	s	c	l

"So there we have it. A sophisticated way of documenting foolishness?"

"Got it."

"Or perhaps of verifying that 'love' and 'fool' are kissing cousins?"

"You're pretty incorrigible."

"You're almost as bad as that long-winded playwright, conjuring up big words no dictionary would dare still carry."

"Give it up, Peter. Come on, give me a word you're really curious about and let's see if the computer can find it. After all, you said I could find anything."

"Welllllll . . . how about 'Diana?' "

" 'Diana?' Why 'Diana?' "

"Now you're being the skeptic. I have this hunch that, in addition to being a well-organized monkey, Old Will was also a psychic."

"I can't believe a cynic like you would think such a thing."

"Yeah, I know it's wild, but so are subliminal messages about 'bangers' and 'mash.' Besides, maybe it will prove my original point that you can find just about anything you're looking for as a code."

"All right. Here we go . . . D . . . I . . . A . . . N . . . A."

The screen blinked a few times and then dropped out the place in *Much Ado* where "Diana" showed up as a code.

"Man. That was fast. So 'Diana' appears as a code starting with the first 'd' in the text, which is only the second letter in Benedick's quote. Then the other letters are 45 spaces apart."

I **D**o much wonder that one man, seeing how much another man **I**s a fool when he dedicates his behaviours to love, will, **A**fter he hath laught at such shallow follies i**N** others, become the argument of his own scorn by f**A**lling in love: and such a man is Claudio. (II, III, 7-12)

"See. I told you, you could find anything."

"Or he was psychic."

"Ha. Ha. Now try 'paparazzi.' " Peter stood back, looking a bit hooked over the possibility it might be in there.

"OK, if that's in there I'll be real surprised. Here goes . . . P . . . A . . . P . . . A . . . R . . . A . . . Z . . . Z . . . I." Flash. Blink. The monitor showed the infamous term for the rabid free-lance photographers as a code.

"Far out. Now try 'Dodi' and 'Fayed' and 'Paris' and 'Mercedes.' "

"Hold it. Hold it. Only one at a time, please." Linda dutifully tapped in each suggested code, and the computer reported back its sighting and location. She quickly scribbled down the letter position of the first letter of each code and how big the skip was between each coded letter. She held up her note pad in astonishment (table 1A).

Table 1A

Word	First Letter	Skip
Diana	2	45
Paparazzi	16	14
Dodi	72	59
Fayed	65	19
Paris	21	7
Mercedes	49	16
Tunnel	83	4
Crash	9	66
Ritz	37	18
Charles	51	15
Princess	4	84
France	88	42
Royal	48	6
Drunk	37	30
Divorce	29	44
Spencer	46	39

With each code the computer fetched, a stunned silence came over them. At last, Peter broke the eerie blanket of speechlessness that had extinguished their typical chatter. "Unreal. Simply un-real."

"No kidding."

They looked at each other in amazement. "Either it's true that you can find anything that you're looking for as a code, OR that old playwright was a prophet. I guess you'd better hurry up and do the math. I'm dying of curiosity."

Linda nodded.

Days later, Linda's bloodshot eyes met her husband's. "This can't be a coincidence. The odds are far too small."

"How small?"

"Well, the real mind-blower is that cluster of all the Diana codes. They all intersect a small passage in *Much Ado*, which only has about 200 letters. I figured the chances of it being a coincidence are about 1 in 1,000,000,000,000,000,000,000,000."

"So what you're saying is that Old Will predicted Diana's death and all its details almost 400 years ago?"

"That's the size of it." Linda studied the display of incredulity raging over Peter's face.

"Nostradamus, move over. You've been outclassed."

Chapter Two

An Irrepressible Urge

The distinction between past, present, and future is only an
illusion, however persistent.

—Albert Einstein

We *Homo sapiens* suffer from an irrepressible urge to probe the
future. Everywhere it is evident. Stock gurus pump out investment
newsletters and watch their herds of believers swell. Farmers snatch
up the latest almanac, hoping to divine the fate of their crops. And
the moods of so many souls rise or fall on the expectations of clouds
or sun foretold by some pupil of satellite weather scans.

When the seer's track record is admirable, attempts to satisfy this
itch for future peek could be considered rational. But even not-so-
reliable clairvoyants keep their jobs. Who hasn't scanned the head-
lines in checkout lines heralding sensational articles by psychics
with lousy records of fulfilled predictions? No matter. The itch must
be scratched. And so another copy is sold.

Marketers of some Bible code (Torah code to Jewish researchers) books took advantage of this human weakness beginning in
1996. The best-selling of these authors is a self-professed atheist
with an irrepressible craving to milk the ancient text of the Hebrew
Bible for hidden messages about future events. This is no mystical
foray into Kabbalah[1] though, he assures us, because the techy tools
of the statistician tell us that these omens are "beyond chance." We
must believe these tea leaves because they pass accepted standards
of "significance."

Our age of instant notoriety thrust Michael Drosnin center stage with astounding speed. His book, *The Bible Code*, was successfully promoted by Simon & Schuster onto the *New York Times* bestseller list for many weeks in 1997 and 1998. Drosnin is no hack journalist. After stints at the *Washington Post* and the *Wall Street Journal*, he penned the bestseller, *Citizen Hughes*. However, Drosnin's book is a double-edged sword. It introduced Bible codes to the world, but used such poor examples that his book was a giant setback for serious code research.

Wasting no time, he kicks off *The Bible Code* with a show-stopping claim: the assassination of Israeli Prime Minister Yitzhak Rabin in November 1995 was foretold by hidden Hebrew codes in the ancient text of the Bible. Not content to let bad enough alone, following the assassination Drosnin hunted through the Hebrew text and found the name of the assassin, Amir, as a code near the original ones, as well as a code which meant, "name of assassin." Furthermore, a code for Tel Aviv, the city where the shooting occurred, was also discovered, as well as a code for the year when it occurred.

A Scrabble-Like Ouija Board?

Curiously, the Yitzhak Rabin code has an oversized skip of 4,772 between its letters. The sheer size of these skips immediately raises the objection that one should have been able to find the same code with a smaller skip than that. If the mere finding of a code somewhere in a text were all there was to it, then we could quickly dismiss Drosnin as the sly inventor of a Scrabble-like Ouija board that will divulge whatever one wishes to find. Waves of criticism have haunted Drosnin's efforts to establish credibility for his views.

Not surprisingly, the view that one can find anything as long as one keeps on searching for it is put forth by skeptics. This is akin to the famous monkeys and typewriters argument. Just give enough monkeys enough time at enough typewriters, and eventually, they will pound out a Shakespeare play or two. (In fact, Bible code researcher Dr. Robert Haralick calls the scrambled text he uses in experiments "monkey text.")

Another detracting opinion from the skeptics is that application of a similar search to other texts would most likely yield similar revelations. Both of these arguments are founded on the notion that there are a nearly infinite number of codes that can be milked from any text of appreciable length. We will later see that this is not true.

Drosnin doesn't stop with the Rabin codes, however. He goes on to present numerous clusters of codes that would be astounding if only they were not coincidental. Here is a sampler of codes that are displayed in crossword clusters:

- Economic collapse, the depression, 1929 and stocks
- Atomic holocaust and 1945
- Watergate and "Who is he? President, but he was kicked out."
- World War, in 2000, in 2006, and atomic holocaust

While all of these are unpleasant events, Drosnin also presents a few positive clusters:

- Wright brothers and airplane
- Shakespeare, presented on stage, Macbeth and Hamlet
- Newton and gravity
- Edison, electricity and light bulb
- Fall of, communism, Russian, in China next

Science Fiction Theology

From his review of all these configurations, Drosnin launches forth with a jaw-dropping assertion: the Hebrew Bible, written 3,000 odd years ago, must have been crafted by intelligence far greater than any human being. Furthermore, that being also knew the future. Of a naturally skeptical bent, however, he doubts that this being could be God. Make way for a batch of high-powered aliens from a science fiction thriller!

He shies away from the God hypothesis because most of the things he has unearthed in Bible codes to date are bad. So if God were the author, "He/She/It" obviously would have prevented them from happening. Thereby, this atheist theologian overlooks all the graphic passages in the surface text of the Bible, where there are numerous accounts of ugly things God allowed to take place, not to mention divine prophecies of future "bad" things. If Drosnin had spent any time seriously studying the ancient text that he believes has such miraculous properties, he would have encountered Jewish prophets warning the people of God that the dreaded Babylonians would invade their country and haul them off to a gruesome captivity for many years. This took place in spite of God's foreknowledge.

Denunciations by the Original Researchers

Needless to say, this kind of showcasing of codes from a religious text that is at least 2,000, if not 3,000 years old, created controversy all over the world. A search of the Internet will turn up dozens of articles, both supportive and critical.

Criticism of Drosnin's book has not been confined to those whom one would ordinarily expect to be skeptical, however. It is noteworthy that the mathematics professor at Hebrew University in Jerusalem who was the key figure in Drosnin's first book is a staunch critic of that book. In June of 1997, Dr. Eliyahu Rips, one of those who introduced the phenomenon in 1994 (Witztum, Rips and Rosenberg, or WRR), posted a press release on his site in which he stated that he did not support Drosnin's work or his conclusions.[2]

By presenting many examples that are quite likely to occur by chance, Drosnin has unwittingly done much to discredit his own efforts. For example, he presents a cluster of codes, or several codes either crossing or in close proximity to each other, suggesting that an earthquake will hit Los Angeles in the year 2010. The chances of this kind of cluster appearing by chance are breathtakingly close to 100% (99.45%, by my calculation). In other words, statistically they are next to meaningless. And the chances that codes for "great earthquake," "China" and the year 1976 would appear as close as they do are 99.30%. Displaying such nearly inevitable examples is a disservice to serious codes analysis.

One of today's foremost Bible code researchers is Doron Witztum, one of the WRR team. On June 4, 1997, he released a public statement on the Internet. Witztum, while happy to see the publicity for Torah codes, expressed that the entire credibility of Torah code research could be ruined by Drosnin due to the lack of scientific methodology employed in his work.[3]

These criticisms also hold true for the books on codes written by Christian authors Grant Jeffrey and Yacov Rambsel.[4]

What Do These Codes Look Like?

So what are these codes that have been there for thousands of years and yet have been so thoroughly hidden that only researchers with recently developed computer software have unearthed them? They are called "equidistant letter sequences," or ELSs.

An ELS begins with one letter. Then skip forward a fixed number of letters, say 10, to the second letter of your proposed code word, skip forward the same 10 letters and grab a third letter, and so forth. If these three or four letters spell something meaningful, you have an ELS. In doing this, spaces between words are ignored, so the process actually begins by eliminating them.

Bible code research is said to date back to at least the 12th century, when rabbinical scholars first wrote about discovering meaningful words hidden in the Hebrew text of the Torah. Tradition among the most devout Jewish scholars holds that everything and everyone that ever was or ever will be was recorded in the text of the first five books of the Bible. Thus, as it was passed down letter by letter from God to Moses, then generation by generation to modern times, great care has been taken to preserve it intact. Rabbis encouraged caution in Torah copyists by reminding them that just one letter lost in their work could bring about the end of the world.

Only very slight changes have occurred in the original text over the 3,200 years since Moses first received it — a wonder that ranks among the great miracles of the ages. As the Torah was preserved by a miracle, so were the Jewish people, despite tremendous persecution and being without a homeland for 19 centuries.

The Father of Bible Code Research

In the midst of the Holocaust, Michael Ber Weissmandl, a Slovakian rabbi, continued his study of ancient writings by scholars who had found secret terms encoded in the Torah.

Rabbi Weissmandl noted that if you start with a ת (tav) in the first verse of the book of Genesis, skip 50 letters, pick up a ו (vav), skip another 50 letters, pick up an ר (resh), skip another 50 letters, and pick up an ה (heh), you have תורה, or Torah. Now this occurs, mind you, not only in the first book of the Torah, but also in the first verse of the books of Exodus and Numbers. It also appears in the first chapter of the Book of Deuteronomy. In each case, there is also a skip of exactly 50 letters.

But the Nazis were descending on the rabbi's village, and the majority of his time was taken up with negotiating for the lives of his people. Weissmandl, in fact, invented an outrageously bold scheme to ransom European Jews by bribing Nazi officials. The plan was workable, but no one could or would provide the $4 million the Germans demanded to save the lives of two million people, a mere $2 per person.

He was ultimately rounded up with his family and put on a death train to the camps. With him, he took only a loaf of bread and three books, two copies of the Torah and a dusty commentary by a 13th century scholar mentioning the hidden codes. Alone, Weissmandl escaped the death train and eventually made his way to the U.S., where he was able to continue his research. And yet, he was tortured by grief. His devastating regret was that he had not been able to rescue even one of his children. He died of a broken heart in 1957.

Ironically, it was a Nazi code system that inspired development of today's code breaking. The system uses statistics to unlock secret messages. In the late 1930s, as German U-boats wreaked havoc on Allied shipping in the North Atlantic, allied intelligence officers discovered that the Nazis were using what they called an "Enigma machine" to create coded messages between Berlin and submarine commanders. It looked something like a typewriter, but used combinations of internal wheels to encode and decode messages. When a captured Enigma machine came into their hands, British mathematicians worked non-stop for months to break the coding system. They used the laws of probability to figure it out. We use the same statistical methods to analyze Bible codes.

Codes Move Into the Spotlight

Some time later, the advent of the personal computer made it possible to carry out searches for codes in seconds that had taken previously hours and even days to do. Researchers inspired by Weissmandl's work, and using it as a starting point, began to develop the software necessary to perform these searches.

Finally, there was an awakening of faith among the brightest minds in Judaism. Previously atheistic or religiously disinterested scientists and intellectuals began to find themselves attracted to the most orthodox beliefs. As word of the codes spread around the world, many of these men began to devote themselves to the study of the Torah and the unraveling of these codes.

Two of these scientists, a former physics graduate student, Doron Witztum, and a world-renowned mathematician, Eliyahu Rips, along with Yoav Rosenberg, an Israeli computer whiz, formed the research team WRR and stunned the scientific world with the publication of their paper on the codes in the journal *Statistical Science*.

The Great Sages Experiment

WRR's paper, "Equidistant Letter Sequences in the Book of Genesis," was based on the original work of Rabbi Weissmandl. It described the discovery of the encoded names of 34 notable figures, the Great Sages in Jewish history, along with the dates of their birth or death, in the first book of the Bible, and the statistical significance of each code. Prior to its publication, the paper was reviewed by a panel of referees, a process that took years to complete. The referees found the math used to compile the probabilities to be ironclad.

Statistical Science courageously published the paper, if somewhat reluctantly, because of the storm of controversy they were sure would result. In the same issue of *Statistical Science*, Editor Robert Kass wrote that the scientists who put the report to the test were baffled by the results. Nothing had prepared them to believe that a book of the Bible could contain references to people living today.[5]

Before the WRR paper was published, a senior cryptologist with the National Security Agency outside of Washington learned of their research. Harold Gans is one of the world's top code breakers. He created a test of the team's data on his home computer to satisfy himself that such codes could not possibly exist in the Bible. Author Jeffrey Satinover does a masterful job of telling the story of how the experiment turned out in his book, *Cracking the Bible Code*.

There was not a doubt in Gans's mind that the tests that the computer had been laboring on for hours would support his doubts. Even so, as he waited in his NSA office for a call from home, he was more nervous about the results than he expected to be.

Then came the call. The computer had finished its work. As Satinover reported it, Gans did not speak, but only listened to the numbers his wife read from the monitor. As he stared out at the imposing marble monuments and buildings, he was struck with the temporal nature of it all — as if like Dorothy, he could suddenly see behind the wizard's curtain. The number his wife had read out to him was incredibly small. He had seldom seen a p-value so astonishingly minute. Such conclusions indicated the obvious and banal. Much less dramatic p-values confirmed positive results in scientific research. The 1 in 62,500 result meant that the research reported by the three Israelis was accurate.

As Satinover described it, his surprising response was to be filled with joy.[6]

Books Bring Codes World Attention

Controversy indeed erupted following the *Statistical Science* publication — not only in the scientific community, but in the religious community as well, and among both Jews and Christians. Books were written about the phenomenon, notably *The Bible Code* and *Bible Code II: The Countdown* by Michael Drosnin, which brought it to the attention of the world.

Christian researchers also began to locate codes in the Bible about Jesus Christ, and books were published about their findings. Among them were Yacov Rambsel's *His Name Is Jesus: The Mysterious Yeshua Codes* and Grant Jeffrey's *The Signature of God*.[4]

Professor Barry Simon, chairman of the mathematics department at Cal Tech and an orthodox Jew himself, organized a statement disputing the codes that has been signed by Ph.D.s all over the world.

A rebuttal of the paper was launched by a group of scientists headed by Brendan McKay, Ph.D., a professor in the department of computer science at the Australian National University. Their rebuttal was published by *Statistical Science* in 1999.

Aish HaTorah, a Jerusalem-based organization that is dedicated to bringing secular Jews to a renewed faith in God through its Discovery Seminars, uses Torah codes to help convince skeptical attendees, and has become one of the leading proponents of the science. In late 1996, the *Wall Street Journal* covered this approach by Aish.

Scientists both Jewish and Christian all over the world are using computer software to search the scriptures for new codes and to compute their statistical significance, which in layman's terms means whether or not they can be considered real. The International Torah Code Society (ITCS) has been formed and held its first meeting in Jerusalem in 1999. Leading code researchers, such as Robert Haralick, Ph.D., distinguished professor at the City University of New York, present new findings and works in progress to the group in annual meetings.

Bible Code Digest (BCD) was founded in 1999 to report on developments in the field of Bible code research, including the results of its own research. BCD is published by the Isaac Newton Bible Code Research Society and www.biblecodedigest.com has become the leading Internet site devoted to Bible codes.

The Clinton-Lewinsky Conjunction?

The discovery of these Torah codes by Weissmandl was not eye-brow lifting, however. Any author, human or otherwise, could have intentionally embedded such codes within a text. What impresses are codes about contemporary people and events. Take former president William Jefferson Clinton as an example. His name appears as an ELS within the Torah four times. One of those times, Drosnin notes, the code is intersected by a code for president.

Had Drosnin researched his book during 1998, he may well have also noted that the same Clinton code is also intersected by another code with a possible Hebrew spelling of Lewinsky (לונסכי — Lamed Vav Noon Samech Kaf Yod). In fact, the intersection is so intimate that the ל of Clinton is the starting letter of the Lewinsky code! Could such a find be akin to the conjunction of Jupiter and Saturn? Republicans might have hailed such a discovery as evidence of a divine verdict, whereas Democrats might have cited it as proof of a vast right-wing celestial conspiracy to fell their leader. As beauty is in the eye of the beholder, so is meaning in the gnarled cranium of the seeker.

Debunking the Diligent Data Diggers?

When I first read Drosnin's book, I was at once intrigued, dumb-founded, and very skeptical. Being a mathematician, I couldn't resist the challenge to attempt to directly calculate the odds myself. This entailed a fresh derivation of numerous formulae and a careful re-view of my work by a statistics professor.[7] To my surprise, these derivations involved only a few things more complicated than high school algebra and the most basic theorems of probability. All that was needed was formulae decent college sophomores could rea-sonably tackle.

Through all this deriving and testing of almost every example Drosnin presented, one question remained: How would the fact that his approach was much less than scientific affect what kind of odds should be viewed as significant? Clearly Drosnin had strayed from the science research fold early in his efforts. Drosnin the Diligent

Data Digger had given himself great freedom in unearthing intriguing findings while not reporting all of his failed attempts to locate what he was looking for. Yes, he found Mozart, but how many other composers did he look for and not locate? And in looking, how many different possible ways of spelling a modern name did he try? And how many loosely related words, with multiple possible spellings, did he attempt? Given such liberties, wouldn't it be more appropriate to raise the ordinary standard of significance from odds of 1 in 50 or 1 in 100 to 1 in 1,000? Or 1 in 100,000? Or 1 in a million?

Clearly, a raising of the bar was needful. After further modeling and analysis, I concluded that a significant threshold in the range of 1 in 100,000 to 1 in a million was appropriate. Anything with odds less than that should be regarded as coincidental. In view of the great liberties Drosnin took in locating his examples, an exacting standard should be demanded.

Can You Find Anything You Want?

So isn't it true that you can find just about anything you want in the way of Bible codes? In reality, it depends on how long the word or phrase is. Let's look at an example. For the sake of simplicity, suppose we assume that all Hebrew letters appear in the Torah with the same frequency. Then the expected number of times a code will appear in the Torah[8] drops rapidly as the number of letters in the code increases. Table 2A shows what I mean.

Table 2A

Number of Letters	Expected Number of Appearances in the Torah
2	192,000,000
3	4,000,000
4	132,000
5	4,500
6	165
7	6

8	0.25
9	0.01
10	0.0004
11	0.000016
12	0.00000066

Let me clarify. If a code has six letters or less, it is nearly certain that you could find it somewhere in the Torah, and probably find it in many places. If it has eight or more letters, it is very likely that you won't find it anywhere in the Torah by chance. The probability that you will not be able to find a word you selected as a code in the Torah is 78.5% if it has 8 letters, 99.0% if it has 9 letters, 99.96% if it has 10 letters and 99.998% if it has 11 letters.

Why does this rapid drop-off in the expected number of occurrences take place? First, the number of possible ELSs that can be found in the Torah is far less than infinite. In fact, the number of possible ELSs made of 15 or fewer letters is less than a trillion. So it is limited, and this kills the typing monkeys analogy. Furthermore, as the number of letters increases, the number of different "words" that can be made with any given number of letters increases exponentially while the total number of possible ELSs declines slowly.

For example, we recently searched for the name of "Judge Roy Moore," a 10-letter string in Hebrew, spelled דיין רוי מור. We were surprised to see that our software found it once in the Bible with a skip of 6,805 letters between each of its letters. The odds were less than one in a million against our making this discovery, according to the probability function of our search software, Bible Codes 2000. Then we tried to find "The Ten Commandments," another 10-letter string, spelled עשרת הדברות. This time our luck was not so good. You can see the full story of our "Judge Roy Moore" cluster on our web site at www.biblecodedigest.com/page.php/195.

Separating Wheat From Chaff

If we had been able to find "Judge Roy Moore" and "The Ten Commandments," or "Ten Commandments," near to each other, we would have had a very interesting linkage. If you find two long "related" codes near one another, or three or more medium length codes, the odds can quickly become microscopic that such occurrences could happen by chance. Most of the examples presented to date that are quite likely to appear by chance involve ELSs with only three or four or sometimes five letters. Such ELSs, as the previous table shows, are bound to show up so many times that being stunned that they are near something else is like being astonished that there are ants in your kitchen or dandelions in your lawn.

While stating that Bible codes cannot be used to predict the future, Michael Drosnin nevertheless gave in to the temptation to use it for that purpose in both of his bestselling books, claiming that such efforts involve only the outlining of future "possibilities." A fundamental problem with most of his examples is that individual years are represented by only three or four Hebrew letters. Because such year codes are so short, they are expected to appear so often that they are likely to be close to just about anything you want. Consequently, his attempts at predicting future dates are basically without any real foundation.

Lacking any real mathematical training, Drosnin had started with some proper tools obtained from Dr. Rips. He then apparently wandered into the conclusion that anything that could be reconfigured into one of his own crossword examples must somehow be significant. Having a love for the sensational, Drosnin started moving further into predicting the future. What started as an innocent foray turned into a dizzying frenzy of alarming future peeks dancing in full apocalyptic technicolor.

As I mentioned earlier, the problem of believing that very short ELSs have significance also plagues the assertions by Christian authors Grant Jeffrey and Yacov Rambsel. For example, they marvel at the location of the Yeshua (ישוע — or Hebrew for Jesus) ELS in many verses that Christians cite as prophecies of the Messiah. However, the Yeshua ELS has only four very common Hebrew letters and would be expected to coincidentally appear as an ELS over 600,000 times in the Torah alone. This difficulty also invalidates the claims of some Jewish code proponents that the codes prove that Jesus was a false messiah. Yes, a Yeshua ELS probably is close to the ELS for false messiah. However, Yeshua ELSs are also close to just about everything because Yeshua is virtually everywhere. Such inferences have no statistical significance.

Although the books of Drosnin, Jeffrey, and Rambsel are unintentionally flawed by talking up examples that are very likely to occur by chance, to my surprise they also disclosed some that were at least moderately interesting. For example, the odds that all of the codes about Rabin's assassination, described earlier, could have appeared by chance are about 1 in 6.2 billion.

Inappropriate Rendering

Michael Drosnin claims that the ELS for Yitzhak Rabin crosses a literal text where the phrase "assassin that will assassinate" appears (Deuteronomy 4:42). Curiously, his translation of the Hebrew phrase crossed by the Rabin ELS is clearly incorrect. The context makes it clear that the slayer in question acted without premeditation. Assassins do not fit that description.

Quite surprisingly, he does not mention that a different letter of the Rabin ELS is crossed by the Hebrew word for killed (stoned) which is in a passage (Deuteronomy 17:2-5) that may well have instigated the assassin's radical belief that Rabin should be killed. The passage calls for any Jew "who transgresses God's covenant" to be stoned to death. That covenant involved God's gift of the land of Canaan to the Jews "as an everlasting possession" (Genesis 17:7-8).

Rabin had been the key proponent of three peace agreements with Yassir Arafat and the Palestinians. These agreements had led to Israel giving up land on the West Bank and the Gaza Strip in exchange for promises by the Palestinians to cease hostilities. While Rabin was hailed as a champion of peace, in Amir's eyes he may have transgressed God's covenant by giving land back to the Arabs. This is much more astonishing than the word for unintentional murder, which Drosnin shifted to mean assassination and then showcased on the cover of his book.

The Surprising Einstein Code Cluster

What is even more amazing, however, is that there are several code clusters in Drosnin's book that are much more improbable than the Rabin codes. The Einstein codes are a prime example. First is the appearance of a nine-letter sequence that is a possible spelling of Einstein (איינשטיין). The chances of this code appearing anywhere in the Torah with a skip of 16,498 or fewer letters is only 1 in 20. Then, there are four codes with words or phrases that could easily be taken as descriptive of Einstein that either intersect or are very near the original Einstein ELS (figure 2B).

The combined probability of all five of these codes appearing anywhere in the Torah is 1 in 110 trillion! However, not only do they all simply appear, they are all right on top of one another. This closeness greatly increases the improbability of these occurrences. The odds of all these codes appearing as they do is 1 out of 5.4 million times 1 billion times 1 billion, or 1 out of 5,385,990,000,000,000, 000,000,000.

Fig. 2B

Code	Number of Letters	Skip	Chances of Appearing Anywhere in the Torah
Einstein	9	16,498	1 in 20
A new and excellent understanding	10	1	1 in 11,968,000
They prophesied a brainy person	8	1	1 in 15,395
He overturned present reality	6	1	1 in 30
Science	3	3	100%

How big a number is 5.4 octillion? Suppose you had sand so fine that if you laid 1,000 grains of it end to end in a straight line it would be only one inch long. Every cubic inch of this sand would have one billion grains. Now, picture covering all 48 states of the continental U.S. one half inch deep with this fine sand. Then, color just one grain of this sand red and randomly place it somewhere in this countrywide sandbox. You then give someone freedom to travel anywhere within the U.S., be blindfolded and given a pair of tweezers to pick up only one grain of that sand. The chances that this person will pick up the one grain of red sand is about the same as all of the Einstein codes described above occurring by chance.

If this was all there was to the probability calculation, these odds would truly be mind blowing. However, there is a catch. What we really want to know are the odds of finding a code cluster similar or comparable to the Einstein cluster. To do that, you would have to factor in the very large number of alternative words and phrases that would be considered to be comparable. For example, instead of finding, "he overturned present reality," you might consider "he dramatically changed theories of physics" to be a comparable phrase.

There may well be millions if not billions of alternative phrases that could instead have been found. Working this into the calculation is very complex, but at the end of the day, after doing that, one would still have to come to the conclusion that the Einstein cluster was quite improbable.

There are more characteristics of this cluster that are highly unusual. First, the three phrases each have skips of only one letter. Second, these three phrases are each formed by taking the last few letters of one original Hebrew word and the first few of the next word (and sometimes part of yet another word) to obtain still another word with clear meaning. Third, the three-letter code for science has only one chance in 595 of having a skip of three or fewer letters and of crossing the Einstein ELS. Fourth, that same science ELS only has one chance in 2,383 of overlapping the phrase, "a new and excellent understanding."

Two Improbable Clusters

The Hitler cluster mentioned in Drosnin's first book is fairly improbable. It includes these words and phrases:

- Hitler, evil man, Nazi and enemy, slaughter, in Germany, Nazis, Berlin, Eichmann, the ovens, extermination, in Auschwitz, final solution, and Zyklon B.

Grant Jeffrey and Yacov Rambsel both wrote about a cluster that Rambsel discovered and that is far less likely to appear by chance than Drosnin's example. Its theme is the life and crucifixion of Jesus of Nazareth.

- Yeshua is my name, the evil Roman city, from the atonement lamb, Mt. Moriah, disciples (the names of all of the disciples except Judas), tremble Mary, Joseph, his signature, Nazarene, Passover, Galilee, let him be crucified, Pharisee, Herod, Annas, his cross, Caesar, messiah, Shiloh, and pierce.

In spite of flaws in the books of Jeffrey and Rambsel, these authors presented this startling cluster of ELSs to the world. This highly improbable cluster is located in a passage that Christians cite as a prophecy about the crucifixion (Isaiah 53).

It is notable because it is comprised of an unusually large number of codes (47). While the majority of the Isaiah codes are very likely to appear by chance, there are so many of them that, after eliminating the highly probable ones, numerous codes remain that are worthy of significant further study. For example, the three most improbable codes in the Isaiah cluster have a combined probability of appearing in a section of text as small as Isaiah 53 that is comparable to that of the Einstein cluster. And this is not all. There are also codes with odds of 1 in 225,000, 1 in 99,000 and 1 in 23,500, and nine more codes in this cluster that have odds between 1 in 2,000 and 1 in 10.

The Jesus codes would seem to fall into a different category than the others. While the first four involve people and events of the twentieth century, Jesus lived much closer to the time of the earliest manuscripts. One might suppose that human authors placed the Jesus codes there after the fact of His life. There are three reasons why this is most unlikely. First, the cluster appears in the Book of Isaiah that scholars believe was written centuries before Jesus lived. Second, the Dead Sea Scrolls include the Great Isaiah Scroll, a nearly complete copy of the entire book that pre-dates the life of Jesus by 100 years.[9]

Third, these clusters appear in the Hebrew part of the Bible — and the Jews did not believe that Jesus was someone that should have been accorded the special status of having many key people and places in His life imbedded as codes within their sacred text. If anything, the authors' and copyists' motives would cause them to try to prevent such codes from being there.

Looking More Deeply

Perhaps the main reason why there are not more compelling codes being announced by researchers is the Hebrew language component. Most do not have sufficient knowledge of the language, or access to someone who does. And so their searches for ELSs are limited to single words or simple phrases that they can pull from dictionaries or interlinear Bibles. This is why a key member of our team is Nathan Jacobi, Ph.D., a retired professor of mathematics and physics and a former Jet Propulsion Lab scientist, who is now a registered investment advisor and part-time Hebrew teacher. With his help, we were able to delve more deeply into Rambsel's Isaiah 53 codes, with simply amazing results. One of the most astounding aspects of this research is that Nathan is a Jewish agnostic who has a great respect for Jesus as possibly the greatest Jewish prophet, but seriously doubts the existence of God and that Isaiah 53 is about Christ.

In early 2001, we began attempting to extend codes. That is, with Nathan's understanding of biblical Hebrew, we began to look at letters before and after words and terms previously discovered. One of the first strings we worked on was the "Yeshua is my name" discovery by Yacov Rambsel. This was its spelling when Rambsel first wrote about it:

ישוע שמי

This code appears in Isaiah 53 using every 20th letter from the Hebrew text, going in a backward direction. Our search software enables us to pick up every 20th letter, both before and after this 7-letter-long code. Later, Rambsel and Jeffrey noticed that additional letters on both sides of the original term read "Exceedingly high. Yeshua is my strong name."

מעל ישוע שמי עז

Author and researcher Truman Blocker extended it in the other direction for "One rushing from above, Jesus is my strong name."

שקק מעל ישוע שמי

Finally, Nathan extended it into a 22-letter code, which at the time was the longest ever discovered, "Gushing from above, my mighty name arose upon Jesus and the clouds rejoiced."

שקק מעל ישוע שמי עז ששו עבים

This ELS is still the most poetically beautiful we have discovered, even though we have found many much longer codes since then. It became the heart of the Isaiah cluster we have continued to research. To date, we have discovered more than 1,600 codes in the cluster, ranging in length from 2 letters to 40 letters long. I'll be devoting a full chapter to the Isaiah 53 cluster later on.

Extremely interesting is that all of the extended ELSs Nathan has discovered are expressed in biblical Hebrew, as opposed to modern Hebrew of the kind that is spoken by the contemporary inhabitants of Israel. The difference is loosely analogous to the difference between 21st century American English and the language that was used in the King James Bible. Fortunately for us, Nathan was schooled in both modern and scriptural Hebrew during his childhood education in Israel.

In this book, we will examine two clusters of codes that are so extensive and complex that it is hard to see how anyone who truly comprehended them could think that they were simply the product of chance. Each cluster includes dozens of lengthy ELSs, all crossing a fairly short portion of the Hebrew Bible that are topically related to one another and to the subject matter of the surface text.

In chapter 4, we arrive at the conclusion that the odds that a cluster as extensive as that found in Isaiah 53 could be due to chance are less than 1 in 2,189,000,000,000,000,000,000,000,000,000,000, 000,000,000,000,000,000,000,000,000,000,000,000,000,000,000, 000,000,000,000,000,000,000,000,000,000,000,000,000,000,000, 000,000,000,000,000,000,000,000,000,000,000,000,000,000,000, 000,000,000,000,000,000,000,000,000.

Odds so remote are virtually impossible for the human mind to comprehend. It is *truly* staggering. Something as improbable as the Isaiah 53 cluster has about the same odds as someone buying only one lottery ticket in each of 33 different states and winning the one-in-a-million jackpot in every state. In other words, the chances are about as zero as you can get.

In chapter 6, we arrive at the conclusion that the odds that a cluster as extensive as that found in Ezekiel 37 could be due to chance are less than 1 in 640,000,000,000,000,000,000,000,000,000, 000,000,000,000,000,000,000,000,000,000,000,000,000,000,000, 000,000,000,000,000,000,000,000,000,000,000,000,000,000,000, 000,000,000,000. Such odds, though less remote than those for the Isaiah 53 cluster, are nevertheless far beyond the range of what chance can produce.

Real or Coincidental?

The code clusters we have researched and verified in the past five years, taken altogether, present strong evidence that the phenomenon of Bible codes cannot be coincidental. This begs us to somehow reckon with it. If the phenomenon is not coincidental, is not the alternative that they are intentional? If that is indeed true, then a new chapter in the saga of the long struggle between science and religion is now being written. I believe that it must be true and that there can only be one creative mind behind the phenomenon — the same Intelligence that created the cosmos, God himself.

There is a growing contingency of mathematicians and intellectuals who have closely examined this phenomenon and are of the opinion that the evidence strongly supports the hypothesis that it is real. They may stop short of claiming publicly that God wrote the Bible, but some have had their lives radically changed by what they have seen in Bible codes.

- The three authors of the paper, "Equidistant Letter Sequences in the Book of Genesis," published in the August 1994 issue of the journal, *Statistical Science* (Dr. Eliyahu Rips, Associate Professor of Mathematics, Hebrew University of Jerusalem; and Doron Witztum and Yoav Rosenberg, researchers at Jerusalem College of Technology — the WRR mentioned earlier). Professor Rips is a top-ranked mathematician who was able to leave Lithuania following the fall of communism. After immigrating to Israel, he became interested in Torah codes. His work with them influenced his decision to transition from atheism to orthodox Judaism.[10]

- Professor Robert Haralick, mentioned earlier, has written an academic paper, "Testing the Torah Code Hypothesis: The Torah Code Effect is Real," showing how the primary skeptic publication refuting the WRR paper in *Statistical Science* used "cooked" data.

- Harold Gans, a senior code-breaker at the National Security Agency,[11] and

- Robert J. Aumann, considered to be Israel's most famous mathematician, one of the world's experts in game theory, and a member of both the Israeli and the U.S. National Academy of Science.[12]

Second are three other authors who have published on the subject:

- Dr. Jeffrey Satinover, author of the excellent *Cracking the Bible Code*, which was published in 1997 by William Morrow and Company, Inc. Dr. Satinover is a practicing psychiatrist and former William James Lecturer in Psychology and Religion at Harvard. He holds degrees from M.I.T., the Harvard Graduate School of Education, and the University of Texas.[13] Satinover is so intrigued with the potential of Bible codes that he has earned a masters in physics since completing his book and is now working on a doctorate in the field.

43

- D.J. Bartholomew, author of the article, "Probability, Statistics and Theology," in a 1988 issue of the *Journal of the Royal Statistical Society*.
- Daniel Michelson, a professor in the Department of Computer Science and Applied Mathematics at the Weizman Institute of Science in Rehovat, Israel, has posted a supportive article at www.600000men.com/book/bo.htm.

Third, it should be noted that the research behind WRR's paper was peer reviewed three times by various mathematicians before the editors of *Statistical Science* would publish it. These unnamed reviewers must have signed off on Dr. Rips' research or it would not have appeared in that professional journal. In addition, four professors (H. Furstenberg of the Hebrew University of Jerusalem, I. Piatetski-Shapiro of Yale, and David Kazhdan and J. Bernstein of Harvard) have issued a joint statement regarding the results of their review of Dr. Rips' research stating that the work was carried out by serious researchers, but that it is a controversial topic that may require a higher level of statistical significance than would be required of more routine research. They also stated that the results deserve further study.[14]

Finally, we have the chairman of Harvard's mathematics department, Dr. Kazhdan stating that Bible codes are a real phenomenon, but that the conclusions derived from them are left to each individual to decide.[15]

Worthy of Further Study

Because this tentative conclusion is so diametrically opposite to the views of millions of the most intelligent people on earth, what is needed is further examination by more leading mathematicians and scientists. The nature of the evidence invites close inspection. The subject data is a text that has not changed in over a thousand years.

There are relatively inexpensive computer programs that can rapidly scan this text and locate any potential codes. This makes verification of past findings relatively easy once one has committed to memory the Hebrew alphabet and purchased a Hebrew-English translation CD or dictionary.[16] We are dealing with cold, hard objective stuff here.

Most of the authors of bestselling books on Bible codes don't have any technical credentials. Because they lack the mathematical expertise, they have gone overboard in their enthusiasm about codes discovered in the last decade. In their enthusiasm, they have not only presented some incredibly shaky code clusters, but many highly unremarkable ones as well. But is this a valid reason for dismissing the entire matter?

Suppose you are a museum's curator. You are inspecting a newly donated rock collection. It is a medley of some hopelessly common river rocks, the Hope Diamond, a chunk of discarded asphalt, a 50-pound nugget of gold, a ragged hunk of granite, and the largest unflawed sapphire in the world. A wise curator would accept the donation, throw out the junk, and display the priceless treasures. While guilt by association may have some validity on occasion when we are dealing with people, it has no place in assessing rocks and gems. The same holds true for code clusters in the ancient Hebrew text of the Bible.

As an orthodox Jew, Dr. Rips believes that God intentionally placed these codes in the text to show that no human could have written it. After all, he might say, the Bible itself claims that its ultimate author has the exclusive power to accurately foretell the future. Can you not picture Dr. Rips dusting off one of the Dead Sea Scrolls and peeling it open with a glint in his eyes? He then proceeds to utter these words of Isaiah, " . . . I am God, and there is no other; I am God, and there is none like me. I make known the end from the beginning, *from ancient times, what is still to come* . . . " (Is. 46:9, 10; emphasis mine).

Baby and Bath Water

Certainly the study of ELSs is still in its infancy. We can choose to focus on the murky condition of the bath water, or we can marvel at the wonders of the baby itself. Should we throw out both merely because early chroniclers got excited about their discoveries and

45

overreached a bit? Witztum's view is that by publicizing examples of poorly researched codes, the integrity of serious research is crippled. In his public statement, he writes that Torah codes are a real scientific phenomenon deserving serious research.

An intriguing question is that of what researchers might unearth in the next decade or more. Are we standing on the threshold of discoveries that could reshape the worldview of millions? What if a way is found to use codes to precisely predict future events? Witztum's views on this are emphatic — it is impossible to make future predictions using the codes. A fundamental problem is that of attempting to interpret text without syntax or punctuation. Without punctuation, one could misread the Ten Commandments and believe the instruction is to steal and murder.[17]

Could such codes provide clear evidence in support of or contrary to one or more of the world's great religions? This would be a disturbing possibility for fundamentalists of any persuasion. It is likely, however, that the same problems of interpreting a text with no syntax or punctuation, and no way to tell who is speaking, will prevent this from taking place. Our research has turned up codes from a terrorist point of view.[18] The surface text may quote anyone, including Satan,[19] but the codes that we have seen don't come with attribution.

The existence of numerous non-random subliminal words within the Bible directly challenges the widely held view that the Bible is basically an anthology of religious myths. As research continues, it will either fail or succeed at unearthing more highly improbable codes. The next decade should be telling. The phenomenon will either be: (1) dismissed as a clever hoax because of the non-scientific approach of some of its main advocates, (2) viewed as an illusory paradox for some yet undiscovered reason, or (3) become a gathering force with which skeptics must reckon.

Just as mountaineers have risked their lives in ascending the heights of Mt. Everest simply because it is there, so some today will step forward to risk their reputations and beliefs in plying the uncharted depths of yet to be discovered codes. Why? Because they are there.

In the following pages, I will share the mountaintop that my colleagues and I have been exploring over the past few years. To share the whole mountain would take several volumes. It may be that we will be able to get to those volumes later, but in the meantime, you can explore most of the research that we have completed on our web site at www.biblecodedigest.com.

R. EDWIN SHERMAN

Chapter Three

The Mega-Cluster of Jesus Codes in Isaiah 53

From its introduction, the phenomenon of Bible codes has been fraught with controversy. At first, it was the question of whether codes were substantive or coincidental. That issue has persisted. As writers and researchers delved into the ancient Hebrew text with efficient computer programs, each came to conclusions supportive of their own predisposed beliefs.

Orthodox Jews claimed support for the notion that Jesus was a false messiah. Christians claimed support for the opposite conclusion. Skeptics were quick to suppose that you could find whatever you were looking for in the codes. With so much at stake, the rhetoric has not become kinder and gentler.

Is it possible that all the ferocity of the various controversial issues surrounding Bible codes could be concentrated in two pages of Hebrew text? That may be the case. The intensity in the Isaiah 53 passage is phenomenal. What are the most heated issues in this debate?

- *First is the intense controversy over whether Bible codes are real.* The mega-cluster of codes in Isaiah 53 has emerged as one of the strongest examples of what code proponents have put forth as evidence of the non-coincidental.
- *Second is the most intense flashpoint of disagreement between Jews and Christians — the messianic claims about Jesus Christ.* That subject thoroughly permeates every aspect of this mega-cluster of ELSs. And it is the essence of the literal text of this

passage, as it depicts a suffering servant whose torture and death will serve as the basis for the healing of many. While many Jews believe this servant is a collective symbol of all of the children of Israel, Christians believe the servant of Isaiah 53 is Jesus. Ask almost any sizeable group of ministers which passages in the Old Testament contain the most important prophecies about Jesus and Isaiah 53 will invariably be at or near the top of the short list.

• *Third is the firm belief of some orthodox Jews that only the Torah was dictated letter-by-letter by God, and thus it is the only part of the entire Hebrew Bible that is encoded.* (Which is why you see the term "Torah codes" sometimes used interchangeably with "Bible codes." Orthodox Jewish code researchers maintain that only the Torah is encoded. Their Christian colleagues believe that the entire Bible contains valid codes.) The remaining books are viewed as being the product of human authorship under the inspiration of God. Furthermore, as a result of this difference in how the different books have been viewed by Jewish scholars down through the centuries, scribes have not been as careful to make sure that copies they have made of books outside the Torah are free of errors. The Isaiah 53 mega-cluster serves as the strongest counter-example to that belief. In terms of its sheer improbability, the total number of ELSs, the number of highly improbable codes, and the intricate spatial relationships between various groupings of topically related ELSs, this mega-cluster outclasses anything found to date in the Torah. Would it not indeed be ironic if the group of people that to date has been the strongest proponents of Bible codes are faced with the possibility that the most conclusive evidence in favor of the authenticity of the codes is a passage that provides the strongest challenge to their skeptical views about Jesus?

Our research has elevated the group of ELSs in Isaiah 53 originally discovered by Yacov Rambsel from being an unusual curiosity of more than 40 ELSs to a mind-boggling web of over 1,600 ELSs packed into the two pages of Hebrew text comprising this passage. It has transformed this code cluster from relative obscurity to center stage in the conflicts between code skeptics and proponents, and in the ongoing debate between Jews and Christians about the identity and office of Jesus Christ.

Figure 3A (page 52) shows what the core of it looks like in a 20-letter-wide matrix, with the 22-letter "Gushing" code as the focal code running up the middle, and a sampling of other codes in the cluster crossing it or running close to it. If all of the codes in this cluster were shown in this matrix, nearly all of the letters would be colored in. Shown is a portion of the Isaiah 53 scripture, with letters running from upper right to lower left. Each row of the matrix contains 20 letters, because the focal code in the middle has a skip of –20 (a minus sign indicates a backward skip).

It is truly astonishing how many letters in this matrix are used twice or more, as indicated by the shading in the last box on the list of ELSs in the matrix. Half of the letters in the focal code are used more than once by codes, which means direct hit crossings by other codes of the focal code. Several of the letters of the focal code in sequence, numbers 4-11 counting from the bottom up, are crossed by other letters. This continuity occurs only with these letters:

מעל ישוע

They spell "Jesus is exceedingly high" or "Exceedingly high is Jesus." Coincidence?

Nestling right up to the focal code with the same skip in an adjacent column on the upper left is the ELS "Lamp (or light) of the Lord." It shows up right next to the letters in the focal code that spell out "The clouds rejoiced."

With its very short skip of +4, the ELS "I fought suffering in God's servant, and in God he slept," wraps itself around the central ELS. We found this ELS when we were searching a code for "Matthew," but the three letters spelling "Matthew" were swallowed up by another, longer word. Here is the Hebrew for the final code, with the letters spelling "Matthew" highlighted:

לחמתי וחלי מעבד יי וג יי נם

Fig. 3A

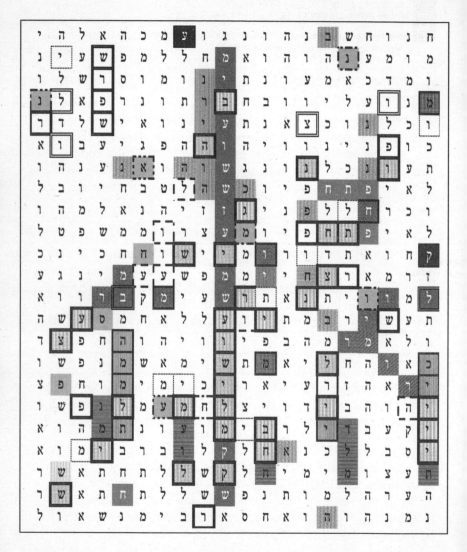

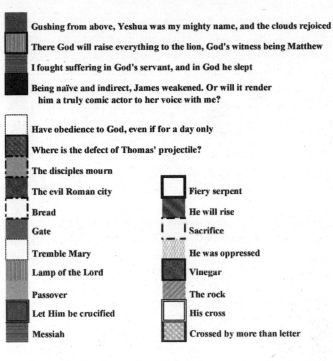

Gushing from above, Yeshua was my mighty name, and the clouds rejoiced

There God will raise everything to the lion, God's witness being Matthew

I fought suffering in God's servant, and in God he slept

Being naïve and indirect, James weakened. Or will it render him a truly comic actor to her voice with me?

Have obedience to God, even if for a day only

Where is the defect of Thomas' projectile?

The disciples mourn

The evil Roman city   Fiery serpent

Bread   He will rise

Gate   Sacrifice

Tremble Mary   He was oppressed

Lamp of the Lord   Vinegar

Passover   The rock

Let Him be crucified   His cross

Messiah   Crossed by more than letter

Does this indicate that Matthew was involved, along with Peter, in attempting to forestall Christ's mission? The Bible is silent on this question.

The Last Days of Jesus

The Isaiah 53 mega-cluster is made up of hundreds of words and phrases, all related to the last days of Jesus Christ, including His actions and characteristics. These ELSs provide an eerie confirmation of the prophecies detailed in the literal text of this passage.

What human being today could assemble a highly coherent surface text of two pages while interlacing the letters beneath with a labyrinth of lengthy ELSs relevant to a topic in the surface text? Even if such a person had the help of some of today's fastest computers and a Pentagon-sized time and expense budget, it is exceedingly doubtful that such a feat would be possible. If you have ever tried to compose a sensible paragraph containing half a dozen thematically related ELSs, you know how difficult it can be. How then can skeptics maintain that such a text could be a happenstance? In reality they cannot. Most likely they will choose to either ignore this book or try to pick at little details in the hope of reducing its credibility. And yet, even if a few of the details presented in this and the next chapter were to be revised, the case would still be conclusive.

The original search for codes about Jesus Christ in the Tanakh was completed by Yacov Rambsel, the author of two books on the subject — *Yeshua: The Name of Jesus Revealed in the Old Testament*, and *His Name Is Jesus* (Frontier Research Publications, Inc., Toronto). Rambsel reportedly did all of his research by hand, not trusting computers to provide accurate counts of the characters in the original Hebrew text.

Rambsel, a Convert

Pastor of a messianic church in San Antonio, Texas, Rambsel is a convert from Judaism to Christianity. His findings have been extensive and are some of the most fascinating in print. He has devoted his life for several years now to a passionate pursuit of codes supporting his belief that Yeshua is the true messiah. It was Rambsel's work that formed the starting point for our research of this cluster. He claims he has found the name Yeshua encoded beneath all of the major prophecies of the messiah. However, the significance of this is open to question. Only four letters long, the ELS for Jesus is expected to appear 5,432 times in the Hebrew Bible with skips of 100 or less simply by chance. A shorter spelling for Jesus (ישי) is expected to appear more than 145,000 times with skips of 100 or less.

By 1997, Rambsel had discovered more than 40 Yeshua codes within Isaiah 52 and 53. These findings are presented primarily in his book, *His Name is Jesus*, with later discoveries included in the book by Grant Jeffrey, *The Handwriting of God* (Frontier Research Publications, Inc., Toronto). Jeffrey largely built this book and an earlier one by the same publisher, *The Signature of God*, on Rambsel's findings. Another Christian author, Chuck Missler, has written *Cosmic Codes: Hidden Messages from the Edge of Eternity* (Koinonia House), which devotes about ten percent of its text to the subject of Bible codes. Missler's findings are presumably based on Rambsel's discoveries and a few of his own. As we began to research this passage of the Bible more intently, we discovered that a number of Rambsel's Hebrew spellings were in error. These errors were repeated by authors using his research.

Checking Out the Findings

Our work on this passage began by merely checking out the findings reported in these books. Although we did find some incorrect Hebrew spellings, most were correct. Our investigation soon expanded, however, to searching for additional words regarding Jesus that might appear as ELSs in this passage. We were astonished at how many ELSs with fairly short skips we were able to locate. Each day we looked for a few more, and we kept a running account of our findings. The result was an expansion of the list of ELSs from Rambsel's more than 40 to our more than 1,600 codes.

In the foreword to his book, *Yeshua*, published in 1996, Rambsel cites one ELS translated as "Yeshua (Jesus) is my name" from Isaiah 53. Grant Jeffrey also refers to this ELS in his 1996 book, *The Signature of God*. These authors cited this ELS as significant evidence that Jesus was the messianic figure prophesied in Isaiah 53. This claim was extensively criticized in a paper, "Jesus Codes: Uses and Abuses," by Rabbi Daniel Mechanic, which is posted on the Aish HaTorah site.[1] We agree with most of the criticisms that Rabbi Mechanic cites in his report, which is now, however, seriously out of date.

Nevertheless, it has to be noted that Rambsel and Jeffrey pioneered this delightful cluster. The "Yeshua (Jesus) is my name" ELS was the foundation of the wonderful 22-letter "Gushing" code that is the focal ELS of the cluster.

Both Rambsel and Jeffrey have disclosed their finding of dozens of "relevant" Isaiah 53 Jesus ELSs in subsequent books. In Jeffrey's 1998 book, *The Mysterious Bible Codes*, he lists 44 ELSs about Jesus in this passage, and addresses most of Rabbi Mechanic's criticisms. In Rambsel's 2001 book, *The Genesis Factor*, he cites 74 ELSs about Jesus that he had found in Isaiah 53.

While the subject of the Isaiah 53 ELSs is the highly controversial one of Jesus Christ, my focus here is not to convince anyone of a particular viewpoint about who Jesus was, but to examine this cluster as potentially compelling evidence of the reality of Bible codes.

It is our general view that ELSs consisting of phrases or statements about Jesus should initially be regarded as no more than simply being ELSs relevant to the topic of Jesus. Unless their statistical significance can be demonstrated, it would be inappropriate to assert that such words or phrases are "proof" of their content. For example, the mere appearance of the ELS "true messiah" in this cluster is not, per se, proof of that belief, but simply is a phrase relevant to the topic of Jesus, because it is well known that some people hold to that belief.

The odds are 1 in 12 that the "true messiah" ELS could appear in the Isaiah 53 cluster simply by chance. Therefore, by itself, the appearance of this ELS within the cluster does not qualify as "proof" of that viewpoint.

What Is So Different About the Isaiah 53 Cluster?

To date, we have discovered that there are five facets of this mega-cluster that push it far beyond the realm of what is potentially coincidental. These facets are:

1. The existence of numerous multi-phrase and multi-sentence ELSs that make sense on their own, and additionally have relevance to the subject of the surface text.
2. The existence of a lengthy focal code that is highly relevant to the topic of Jesus and that exactly overlaps with or is very near to a large number of other lengthy, topically relevant ELSs.
3. The presence of an exceptionally large number of visual crosses formed by intersections of two ELSs of the Hebrew

word for prophecy — which if viewed in reverse is the Hebrew word for guilt offering.

4. The presence of ELSs that appear many more times than expected within the passage.

5. The apparent topical arrangement of portions of this mega-cluster into sub-clusters focused around specific subtopics.

Our calculations of the combined probability of this or any comparable mega-cluster appearing by chance only take into account the first facet of non-randomness. We have not factored in the additional improbability of the other facets since the improbability of the first facet is so great that there is no need to try to modify the calculations for them. Obviously, if we were to do so the chances would be even more remote.

The First Non-Random Facet: Numerous Multi-Word ELSs That Make Sense

First, there is the presence of numerous, topically specific, multi-phrase and multi-sentence ELSs that make sense. It is one thing to find a longer ELS that represents grammatically reasonable Hebrew, but that appears random in its content. It is another to find a longer ELS with content that clearly ties to the topic or theme of the literal text. Logically, the latter should only occur now and then if Bible codes were a random phenomenon. Nevertheless, as we can see from the following compilation, there are far too many long ELSs with content that clearly ties to the substance of the text of Isaiah 53 to dismiss this cluster as coincidental in nature.

We have grouped the ELSs found in this cluster that are three or more words long according to the level of their relationship to the topic of Christ reflected in their content. Within each category the ELSs appear in alphabetical order. Obviously, this is to a fair degree a subjective exercise. Because of that the reader is invited to re-categorize any of the longer ELSs shown below according to the degree of relatedness that they believe is reasonable. In appendix 3, commentary is offered on possible connections between key words and phrases in many of these long ELSs with the topic of Jesus Christ.

Relevant Codes

And brother of the gospel, where has the manna spread?
And command that we skip everything but the gem of ascension.
And in his name, as he commanded, Jesus is the way.
And thirst for all of him is the faith of Mary the mother.
And where are they? The Sanhedrin is finished.
Ascension, considering God's hands under me.
Ascension, we will thank God, and they will be near my shelter.
  Recognize her blood.
Bemoan the prince, Jesus the king
Captain of the army of the Lord, carry the ark of sight.
Dreadful day for Mary
Evil Roman city
Father, the ascension of Jesus is heavenly.
From the joy of God my friend
Give them a Jewish messiah who will become a priest.
God is for them and long live the exalted flame. God is Jesus.
God will have his own day.
God's miracle to us is appropriate for them in the temple.
Greed, according to Matthew, was the rule.
Gushing from above, my mighty name arose upon Jesus, and the
  clouds rejoiced.
He offended. The resurrection of Jesus. He is risen indeed.
Her struggle is for them; God has graced them; Lord of Hosts.
Hurry to pay heed about giving, for in it hearing will be given to
  you.
If the friend of evil will thirst for the end of righteous purity, his
  home is an urn. Let Judas have his day. To me, the elevated one,
  they fasted. Where are you? Its content will be written from my
  mouth. Father, indeed you will raise the dead over there.
In his name, as he commanded, Jesus is the way.
It will be understood. Jesus created.
Jesus created a high gift.
Jesus created to the Father.
Jesus the gift is master and my Lord.
Know who the chosen people are or God will be angry.
Long live the ascension coming from God.

My shepherds are among the disciples.
Have obedience to God, even if for a day only — Peter.
Shed light on ark of the covenant and fade away.
The ascension of Jesus: for the sleeping one will shout. Listen!
The ascension of Jesus is the death of the witness.
The man and the God alive
The rabbi from the glory of God
The value of resurrection is thus dear.
There God will raise everything to the lion, God's witness being
   Matthew.
Who is Jesus? Master.
Who will it be that God's miracle will save?
Wonder! Jesus is the truth.

Plausible Codes

And command fleets of resurrection from above to flee with raging
   excitement.
Ascension, be a cause for my heart, and render my Father trans-
   formed. I will be ashamed, and will divide the temple of the
   messenger.
He waited. He will emit my very light thunder in them proudly from
   Armageddon. And they will crush the echo.
If indeed all the detail of this one is a string, does Peter despise the
   burden of the extra ships, and does my throne rest? So spoke
   God's poor.
I fought sickness in God's servant, and in God he slept.
I will cool the priest from his faith. Since Babylon has fallen, His
   lamb is under the storm.
Smile, I see Matthew there. Let go!
We will advise the dove. He will place in me the multitude of Gog.
   You will be weakened.

Mysterious (but potentially sensible) Codes

Ascension, monument of the saturated. And the hand of the monument is the daughter of the cedar supporter.

Being naïve and indirect, Jacob (James?) weakened, or will it render him a true comic actor to her voice with me.

Come as my fire from my cell. Kidron is my life.

From my fear of resurrection he made a monument, or the power of the mouth.

Kidron calmed down and went.

My bride is dead. Let all the sweetness in me come forth.

Where is the defect of Thomas's projectile?

Of the 57 extended codes found in the Isaiah 53 cluster, an astonishing 73.7% (42) can be categorized as topically "relevant." Table 3B summarizes the total number of codes in each category.

Table 3B

Category	Number in Isaiah 53	%-age From Isaiah 53
Relevant	42	73.7%
Plausible	8	14.0%
Mysterious	7	12.3%

If the above codes were the result of chance, we would intuitively expect that the content of relatively few of them would seem relevant to the content of the literal text. Most of them would fall in the plausible or mysterious category. To get a better idea of what to expect from a non-encoded text, we examined the extended codes found in a Hebrew translation of Tolstoy's *War and Peace* in the Islamic Nations Experiment (see table App5D, page 272). The results appear in table 3C.

Table 3C

	War and Peace	%-age of Total
Relevant	1	4.2%
Plausible	8	33.3%
Mysterious	15	62.5%
TOTAL	24	

This kind of distribution of codes seems to be in line with what one would expect from a non-encoded text. Occasionally, by chance, an entire long code consisting of grammatically reasonable Hebrew will appear to have content relevant to that of the literal text in one of these books. But one would not expect that to happen very often.

Table 3D

	Ezekiel	%-age of Total
Relevant	3	7.9%
Plausible	17	44.7%
Mysterious	18	47.4%
TOTAL	38	

As shown in table 3D, a similar distribution emerged from the Islamic nation extended codes found in the book of Ezekiel — which some code researchers would consider to be an encoded text.

If the 57 extended codes found in the Isaiah 53 cluster behaved in a similar manner to the extended codes from *War and Peace*, we would expect that only two of them would be relevant, while 19 would be plausible and 36 would be mysterious in content. Table 3E provides a side-by-side comparison of these expected numbers with the actual results for the Isaiah 53 codes.

Table 3E

Category	%-age From *War and Peace*	Expected From Non-Encoded Text	Number in Isaiah 53	%-age From Isaiah 53
Relevant	4.2%	2	42	73.7%
Plausible	33.3%	19	8	14.0%
Mysterious	62.5%	36	7	12.3%

As I mentioned earlier, some level of subjectivity is inherently involved in categorizing codes in this manner. It should be evident from this comparison that the Isaiah 53 code cluster must largely be intentional in nature. It cannot be the result of chance. One would have to seriously downgrade a large number of these codes before the hypothesis that they were coincidental would even be a very remote possibility.

The obvious presence of a very high percentage of extended codes that are related to the content of the literal text is one of the most convincing ones to me as an expert in statistical analysis.

Meaningful Two-Word ELSs

What is also remarkable is that the above list of 57 extended codes emerged from the examination of only 86 initial one or two-word ELSs for the possibility of their being part of longer ELSs.

It is also intriguing that there were numerous highly meaningful two-word ELSs that we looked for and found in the Isaiah 53 cluster. The English translations of these ELSs are listed below in alphabetical order. If there is more than one appearance of one of these two-word ELSs, the total is in parenthesis after it. (The Hebrew spellings of these codes and other information can be viewed on our web site at www.biblecodedigest.com/page.php/14.) There is

much more research that could be completed on these ELSs, including examination of each one for the possibility that it is part of a
longer ELS that consists of grammatically reasonable Hebrew.

Angel of the Lord
Ascension of Jesus
Deer of the Dawn *(see Psalm 22)*
God has atoned
Have hemmed me in
His spirit on a tree
Jesus, be judged
Jesus is salvation
Jesus is truth (2)
Jesus reigns
Jesus the messiah
Jewish messiah
King of light (3)
Lamp of the Lord
Living water (2)
Mother of God *Yed-bahz*
Mother of God (7) *Ah-mahl*
Mt. Moriah (2) *Ha-Moriah*
Much weeping (2)
Resurrection of Jesus (4)
Shiloh is a guilt offering
Son of a virgin (2)
Son of God *Eloheem*
Son of God (2) *Yahweh*
Son of man
Son of Mary
Struck by God
The king of light
The priestly tribe
Third temple
True messiah
We are healed (2)
Who is the messiah?
Will make intercession

For a listing of the large number of one-word ELSs found in the Isaiah 53 text, see appendix 4.

The Second Non-Random Facet: An Obvious Focal Code Surrounded by Numerous Improbable ELSs

There is also the existence of an extremely improbable focal code that is highly relevant to the topic of Jesus and that exactly overlaps with, or is very near to, a large number of other improbable ELSs. What could be more relevant to Jesus than a code that, translated, states, "Gushing from above, Jesus is my strong name, and the clouds rejoiced"?

When we calculated the odds of a cluster similar to that of Isaiah 53 occurring by chance, we ignored a critical factor — how tightly packed many of the most improbable codes are around a focal code. If we were to reflect this in our calculation of the odds, the chances of it being a coincidence would be far more unlikely.

Table 3F

Nearness of Top ELSs to 22-Letter Focal Code *(ELSs less than 10 letters away)*			
Minimum Distance	**ELS**	**Letters**	**Skip**
0	And command that we skip everything but the gem of ascension.	22	158
0	It will be understood. Jesus created.	9	4,906
0	I fought suffering in God's servant, and in God he slept.	21	4
0	Where is the defect of Thomas's projectile?	14	62

0	There God will raise everything to the lion, God's witness being Matthew.	22	5
0	Have obedience to God, even if for a day only — Peter.	19	42
2	Being naïve and indirect, James (Jacob) weakened. Or will it render him a truly comic actor to her voice with me?	33	188
4	Hurry to pay heed about giving, for in it hearing will be given to you.	19	762
4	We will advise the dove. He will place in me the multitude of Gog. You will be weakened.	24	23,843
4	Bemoan the prince, Jesus the king.	14	16,384
7	If indeed all the detail of this one is a string, does Peter detest the burden of the extra ships? And does my throne rest? So spoke God's poor.	47	148
7	Kidron calmed down and went.	12	219
7	Jesus the gift is master and my Lord.	12	9,140
8	If the friend of evil will thirst for the end of my innocence, his home is an urn. Let Judas have his day. To me, the exalted one, they fasted. Where are you? Its content will be written from my mouth. Father, indeed you will raise the dead over there.	73	738
8	And brother of the gospel, where has the manna spread?	16	489
8	The rabbi from glory of God	11	544
8	Her struggle is for them; God has graced them; Lord of Hosts.	21	45,646
9	The value of resurrection is thus dear.	12	260

Reflecting this is quite complicated, and the odds are already extremely small, so we will just display in table 3F the minimum distance (in letters) between the letters of the most improbable ELSs and any of the letters of the 22-letter "Gushing from above . . . " code.

The existence of this highly organized group of improbable ELSs so close to an extremely improbable focal code is so utterly non-random that it defies description.

In table 3F, we can see that 18 of the 75 most improbable ELSs either share a common letter with the focal code or are less than ten letters away from it. This focal code is located in the last third of the 1,584-letter-long text crossed by each of the more improbable ELSs.

The closeness of ELSs that are tightly related thematically is common in Isaiah 53. Table 3G provides an example drawn from only four consecutive letters from Isaiah 53:12 (column 1 shows chapter, verse, word, and letter) where the literal text reads, "He poured out to death his soul."

Table 3G

Ch./Vs./Wd./Ltr.	ELS (with skip)
53:12:11:3	Mary (16), Mary (46), and Virgin (17)
53:12:11:4	The blessed (28)
53:12:12:1	Two visual crosses of the prophecy/guilt offering ELS stacked on top of one another (3 & 11 and 3 & 60)
53:12:12:2	Mary (13), Mary (16) and Mother of God (8)

"Mary" (skip of 3) and "Mother of God" (skip of 33) also exactly overlap at Isaiah 53:3:10:2. The intersection of these two ELSs is at the center of another thematically arranged collection of dozens of ELSs that intersect a very short set of consecutive letters.

The Third Non-Random Facet:
Excess Occurrences of Prophecy/Guilt Offering ELS Crosses

An ELS cross occurs when the ELS appears with a short skip such as five or less, and its middle letter coincides with the middle letter of another ELS of the same word with a longer skip (e.g., up to 100).

Figure 3H is an example using the Hebrew word, a'sham (אשם).

Fig. 3H

In this example, the horizontal beam of the cross is made up of an appearance of the ELS with a skip of +1, while the vertical up right is made up of another ELS of the same word, with a skip of, say 48. In Isaiah 52:11-53:12, we would expect 3.6 of these visual crosses to appear by chance. Instead, there are 21 of them. The odds of this just happening by chance are about 1 in 3.2 billion.

This extraordinary excess of visual crosses is not due to a repetition of words or phrases (that contain the letters of the ELS) appearing in the literal passage. What makes it unusually pertinent are the meanings of the word — אשם (a'shem) means "guilt" in contemporary and biblical Hebrew, but it also is a short form for "guilt offering" (a'sham) in various passages in the Hebrew Bible. Spelled backwards — משא (ma-sa), the same letters mean "prophecy" or "burden." What is Isaiah 53 about? It is a prophecy of a guilt offering. What could be a more succinct and appropriate summary of the literal passage than this little three-letter word! And to have it cross itself 21 times in forming visual crosses would seem to be a form of intentional repetition that stresses the importance of the theme of the passage.

The Fourth Non-Random Facet:
ELSs That Appear Many More Times Than Expected

Fourth is the presence of some ELSs that appear many more times than expected within the passage. For example, the ELS for "Mary" appears 16 times with skips of 1-50 in Isaiah 52:12-54:3.

The short ELS was expected to show up only 4.76 times within the search area. And the odds of this occurring were less than 1 in 25,368.

To verify this startling result, we scrambled the letters of Mary and looked for each of these possible rearrangements as an ELS. None of the alternative "words" appear an unusual number of times. There really is no comparison. All of these other results fell well within the bell-shaped curve describing the number of times we would expect that the ELS would show up. On the other hand, the number of "Mary" ELSs was way off the charts, far to the right of the bell-shaped curve.

As another example, the ELS for "remorse" appears 12 times within Isaiah 52:13-53:12. According to the Bible code search software Bible Codes 2000, it is expected to appear only 6.05 times in this passage and the odds are only 1 in 100 that remorse could appear 12 or more times within this passage.

The Fifth Non-Random Facet:
Very Compact Sub-Clusters on a Single Topic

Fifth is the apparent topical arrangement of portions of this mega-cluster into sub-clusters focused around specific subtopics. The Judas cluster is a clear example of this. Included in this very tight cluster are ELSs for "Judas," "zealot," "thirty (pieces of)," "silver," "shekels," "field of blood," "money" (mammon), "execute," "potter's field," "deceived," "darkness," "whipping," "Caesar," "enemy," and "dreadful day for Mary."

If we were able only to say that we had found all of these ELSs in the entire Hebrew Bible, you would yawn. And you should. If we were only able to say that we had found all of these ELSs in only one book of the Bible, you should still yawn, but not quite as deeply. However, when we say that all of these discoveries cross a tiny span of only 18 letters of text in the 13th and 14th verses of chapter 52, you should be astonished. Finding that many thematically-related ELSs in one small space is almost certainly not coincidental.

These 18 letters are composed of the last letter of one word, four subsequent complete words, and the first two letters of the sixth word.

ה מאד כאשר שממו עליך רב

What does the literal text say? We have put the English equivalents of this 18-letter section in capital letters from the text of verses 13 and 14:

"Behold, My servant shall rule wisely; he shall be exalted and lifted up AND BE VERY HIGH. JUST AS MANY WERE ASTONISHED OVER YOU — so much was the disfigurement from man, His appearance and His form from sons of mankind — "

The locations of the key letters of these ELSs in the 13th and 14th verses of Isaiah 52 are shown below. We then show the Hebrew letter of the ELS, then the English for the ELS, and then the size and direction of its skips:

(13:6:4) ה Resurrected (-144)

(13:7:1) מ Execute (-88); Blood (-2); Abraham (-419)

(13:7:2) א Zealot (+223)

(13:7:3) ד Field (+30); Blood (–2); Blood (+6); Blood (+7).

(14:1:1) כ Dreadful day for Mary (-13); Silver (-40); The way (+4)

(14:1:2) א Darkness (-186)

(14:1:3) ש Thirty [pieces of] (+106)

(14:1:4) ר

(14:2:1) ש Simon (+7); Caesar (-89); Enemy (-15)

(14:2:2) מ Blood (+6); Money [mammon] (+13); Deceived (-131)

(14:2:3) מ Shekels (-642); Field (+135); Blood (+7); Lots (+93)

(14:2:4) ו Foundation (+270)

(14:3:1) ע Darkness (-63); Seed (-19); Savior (+99)

(14:3:2) ל Whipping (+475), Savior (+42)

(14:3:3) י Judas (-531)

69

(14:3:4) כ Silver (-143)

(14:4:1) ר Master (-37)

(14:4:2) ב Dreadful day for Mary (-13); Archenemy (-29)

It seems unusual that only one of the 18 letters has not been crossed by any of the 31 ELSs we located (these 31 ELSs cross this section a total of 35 times). And it is unusual. The probability of that happening by chance is about 7.6%.

To find over 30 ELSs that are tightly related thematically and that cross such a short segment of text is, to say the least, extremely unusual. According to our calculations, the odds of such a cluster, or one we would consider to be comparable to it, being this compact, are about 1 in 490 million! That's assuming that for every ELS we have found, we could instead have found nine other ELSs that we would agree are equally as relevant to Judas's act of betrayal as the ones we did locate.

Look now at how some of these ELSs are topically related. The first relevant passage of Matthew 27:1-8 reads as follows:

> Early in the morning, all the chief priests and the elders of the people came to the decision to put Jesus to death. They bound him, led him away and handed him over to Pilate, the governor. When Judas, who had betrayed him, saw that Jesus was condemned, he was seized with remorse and returned the thirty silver coins to the chief priests and the elders. "I have sinned," he said, "for I have betrayed innocent blood."
>
> "What is that to us?" they replied. "That's your responsibility." So Judas threw the money into the temple and left. Then he went away and hanged himself. The chief priests picked up the coins and said, "It is against the law to put this into the treasury, since it is blood money." So they decided to use the money to buy the potter's field as a burial place for foreigners. That is why it has been called the Field of Blood to this day.

This may be related to Zechariah 11:12-13, where there is a prophecy about the significance of thirty pieces of silver:

I told them, "If you think it best, give me my pay; but if not, keep it." So they paid me thirty pieces of silver. And the Lord said to me, "Throw it to the potter" — the handsome price at which they priced me! So I took the thirty pieces of silver and threw them into the house of the Lord to the potter.

The last letter of the "blood" ELS with a skip of +6 is the same letter as the first letter of the "money" (mammon) ELS with a skip of +13. This could be seen as a linkage indicating the phrase, "blood money."

The first letter of this span is shared by all of the following ELSs: "blood" (3 times) with skips of +2, +6 and +7, and "field" with a skip of +30. This could be seen as a linkage indicating the phrase, "field of blood."

The last letter of this span is shared by all of the following ELSs: "blood" with a skip of +7, "field" with a skip of +135 and "shekels" with a skip of -642. This could be seen as a linkage indicating the phrase, "field of blood." In other words, there is an eight-letter span of text that begins and ends with the exact intersection of "field" and "blood."

In figure 3I, a trapezoid is formed by these ELSs, the fourth side of which is defined by the ELS for "potter." This indicates the phrase, "potter's field."

One side of the trapezoid is the short eight-letter span of text just described. Two of the sides of the trapezoid are the two ELSs for "field." And the final side is the ELS for "potter." The first letter of the ELS for potter is only one letter away from the first letter of the ELS for "field" (skip of +30). The second letter of the ELS for "potter" is only 2 letters away from the second letter of the ELS for "field" (skip of +135).

The third letter of the ELS for "execute" with a skip of +88 is the first letter of the ELS for "blood" with a skip of +2.

Only four letters away from the first letter of the ELS for "thirty" (Isaiah 52:7, Word 8, Letter 1) is the first letter of the ELS for "bribe" (Isaiah 52:7, Word 7, Letter 2) with a skip of only −15.

Fig. 3I

```
                 Execute
                  Zealot
                  Blood
                  Blood
                  Blood
Field ....... Field ........ Field ....... Field ...... Field
Dreadful day for Mary ......................... Potter
Silver .................................................
Darkness ............................................ Potter
Thirty ................................................
Simon ................................................ Potter
Caesar ...............................................
Enemy ................................................ Potter
Blood money (Mammon)..........................
Deceived ............................................ Potter
Shekels ..............................................
Field ....... Field ........ Field ....... Field ...... Field
                  Judas
                  Silver
```

The ELS for "Simon" is relevant because of Simon Peter's central role in the action when Judas led the soldiers to capture Jesus. In John 18:10-11, Peter drew his sword and cut off the ear of one of these soldiers. Because of this, Peter was probably one of the most prominent disciples (apart from Judas) who was mentioned in the story of the betrayal. Peter was also prominent in terms of his forceful claims that he would never deny Jesus and that he would die for him.

The ELS for "whipping" or "flogging" is relevant because of Matthew 27:26: "Then he released Barabbas to them. But he had Jesus flogged, and handed him over to be crucified."

The ELS for "lots" is relevant in view of Matthew 27:35: "When they had crucified him, they divided up his clothes by casting lots."

Intriguingly, an ELS for "resurrected" (תחיה) crosses right through the Hebrew word (גבה) for "and be high" at the end of verse 13. The "resurrected" ELS has a skip of 144, which is the product of

12 times 12. Twelve is widely recognized as a biblically significant number, given that there were 12 tribes of Israel and that Jesus had 12 disciples. This verse, right at the beginning of the passage extending from Isaiah 52:13 through Isaiah 53:12, is one that Christians regard as being highly prophetic of Jesus and his crucifixion. It should be noted that 144 is a fairly large skip, and the chances of the resurrected ELS crossing the 18-letter section with a skip of 144 or less is about 55%. Consequently, by itself this crossing is not remarkable mathematically.

The ELS for "Abraham" crosses the second letter of the 18-letter section of text. It appears only one letter after the letter crossed by the "resurrected" ELS. Two different ELSs for "savior" appear later in the 18-letter section of text. The ELS for "the way" also appears, as do ones for "foundation," and "master." How are these topically related? The apostle Paul cited Abraham as the prime example of salvation by faith (as contrasted with deeds) in Romans 4:7-22. Paul then claims that by faith in Jesus and his resurrection people would receive salvation. This is "the way" that he pronounced, and it is what Jesus referred to when he said in John 14:6, "I am the way and the truth and the life." "The Way" was also the term used for the Christian faith long before the word "Christianity" came into use. According to Paul, the "foundation" of the Christian faith is the claim that Jesus was resurrected, as he explained in 1 Corinthians 5:12-23.

Many Christians believe that Isaiah 53:5 refers to this "way": "But he was pierced for our transgressions, he was crushed for our iniquities; the punishment that brought us peace was upon him, and by his wounds we are healed." They would also cite Isaiah 53:12 in this regard: "Therefore I will give him a portion among the great, and he will divide the spoils with the strong, because he poured out his life unto death, and was numbered with the transgressors. For he bore the sin of many, and made intercession for the transgressors."

Jesus used the phrase, "Abraham's bosom," to refer to paradise in Luke 16:22-23. In this way, the "Abraham" ELS could also relate to the "resurrected" ELS. In various rabbinical texts, as well as in the Apocrypha (4 Maccabees 13:17), descriptions are made of the just being welcomed at death by Abraham, Isaac, and Jacob. An ELS for "bosom" comes within one letter of the "Abraham" ELS which crosses the 18-letter section. The first letter of the "bosom" ELS with a skip of –176 appears at Isaiah 54:2, Word 1, Letter 3. It is right next to the third letter of the "Abraham" ELS at Isaiah 54:2, Word 1, Letter 2.

How does the ELS for "seed" relate? In the literal text of Isaiah 53:8-12, specific reference is made to the death (verse 8) of the "suffering servant," but it also refers in verse 10 to this servant subsequently seeing his seed (descendants). This reference would seem to imply the return to life of the suffering servant. It is more directly referred to in verse 11, "After the suffering of his soul, he will see the light of life and be satisfied."

What Are the Chances?

While many of the shorter ELSs we discovered in Isaiah 53 could reasonably have occurred by chance, the large number of long, topically relevant ELSs regarding Jesus Christ that we found in this text is far beyond the workings of coincidence. We have estimated that the odds of chance occurrence of the collection of long ELSs located in Isaiah 53 are so incredibly remote that the only rational conclusion is that this text was intentionally encoded. In the next chapter, we will describe how we arrived at this conclusion.

What we are talking about here is nothing short of a proof of the miraculous that directly challenges the wisdom of our scientific age, a "wisdom" that denies all miracles. While the combined probability of this mega-cluster will vary depending on a few key assumptions, *any* choice of reasonable assumptions results in odds that are astronomically beyond chance. Most of them had to be intentionally encoded within this prophetic passage of the Old Testament.

It only makes sense that you could find a few shorter terms about many subjects in the text of any book. What makes no sense whatsoever is that you could find such an overwhelming collection of topically related, lengthy ELSs congregating within a few pages of text. While the chance re-acquaintance of two long lost friends may be a coincidence we all know happens, when dozens of long lost friends all happen to bump into one another at the same place on the same day, we know that the reunion was planned. When too many coincidences congregate together, we know it had to have been orchestrated.

What Does It All Mean?

We have seen that it is a virtual certainty that the transcendent intelligence that authored the Isaiah 53 passage intended to link its prophetic surface text with Jesus Christ. This is evident in the extreme improbability that a cluster like this could occur coincidentally. And yet, what does it all mean?

The New Testament frequently quotes prophecies from the book of Isaiah that it claims are references to Jesus Christ. Many Christians claim Jesus precisely fulfilled the description of the messiah in these few verses written at least a century before his birth. They see a number of predictions here that were fulfilled by Christ:

- He would be rejected by Jews (Isaiah 53:3).
- He would suffer for the sins of others, and His wounds would result in the healing of sinners (Isaiah 53:4-5).
- He would be silent when accused (Isaiah 53:7).
- He would be executed with sinners (Isaiah 53:12).
- He would be buried with the rich (Isaiah 53:9).
- He would return to life after His execution (Isaiah 52:13 and 53:11-12).

The majority of Jewish sects view these scriptures as prophetic of the messiah, or at least of a messianic figure, but they do not see any connection between them and Jesus Christ. From a Christian viewpoint, this is a continuing fulfillment of the prophecy that Christ would be rejected by Jews.

There are other prophecies in these chapters that are not widely cited by Christian biblical scholars. Beginning in 52:13, Isaiah speaks in Hebrew verse as he quotes God referring to "My servant" as one who will act wisely and be raised and lifted up and highly exalted. Christians believe that Jesus fulfilled this prediction, although he was not truly raised, lifted up and highly exalted until he rose from the dead. Now even secular commentators agree that Jesus is the most significant man who ever lived.

Isaiah goes on to quote God as promising that "there were many who were appalled at him — his appearance was so disfigured beyond that of any man and his form marred beyond human likeness." Indeed, Christ was flogged by Roman soldiers with a cat-o'-nine-tails, a whip of leather thongs with pieces of sharp metal attached at their ends. They also plucked out his beard, a particularly cruel torture that pulls not just hair from a man's face, but huge chunks of flesh as well. This kind of torture would certainly qualify as "disfiguring" and "marring."

"He had no beauty or majesty to attract us to him, nothing in his appearance that we should desire him. He was despised and rejected by men, a man of sorrows and acquainted with grief," another "unofficial" prophecy in Isaiah 53 states. Despite the hopeful depictions of Christ by many old masters and most movie directors, Jesus was never pictured in the Gospels as more than an ordinary man. But these same Gospels do make clear that he was hated and rejected by his contemporaries.

Disappointed Expectations

The fact that Christ did not come as a conquering hero on a white horse disappointed the expectations of a Jewish people looking for a messiah much more on the order of David, Gideon, or Joshua — victorious Jewish characters of ancient Israel. They "stumbled over," as the Bible describes it, this "nebbish," or nobody. Earlier in the book of Isaiah, in fact, the prophet foretells that the messiah would be to the Jewish people "a stone that causes men to stumble and a rock that makes them fall." (Isaiah 8:14) Here, then, from the Christian viewpoint, is another fulfilled prophecy.

Rather than leading a mighty army that would deliver them from the oppression of the Romans, the Jews of first century Jerusalem saw Christ arrive seated on a borrowed donkey along with a group of poor working men, His disciples. He angered the rich and powerful by publicly pointing out their evils and by spending time with the sick and poor. Far from preaching the overthrow of the hated Roman government, He taught meekness and gentleness and a creed that promised the last would be first, and the first, last.

With few exceptions, Jewish people have never been able to accept this "suffering messiah" as theirs, and so disregard these two chapters of Isaiah as irrelevant. They are rarely read in synagogues. The very fact that the writings of Isaiah go on to say that the messiah would take man's sins upon himself and be "pierced" and "crushed" for them, a cornerstone belief of the Christian faith, is beyond possibility in their minds.

The Christian point of view about the link between the prophecies in these chapters and Jesus Christ is bolstered significantly by the discovery of the great number of codes in this section. There is simply overwhelming evidence of a prophetic concurrence beyond human capability in the huge number of phrases and words straight out of the Gospel's account of Christ's execution that appear in these two chapters of Isaiah. The fact that so many codes in the underlying Hebrew text contain the details of the playing out of the prophecy of Isaiah, Moses and many other Old Testament prophets is totally beyond human comprehension.

Could Not Have Been Written After Christ's Death

The existence of so many ELSs in this passage also argues vehemently against the possibility that the text of Isaiah 52 and 53 was written following the death of Jesus. If this passage in Isaiah was written after Jesus had died, then why did its author implant such an amazingly complex web of underlying codes authenticating Jesus as the messiah? Such a possibility makes no sense whatsoever. Not only that, but the Dead Sea Scrolls contain complete copies of this passage made 100 years before Jesus was born.

In *The Dead Sea Scrolls Bible*, the authors note that an intact scroll containing the entire Book of Isaiah was found in Cave 1, and that Isaiah and Psalms both have very large manuscripts preserved.[2] Other comments make it clear that Isaiah is the only book for which the complete manuscript was found.

Is it not ironic that Jewish people, who to date have been the strongest proponents of Bible/Torah codes, are faced with the possibility that the most conclusive evidence in their favor was a passage that provided the strongest challenge to their skeptical views about Jesus? What other ironies await us as we continue to explore this incredible labyrinth of ELSs? All that is certain is that the controversies will rage on.

Some Closing Precautions

It is important to close with a summary of what has been proved and what has not so far been demonstrated with these Isaiah 53 code findings. First, what has been proven through examination of this mega-cluster is that:

- It would be a widely held belief that the suffering servant described in Isaiah 53 is Jesus of Nazareth.
- Because of the existence of a copy of the entire book of Isaiah among the Dead Sea Scrolls that clearly predates the life of Jesus, it can be concluded that the author of Isaiah 53 had extensive foreknowledge of the details of the life and crucifixion of Jesus. This is tantamount to scientific proof of the occurrence of a miracle.

What has not been proven by these findings (although this does not mean that these assertions might not otherwise be entirely true) are such possible claims as:

- Jesus is the true Messiah. It is not undisputed that there might be more than one Messiah.
- Jesus was resurrected. Though ELSs for "resurrected" and "raised" do appear within this passage, they are not so improbable as to statistically demonstrate this assertion.
- Jesus is the Son of God. Again, though ELSs that support this assertion appear within the passage, they are not so improbable as to statistically demonstrate this assertion.
- The entire Hebrew Bible was written by God. All we have shown *in this chapter* is that a two-page section of one book of the Hebrew Bible was written by an author who foreknew much of the life and death of Jesus.

In summary, what has been mathematically proven is this: it is an established fact that the author of Isaiah 53 knew at least a century in advance the key details of the life and death of Jesus. In other words, the occurrence of this miracle has been scientifically established.

Chapter Four

Using the Isaiah 53 Cluster to Answer Code Skeptics

There is no way the Isaiah 53 cluster could be the product of chance. In a word, this cluster is packed. It is packed with very long, highly improbable ELSs, most of which are clearly relevant to a single topic. That kind of thing cannot simply "happen." It must be intentionally embedded in the text. Furthermore, the large number of lengthy codes discovered to date were unearthed with a relatively small amount of searching.

Ever since Bible codes were first introduced to the world in the late 1990s, skeptics have been saying, "Oh, well, you can find codes like that in books like *War and Peace* and *Moby Dick*." In fact, skeptic Brendan McKay went so far as to collect a fairly impressive-looking cluster of codes about Hanukah from a Hebrew translation of *War and Peace*. His findings have been posted for some time on his web site (www.wopr.com/biblecodes/TheCase.htm).

The argument that you can find meaningful code clusters in books other than the Bible — and the presentation of the Hanukah cluster — has done much to reduce the credibility of Bible codes in the eyes of many. In the case of some codes presented in bestselling books, this was appropriate, because it would be misleading to attach significance to clusters that are comparable to the Hanukah example. For this contribution, Dr. McKay is owed a debt of gratitude. However, when the Hanukah example is used to dismiss the potential validity of all Bible codes, it is totally inappropriate and unfounded. The skeptics will never be able to come up with a counter-example that would begin to compare with the Isaiah 53 cluster, no matter how hard they try, because it doesn't exist. That will be made evident in this chapter.

Taking Length Into Account

Leading skeptics would have us believe that all purported codes are the product of chance. In order to do this, they have quietly pushed the idea that all ELSs are very likely to be coincidental. *The truth is that ELSs vary tremendously in their improbability.* Some ELSs are as common as crabgrass, while others are as rare as the Hope Diamond. Just throwing them all into the same basket, as skeptics would like us to do, is like parking your brains at the door as you consider whether or not Bible codes have any validity. In this chapter, some tools will be applied to take off the blinders and un-mask the truth about the reality of Bible codes.

The biggest factor affecting the improbability of a given ELS is its length, as we learned in chapter 2. The real question is, "Given a word or phrase that you are looking for as an ELS, how likely is it that you will be able to find it in any two-page-long section of Hebrew text?" Those odds are shown in table 4A.

Table 4A

Letters in ELS	Odds of Appearing by Chance in Any Two-Page-Long Section of Text
6 or Less	100%
7	1 in 5
8	1 in 77
9	1 in 1,475
10	1 in 28,850
11	1 in 572.800
12	1 in 11,476,500

Understanding and appreciating the above table is critical to grasping what separates coincidental examples of Bible codes from substantive examples. If you look for an ELS that is six or fewer letters long you are almost certain to find it in any two-page-long section of Hebrew text that you select. It doesn't matter what the text is. It could be the Jerusalem phone book, or it could even be a scrambled string of Hebrew letters. Seek and you shall find it. So if you want to engage in an exercise of wish fulfillment, just look for short words as ELSs, and you will almost certainly be able to compile a collection of them that looks like it could have some earth-shaking significance. Nonetheless, if you can do that with any varying string of Hebrew letters, all you are doing is fooling yourself and perhaps others as well.

Another key finding from table 4A is that if you want to search for something that is unlikely to be just a coincidence, the longer the ELS is that you are looking for, the better. If you look for a 10-letter-long ELS, the odds are about 1 in 28,850 that you will find it in any two-page-long section of Hebrew text that you pick. But if you look for a 12-letter-long ELS, the odds are about 1 in 11,500,000 that you will find it.

Why do the odds get worse and worse as the ELS you are searching for gets longer? It is because, as the number of letters increases, the number of alternative "phrases" that can be found (instead of what you are looking for) increases dramatically. Every letter that is added multiplies the number of alternatives by a factor greater than 20 — because there are 22 letters in the Hebrew alphabet.

Because of this, Dr. McKay was able to readily put together the Hanukah cluster as a counter-example — because all of its ELSs are quite short. If he had instead sought to find a cluster of lengthy ELSs from *War and Peace*, he would have had to work very hard and long to come up with anything of interest. Even then, most of his "codes" would most likely be classic examples of ELSs whose content was generally nonsensical. I doubt he would waste time trying to do this, because he is far too intelligent to believe that his findings will be at all impressive.

In this chapter, we will compare the Hanukah cluster with the Isaiah 53 cluster. The results, detailed in table 4B, reveal the complete irrelevance of the Hanukah cluster as a counter-example of what can be found in a non-encoded text. We will also see how utterly improbable the Isaiah 53 cluster is.

Table 4B

How They Compare		
Feature	Isaiah 53 Cluster	Hanukah Cluster
Total Number of ELSs in the Cluster	1,600+	7
Number of ELSs 7 or More Letters Long	61	1
Number of ELSs 15 or More Letters Long	27	0
Longest ELS	73 Letters	7 Letters
Length of Surface Text	1,584 Letters	1,123 Letters
Cluster Appearance	Dense	Sketchy
Relevance to Literal Text	Strong	None
Odds Against a Comparable Cluster Appearing	Less Than 1 in 2,189,000,000,000,000, 000,000,000,000,000,000,000, 000,000,000,000,000,000,000, 000,000,000,000,000,000,000, 000,000,000,000,000,000,000, 000,000,000,000,000,000,000, 000,000,000,000,000,000,000, 000,000,000,000,000,000,000, 000,000,000,000,000,000,000, 000,000,000,000	Less Than 1 in 5

A comparison of the sheer number of ELSs is only part of the story, and a potentially misleading one at that — as will be discussed further. What actually counts is the presence (or absence) of lengthy ELSs. While the Hanukah cluster includes one 7-letter-long ELS, the Isaiah 53 cluster includes 61 ELSs that are seven or more letters long. Of these 61 ELSs that have some improbability of occurrence, 27 of them are 15 or more letters long, making each one fairly unlikely.

And five of them are 30 or more letters long, indicating that each of these is extremely unlikely. The longest ELS in the Isaiah 53 cluster is 73 letters long, more than 10 times the length of the longest Hanukah cluster ELS.

The seven Hanukah ELSs appear within a 1,123-letter-long section of text, which is somewhat smaller than the 1,584-letter-long section that is crossed by all of the Isaiah 53 ELSs that are at least as significant as the Hanukah finds. So the two source texts are fairly comparable in size. In reality, most of the Isaiah 53 cluster is concentrated in the last half of the 1,584-letter-long section. Most of the ELSs cross this latter section of text, which is only 700 letters long.

Does the Hanukah example call into question the validity of all Bible codes? Anything but that. The Hanukah example looks like a tiny bump of sand next to the Isaiah 53 mountain. To appreciate this visually, suppose we display each of the Hanukah ELSs in separate vertical columns, so that it will look a bit like the skyline of the

Figure 4A

Figure 4B

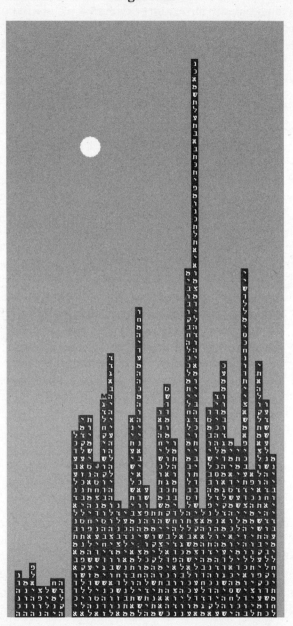

center of a small city, with each letter representing one story of a building. The Hanukah cluster would then look like what is presented in figure 4A.

Figure 4B is a comparison of the chance Hanukah skyline (lower left) with that of the Isaiah 53 cluster. The Isaiah 53 skyline is more like that of a Philadelphia or a Dallas. It towers over the Main Street, USA skyline of the Hanukah cluster, which is the best example of a cluster presented by code skeptics. Another side-by-side comparison of the two clusters in matrices shows a packed frame for the Isaiah 53 codes and a skimpy layout of the Hanukah cluster, with only 35 letters colored in. You can see these matrices in color at www.biblecodedigest.com/page.php/10. A black-and-white version of the Isaiah 53 matrix appears as figure 3A in this book.

The above comparisons should cause all skeptics to reconsider their views about the reality of Bible codes.

Comparing ELSs

There are seven ELSs in the Hanukah example. This compares with more than 1,600 ELSs, or 400+ distinct terms, about Christ from Isaiah 53. In other words, for every Hanukah ELS, we have found over 225 ELSs in Isaiah 53. In the last chapter and in appendix 4, we have provided a complete listing of the ELSs found in the Isaiah 53 cluster. Here are English translations of the ELSs in the Hanukah cluster.

God's miracle	Lighting
Hanukah candle	Menorah
Hashmani	Night
Hidden code	

The contrast between what can be gleaned from an encoded text like Isaiah 53 with a non-encoded text is astonishing. In table 4C, we have a listing of all the ELSs consisting of four or more letters that have been found in both texts, presented in descending length. In reviewing this table, bear in mind that the longer a code is, the more unlikely it is to be the result of chance, as table 4A indicates.

Table 4C

Isaiah 53 Codes — English Translation	Letters	Hanukah Code	Letters
If the friend of evil will thirst for the end of righteous purity, his home is an urn. Let Judas have his day. To me, the elevated one, they fasted. Where are you? Its content will be written from my mouth. Father, indeed you will raise the dead over there.	73		
If indeed all the detail of this one is a string, does Peter despise the burden of the extra ships, and does my throne rest? So spoke God's poor.	47		
Ascension, be a cause for my heart, and render my father transformed. I will be ashamed, and will divide the temple of the messenger.	39		
Being naïve and indirect, Jacob (James?) weakened, or will render him a true comic actor to her voice with me.	33		
Ascension, we will thank God, and they will be near my shelter. Recognize her blood.	30		
And command fleets of resurrection from above to flee with raging excitement.	26		
Ascension, monument of the saturated. And the hand of the monument is the daughter of the cedar supporter.	24		
And command that we skip everything but the gem of ascension.	22		
Gushing from above, Jesus is my mighty name, and the clouds rejoiced.	22		
There God will raise everything to the lion, God's witness being Matthew.	22		
From my fear of resurrection he made a monument, or the power of the mouth.	21		
I fought sickness in God's servant, and in God he slept.	21		
Her struggle is for them; God has graced them; Lord of Hosts.	20		
God is for them, and long live the exalted flame. God is Jesus.	19		
Obedience to God, even if for a day only, Peter.	19		
The ascension of Jesus: for the sleeping one will shout. Listen!	19		
God's miracle to us is appropriate for them in the temple.	18		
Hurry to pay heed about giving, for in it hearing will be given to you.	18		
And thirst for all of him is the faith of Mary the mother.	17		
He offended. The resurrection of Jesus. He is risen indeed.	17		
And in his name, as he commanded, Jesus is the way.	16		
Ascension, considering God's hands under me.	16		
Captain of the army of the Lord, carry the ark of sight.	16		
Long live the ascension coming from God.	16		
Shed light on ark of the covenant and fade away.	16		
Smile, I see Matthew there, let go!	15		
Who will it be that God's miracle will save?	15		
And where are they? The Sanhedrin is finished.	14		
Father, the ascension of Jesus is heavenly.	14		
Know who the chosen people are or God will be angry.	14		
My shepherds are among the disciples.	14		

Where is the defect of Thomas's projectile?	14		
From the joy of God my friend	13		
God will have his own day.	12		
The value of resurrection is thus dear.	12		
Greed, according to Matthew, was the rule.	11		
Jesus created a high gift.	11		
Jesus the gift is master and my Lord.	11		
The ascension of Jesus is the death of the witness.	11		
The rabbi from glory of God	11		
Wonder! Jesus is the truth.	11		
Evil Roman city	9		
It will be understood. Jesus created.	9		
Jesus created to the Father	9		
And treasure in it	8		
Deer of the Dawn	8		
His spirit on a tree	8		
Jesus is salvation.	8		
Mary is the mother of God.	8		
Son of Elohim	8		
Angel of the Lord — 1st Occurrence	7	God's miracle	7
Angel of the Lord — 2nd Occurrence	7		
Angel of the Lord — 3rd Occurrence	7		
Dreadful day for Mary	7		
It Is finished.	7		
Jesus (Yeshu), be judged.	7		
Jesus reigns.	7		
Piercers of my feet	7		
She weeps much.	7		
Shiloh is a guilt offering.	7		
True messiah	7		
Have hemmed me in	6	Hanu-kah candle	6
King of light	6		
Lamp of the Lord	6		
Matthew	6		
Second Adam	6		
Thirty	6		
Andrew	5	Hash-mani	5

Blasphemy (Insult)	5	Lighting	5
Bribe	5	Menorah	5
Carpentry	5		
Controversial — 1st Occurrence	5		
Controversial — 2nd Occurrence	5		
Fulfillment	5		
God has atoned.	5		
Humiliation	5		
Jewish	5		
John	5		
Last (Terminal, Final)	5		
Lazarus	5		
Meal	5		
Meal/Feast	5		
Only way	5		
Paul	5		
Simon	5		
Spitting	5		
The blessed	5		
Who is Jesus? Master.	5		
Wonderful	5		
(His) Cross	4	Hidden code	4
Deception	4	Night	4
Foundation	4		
Glorify	4		
Heaven	4		
Jesus	4		
Mary [Appears 16 times — Vs. 4.76 Expected by chance]	4		
My servant	4		
Prince	4		
Saul	4		
Savior	4		
Scoffer — 1st Occurrence	4		
Scoffer — 2nd Occurrence	4		
Sponge	4		
The vine	4		
Treasure	4		

90

In table 4C there are 50 ELSs from the Isaiah 53 cluster that are each longer than the longest ELS in the Hanukah cluster. Furthermore, ten of the Isaiah 53 ELSs are more than three times longer than the longest Hanukah ELS. And 27 of the Isaiah 53 ELSs are more than twice the length of the longest Hanukah ELS.

In table 4D there is a comparison of the three longest ELSs in each cluster, together with an estimate of the probability of the chance occurrence of each ELS.

Table 4D

Top Three Codes in Hebrew Text of Isaiah 53				Top Three Codes in Hebrew *War and Peace*			
Isaiah 53 Codes English Translation	Letters	Size of Skips	Odds of Appearing by Chance	Hanukah Code English Translation	Letters	Size of Skips	Odds of Appearance by Chance
If the friend of evil will thirst for the end of righteous purity, his home is an urn. Let Judas have his day. To me, the elevated one, they fasted. Where are you? Its content will be written from my mouth. Father, indeed you will raise the dead over there.	73	738	1 in 71.6 billion times 1 billion	God's Miracle	7	48	1 in 1
If indeed all the detail of this one is a string, does Peter despise the burden of the extra ships, and does my throne rest? So spoke God's poor.	47	148	1 in 1,120,750	Hanukah Candle	6	182	1 in 1
Ascension, be a cause for my heart, and render my father transformed. I will be ashamed, and will divide the temple of the messenger.	39	53	1 in 95,124	Lighting	5	4	1 in 1

The above odds are those of finding a code of comparable length. It fully reflects the existence of the large number of alternative ELSs that could have been found, and that would have been of comparable length and relevance to the topic as the code that *was* found.

What is immediately evident is that none of the Hanukah ELSs are unusual in any way. The bottom line is that there is a vast disparity between the two clusters. The skeptics will never be able to come up with an example cluster from a non-encoded book that would even begin to compare with the Isaiah 53 cluster, in terms of the length of its codes and the relevance of those codes to a single topic, because it simply doesn't exist.

What the odds in the table 4D represent are the chances that a Hebrew expert looking for extensions of an initial ELS would end up with a final ELS as long as the example code, given that they had only examined the letters before and after only one initial ELS. In such a case, the odds a Hebrew expert would end up with a final ELS consisting of one relevant or plausible extension are 1 in 8; 1 in 73 for two extensions, 1 in 755 for three extensions, and so forth.

An Unfair Comparison?

An astute skeptic would probably assert that the above comparison is not a fair one. After all, we conducted a far more extensive search for long ELSs in Isaiah 53 than did Dr. McKay in checking out the *War and Peace* text for potential codes. However, the purpose of the above comparison is to emphasize how inadequate Dr. McKay's example is as "proof" that Bible codes have no validity. His example carries absolutely no weight.

Nevertheless, there is a clear need to determine how extensive a cluster one would find if a non-encoded text had been searched as extensively as Isaiah 53. To establish this kind of benchmark, we "blindfolded" Dr. Jacobi and gave him a series of initial ELSs, together with the Hebrew letters that would appear before and after each initial ELS if it were part of a longer code. We looked for the names of Islamic nations within the book of Ezekiel and within a Hebrew translation of Tolstoy's novel *War and Peace*.

What we learned from this experiment (further described in chapter 6) was that there is about a 20% chance that a Hebrew expert will find a phrase consisting of intelligible Hebrew as an extension of a previously discovered existing ELS. We can use this finding, and a mathematical model described in appendix 5, to determine how many longer codes we would expect to find in Isaiah 53, given how many initial ELSs we have researched for extensions.

As of this writing, we have only examined 86 initial ELSs to see if each is part of a longer ELS consisting of reasonable Hebrew. Given that, and a 20% chance of finding an extension each time there is an opportunity to do so, we would expect to find nine final ELSs consisting of two or more extensions. In actuality, we found 41 such final ELSs — 4.6 times the benchmark. Against a benchmark of 2.34 final ELSs of three or more extensions, we found 15 — six times the benchmark. Against a benchmark of 0.6 final ELSs with four or more extensions, we found four — 6.9 times the benchmark. Table 4E summarizes these comparisons.

Table 4E

Number of Extensions	Expected	Actual	Ratio of Actual to Expected
0	55.0	31	0.6
1+	31.0	55	1.8
2+	8.9	41	4.6
3+	2.3	15	6.4
4+	0.58	4	6.9
5+	0.14	3	21.8
6+	0.032	2	62.7
7+	0.0073	1	137.6
8+	0.0016	1	613.8
9+	0.00036	1	2,769.6
10+	0.000079	1	12,617.1

Table 4F provides a comparison similar to that presented in table 4E — except that the results are shown separately according to each distinct number of extensions.

Table 4F

Number of Extensions	Expected	Actual
0	55.04	31
1	22.02	14
2	6.60	26
3	1.76	11
4	0.44	1
5	0.106	1
6	0.0247	1
7	0.0056	0
8	0.0013	0
9	0.00028	0
10	0.000062	1
11+	0.000016	0
	86.00000	86

A standard statistical procedure (chi-square) provides a method of estimating the probability of chance occurrence of actual differences with each benchmark expected number for all categories. It indicates that the odds of a cluster such as Isaiah 53 having as many (or more) long ELSs as is the case are less than 1 in 2,189,000,000,000,000,000,000,000,000,000,000,000,000,000, 000,000,000,000,000,000,000,000,000,000,000,000,000,000, 000,000,000,000,000,000,000,000,000,000,000,000,000,000, 000,000,000,000,000,000,000,000,000,000,000,000,000,000, 000,000,000,000,000, or 1 in 2,189 followed by 192 zeroes.

Can we appreciate how small the odds are in this case? Let's look at an illustration that will give it some perspective. Suppose you bought 33 lottery tickets, one at a time at the beginning of each of the past 33 months. The odds against your winning the one-in-a-million jackpot every one of the 33 times you played would be about as improbable as the number above. If you did win the jackpot five times in a row, the police would come and arrest you. The circumstantial evidence would be overwhelmingly conclusive. You had found a way to beat the system.

We believe the approach taken to calculate these odds fully addresses the objections skeptics have raised regarding the odds of chance occurrence of various Bible code examples that have been cited in different published books. They are the result of a relatively simple approach that nevertheless reflects the realities of the code extension review process. For the technical reader, this is described in the technical addendum to this chapter and in appendix 7.

What has emerged from the Isaiah 53 cluster has to be reflective of an extensive amount of intentional encoding. There is no other explanation. This is nothing short of compelling evidence of a miracle — since the text was certainly written at least a century before Jesus lived.

Presentation of Each Long Code as an Initial ELS and One or More Extensions

In examining each initial ELS for the possibility that it is part of a longer ELS, the starting point is the initial ELS itself. For example, we found the name Matthew, in Hebrew, as an ELS in Isaiah 53 with a skip of five between its successive letters. Next, every fifth letter before and after the Matthew ELS was recorded. This string of longer Hebrew letters, each five letters apart in the literal text, was examined by a Hebrew expert (Dr. Jacobi) to see if any intelligible phrases or sentences could be found within that extended string. In this example, three phrases were found as extensions of the initial ELS before Matthew, but nothing intelligible appeared after Matthew. So the final ELS is as follows, with the initial ELS being underlined and each extension shown in italics.

Extensions found before original search term	Original search term
There God will raise	
Everything to the lion	
God's witness being	Matthew

Table 4F previously provided a summary of the number of final ELSs consisting of different numbers of extensions, together with a comparison of the number of final ELSs expected to have a given number of extensions — if a non-encoded text had been searched. Next, each final ELS is presented in the same fashion as the extended Matthew code. These final codes have been grouped according to the total number of extensions — from the longest down to the shortest. For each category, a comparison of the benchmark number of coincidental final ELSs with the actual number is also shown.

In reviewing these codes, it is intriguing to consider the degree of potential relevance of each code to the topic of Jesus Christ. There is much that is obviously relevant, and very little that is nonsensical. In appendix 3, commentary is provided on the potential relevance of parts of these long ELSs to the topic of Jesus Christ.

Ten Extensions
[Expected with 7+ Extensions: 0.0073; Actual: 1]

Extensions found before original term	Original term	Extensions found after original term
If the friend of evil will thirst		
For the end of righteous purity		
His home is an urn		
Let...		
	Judas	*Have his day*
		To me the elevated one they fasted
		Where are you
		Its content will be written
		From my mouth. Father
		Indeed you will
		Raise the dead over there

Six Extensions [Expected: 0.0247; Actual: 1]

Extensions before	Original term	Extensions after
If indeed all the detail		
Of this one is a string		
Does	Peter	*Despise*
		The burden of the extra ships
		And does my throne rest?
		So spoke God's poor

Five Extensions [Expected: 0.106; Actual: 1]

Original term	Extensions after
Ascension	*Be a cause for my heart*
	And render my father transformed
	I will be ashamed
	And will divide
	The temple of the messenger

Four Extensions [Expected: 0.44; Actual: 1]

Extension before	Original term	Extensions after
Being naïve and indirect	Jacob (James?)	*Weakened, or*
		Will render him a true comic actor
		To her voice with me

<u>Three Extensions</u> [Expected: 1.76; Actual: 11]

1.

Extension before	Original term	Extensions after
And command fleets of	<u>Resurrection</u>	*From above to flee*
		With raging excitement

2.

Extensions before	Original term
And command that	
We skip everything but	
The gem of	<u>Ascension</u>

3.

Original term	Extensions after
<u>Ascension</u>	*Monument of the saturated*
	And the hand of the monument
	Is the daughter of the cedar supporter

4.

Original term	Extensions after
<u>Ascension</u>	*We will thank God*
	And they will be near my shelter
	Recognize her blood

5.

Original term	Extensions after
God's miracle	*To us*
	Is appropriate for them
	In the temple

6.

Extension before	Original term	Extensions after
From my fear of	Resurrection	*He made a monument*
		Or the power of the mouth

7.

Extension before	Original term	Extension after
Gushing from above	Jesus is my mighty name	*and the clouds rejoiced*

8.

Extensions
Hurry to pay heed about giving
For in it hearing
Will be given to you
[Started with Gospel, but this word could not be used in the longest ELS that made sense.]

9.

Extensions
I fought sickness
In God's servant
And in God he slept
[Started with <u>Matthew</u>, but this word could not be used in the longest ELS that made sense.]

10.

Extensions before	Original term
There God will raise	
Everything to the lion	
God's witness being	<u>Matthew</u>

11.

Extension before	Original term	Extension after
We will advise the dove		
He will place in me the	<u>Multitude of Gog</u>	*You will be weakened*

Two Extensions [Expected: 6.60; Actual: 26]

1.

Extension before	Original term	Extension after
And brother of the	<u>Gospel</u>	*Where has the manna spread?*

101

2.

Extensions before	Original term
And in his name	
As he commanded	Jesus is the way

3.

Extensions before	Original term
And thirst for all of him	
Is the faith of	Mary the mother

4.

Extension before	Original term	Extension after
And where are they? The	Sanhedrin	*Is finished*

5.

Original term	Extensions after
Ascension	*Considering God's hands*
	Under me

6.

Extension before	Original term	Extension after
Come as my fire from my cell	Kidron	*Is my life*

7.

Original term	Extensions after
Father	*The ascension of Jesus*
	Is heavenly

8.

Extension before	Original term	Extension after
From the	Joy of God	*My friend*

9.

Extension before	Original term	Extension after
Give them a	Jewish messiah	*Who will become a priest*

10.

Extensions before	Original term
God is for them	
And long live the exalted flame	God is Jesus

11.

Extension before	Original term	Extension after
Greed	According to Matthew	*Was the rule*

12.

Extension before	Original term	Extension after
He offended	The resurrection of Jesus	*He is risen indeed*

13.

Extensions before	Original term
Her struggle is for them *God has graced them*	Lord of Hosts

14.

Extensions before	Original term
And in his name *As he commanded*	Jesus is the way

15.

Original term	Extensions after
Jesus the gift	*Is master* *And my Lord*

16.

Original term	Extensions after
Kidron	*Calmed down* *And went*

17.

Extension before	Original term	Extension after
Know who the	*Chosen people*	*Are or God will be angry*

18.

Extension before	Original term	Extension after
Long live the	Ascension	*Coming from God*

19.

Extensions
My bride is dead
Let all the sweetness in me come forth
[Started with Came forth sweetness from the riddle of Samson in Judges 14:14]

20.

Extensions before	Original term
Obedience to God	
Even if for a day only	Peter

21.

Extension before	Original term	Extension after
Shed light on the	Ark of the covenant	*And fade away*

22.

Extension before	Original term	Extension after
Smile, I see	Matthew	*There. Let go!*

23.

Original term	Extensions after
The ascension of Jesus	*For the sleeping one will shout*
	Listen!

24.

Extension before	Original term	Extension after
The value of	Resurrection	*Is thus dear*

25.

Extension before	Original term	Extension after
Where is the defect of	Thomas's	*Projectile?*

26.

Extension before	Original term	Extension after
Who will it be that	God's miracle	*Will save?*

One Extension [Expected: 22.02; Actual: 14]

1.

Extension before	Original term
Bemoan the prince	Jesus the king

2.

Original term	Extension after
Captain of the army of the Lord	*Carry the ark of sight*

3.

Extension before	Original term
Dreadful day for	Mary

4.

Extension before	Original term
Evil	Roman city

5.

Original term	Extension after
God will have	*His own day*

6.

Extension before	Original term
It will be understood	Jesus created

7.

Original term	Extension after
Jesus created	*A high gift*

8.

Original term	Extension after
Jesus created	*To the father*

9.

Extension before	Original term
My shepherds are among	The disciples

10.

Original term	Extension after
The ascension of Jesus	*Is the death of the witness*

11.

Original term	Extension after
The man and the God	*Alive*

12.

Extension before	Original term
The rabbi from the	Glory of God

13.

Original term	Extension after
Who is Jesus?	*Master*

14.

Extension before	Original term
Wonder!	Jesus is the truth

True Odds Even More Impossible

Even though the odds we have calculated against a chance occurrence of a cluster as extensive as Isaiah 53 are unbelievably small, there are compelling reasons to believe that the actual odds are far smaller yet. In determining the benchmark numbers, we assumed there was a 20% chance that an extension would be found with each opportunity to do so. However, that was for ELSs that met only the minimal standard — that is that they consist of reasonable Hebrew. The chances of an extension consisting of reasonable Hebrew, and that is also topically relevant, are much smaller. This is also true, to a lesser degree, for extensions with plausible content. In the last chapter, we noted that a surprisingly high percentage of final ELSs in Isaiah 53 were either relevant or plausible in content. *If this had been reflected in the above estimate of odds of chance occurrence, rather than being ultra-conservative to avoid criticism by skeptics, the odds would have been vastly more remote.*

The chances of finding an extension that is also relevant to the topic of the literal text must clearly be something quite a bit less than 20%. But how much less is arguably subject to a fair amount of uncertainty — if only because of the subjective assessments that go into deciding whether a phrase is relevant.

To get a handle on this, we took the extensions from the Islamic Nations Experiment (described in chapter 6) and categorized them according to the same scheme as was used in chapter 3 (i.e., relevant, plausible and mysterious). Table 4G, which presents these results, and a comparison with the comparable tally from Isaiah 53, is repeated below, after excluding two plausible codes that originated from the examination of initial ELSs from another code cluster.

Table 4G [1]

Category	%-age From *War and Peace*	Expected From Non-Encoded Text	Number in Isaiah 53	%-age From Isaiah 53
Relevant	4.2%	2	41	74.5%
Plausible	33.3%	19	7	12.7%
Mysterious	62.5%	36	7	12.7%

If the Isaiah 53 cluster were the product of chance, we would expect to find only two long ELSs that were relevant in content. In actuality, we found 41. If it were chance, we would expect 36 final ELSs that were mysterious in content. Instead, we found only seven. Such a radical departure from what should emerge from examination of a non-encoded text is very compelling evidence of intentional encoding.

In appendix 6, we concluded that the chances of finding an extension of an initial ELS that is relevant in content is only 2%

(versus 20% for finding an extension that merely consists of reasonable Hebrew, regardless of its seeming relevance or lack thereof). If we start with this 2% assumption, and apply it to the entire group of 73 codes that were categorized as relevant, we would not expect to have many final ELSs that were of any length. Table 4H provides a comparison of how these final ELSs would end up in different extension categories.

Table 4H

Extensions	Expected	Actual
0	70.1	32
1	2.8	14
2	0.08	20
3	0.002	6
4	0.0001	0
5	0.000001	0
6	0.00000003	0
7+	0.000000001	1

What table 4H is saying is that we should not expect to find any final ELSs with two or more extensions whose content is relevant to the topic of Jesus Christ. Yes, there is some small chance that we might find one or two such longer ELSs if Isaiah 53 were a non-encoded text. But it is truly mathematically impossible for 27 final ELSs to be relevant in content. Table 4H indicates there were 27 such ELSs — 20 with two extensions, plus six with three extensions, plus one with 11 extensions.

The chi-square probability of chance occurrence of the very large number of relevant long ELSs in Isaiah 53 is so small that the spreadsheet program Microsoft Excel cannot compute it. Excel cannot compute probabilities that are less than 1 in 1 followed by 308 zeroes. Although we used the 2% probability of finding a relevant extension in the above compilation, any probability up to 14.8% that we could have used would have resulted in a probability of chance occurrence so remote that Excel could not compute it. And we could use any probability up to 30.5% before the probability of chance occurrence would be greater than 0.1%. So even if it turned out that we were a bit inaccurate in deriving the 2% assumption, the conclusion remains the same: *the Isaiah 53 cluster must include a substantial amount of intentional encoding*.

We can go through the same exercise with ELS extensions that are either relevant or plausible. That gives us the following comparison:

Table 4I

Extensions	Expected	Actual
0	64.8	32
1	13.0	14
2	1.94	22
3	0.259	9
4	0.032	0
5	0.00389	1
6	0.000454	1
7+	0.000058	1

According to the data in table 4I, we should not expect to find more than two or three final ELSs in the cluster with two or more extensions whose content is plausible or relevant to the topic of Jesus Christ. Yes, there is some small chance that we might find three or four or five such longer ELSs if Isaiah 53 was a non-encoded text. But it is truly impossible for 34 final ELSs to be relevant in content.

Again, the chi-square probability of chance occurrence of the great number of long ELSs in Isaiah 53, ELSs that are either relevant or plausible is so small that Excel cannot compute it. Although we used the 10% probability of finding a plausible or relevant extension in the above compilation, any probability up to 15.1% that we could have used would have resulted in a probability of chance occurrence so remote that Excel could not compute it. And we could have used any probability up to 32.6% before the probability of chance occurrence would be greater than 0.1%. So even if we are somewhat inaccurate in deriving the 10% assumption, the conclusion remains the same: the Isaiah 53 cluster must include a substantial amount of intentional encoding.

So we see that if the increased unlikelihoods of finding extensions that are either relevant or plausible are factored in to the probability calculations, the indicated odds are impossibly remote. So it is evident that the Isaiah 53 cluster cannot be explained by chance. We are left to conclude that whoever composed this passage of the Old Testament included these anomalies purposely. To do so, the author had to possess an intelligence far beyond the capabilities of any computer or grouping of computers ever made. Not only that, but because of the length of some of the ELSs in this cluster that reach backward and forward into many other books of the Old Testament, it has to be assumed that this intelligence composed the whole of which this cluster is just a small part.

I believe that the being who created this cluster and the rest of the Old Testament is God. I do not see how there can be any other reasonable explanation for these phenomena.

Dealing With "Wiggle Room"

As we have seen, the odds of finding a cluster similar to the Isaiah 53 example are so astronomically remote as to rule out chance as a rational explanation. That this is so will motivate skeptics to immediately suspect that these odds have not been adjusted for "wiggle room." However, that has been fully factored into our calculations. And we painstakingly recorded all initial ELSs that we searched and noted those where no extension was found. Yes, there is subjectivity involved in deciding what initial ELSs to examine for extensions, but once one was selected, the results were accurately recorded.

Any method of estimating the odds of these configurations happening by chance is bound to be very complicated. That makes it easy for an opposing expert to claim that we should have done our calculations a bit differently than we have. After all, how is the average man on the street going to decide which expert is right?

The reality is that the simple dictates of common sense also lead to the same conclusion — the Isaiah 53 cluster is far too dense and extensive to be explained by chance. Finding a few long ELSs that seem to make sense is one thing, and could be chalked up to happenstance. But that is not the case when a large number of long ELSs quite plausible or relevant to a single topic crosses a short section of the Hebrew Bible.

Proof That Bible Codes Are Real

Given our demonstration that a large number of codes about Jesus of Nazareth were intentionally embedded within the Hebrew text of Isaiah 52-53, what is the bottom line?

First, the Dead Sea Scrolls include virtually complete copies of the book of Isaiah that date back at least a century before Jesus lived. Thus, this cluster evidence shows that the author of Isaiah 53 had prior knowledge of the life of Christ at least 100 years before He was born. According to tradition, and to the literal text, the Book of Isaiah was written by that prophet seven centuries before the birth of Jesus. If that is true, the prior knowledge of its author should be viewed as being even more far reaching.

In either case, what we have here is proof that the Bible codes are real.

Second, the literal text of Isaiah 53 describes a suffering servant who would be humiliated and executed as a "guilt offering" for the wrongdoings of others. The intentional placement of hundreds of codes about Jesus of Nazareth in the heart of this text is compelling evidence that He was the one prophesied in the literal text — or at least that some day this would be a widely held belief. That the latter is true is indisputable.

Whether the suffering servant described in Isaiah 53 was or was not the messiah is a matter Jewish and Christian scholars have hotly debated for centuries. We leave that question to the reader to decide.

Third, this cluster is compelling evidence that significant encoded material exists in the Hebrew Scriptures outside the Torah. This conflicts with the belief of orthodox Jewish code researchers that only the first five books of the Bible are encoded. However, the evidence is exceptionally extensive and substantive.

At the outset of this report, we commented that the mere appearance of the ELS "true messiah" in this cluster is not, *per se*, proof of that belief but is only a phrase relevant to the topic of Jesus, because it is well known that some people hold to that belief. The odds are about 1 in 12 that the "true messiah" ELS could appear in the Isaiah 53 cluster simply by chance.

One aspect of the "true messiah" ELS that makes it more intriguing is that it is only two letters away from the "My name is Yeshua" portion of the 22-letter focal code. In contrast, no "false messiah" ELSs with skips of any size (including those up to a maximum skip of 199,486) appear anywhere in the vicinity of Isaiah 53.

It is entirely possible that subsequent discovery and mathematical analysis will provide an ELS that is so improbable that it could be regarded as both intentional and unambiguous in its message. Such an example might include a definitive doctrinal statement. For instance, some day someone may find an incredibly long ELS with a message saying something like, "Let there be no doubt, such and such is absolutely true — no ifs, ands or buts."

It would be hard to dismiss such an extremely improbable code as mere coincidence.

Chapter Five

The Overwhelming Ezekiel 37 Cluster

As difficult as it is for our finite minds to process, the enormous Ezekiel 37 cluster provides very strong proof that there is no possible way that the Bible could have been conceived and inspired by humans. Certainly Moses, David, Isaiah and the rest of the Old Testament prophets put the words on papyrus, but their inspiration was unquestionably divine.

There is a scripture near the middle of the Old Testament that reads, "The mind of man plans his way, but God directs his steps" (Proverbs 16:9). To paraphrase this scripture in the case of the Hebrew Bible, "The minds of the prophets thought of the words to write, but God put them in their minds to begin with."

The book of Ezekiel was written about 26 centuries before the events of 9/11. Only God could have foreseen them and composed codes using the letters of not only Ezekiel, but in the case of longer skip ELSs, the letters of much of the entire Hebrew Old Testament, as we now have it, to reflect events in 2001 and beyond.

"As we now have it" is an important phrase, because there are those who say that codes are not possible in the text of the 21st century A.D. (or C.E. — Common Era, as Jewish scholars express it). Their contention is that too many changes have occurred to the text — what with copying errors and minor corrections to letters of earlier manuscripts — for it to be a reliable source.

While this is certainly possible, alternative views are also feasible. If God was able to transmit an encoded text to various prophets and scribes in ancient Israel, could not that same God guide the medieval rabbis who finalized the Masoretic text that is used today for code searches? Now there are a few different versions of that text, but who is to say but what one of them might be the one God intended for contemporary code researchers to examine?

By the same token, God also knew exactly what texts — warts and all, as they say — that we would be using for computer searches in the late twentieth and early twenty-first centuries, and encoded not the early texts, but these more recent versions with the ELSs researchers are finding.

Possible Involvement of Saddam

Undoubtedly, the next most significant aspect of the "terrorism" cluster we discovered in Ezekiel 37 was the implied role of Saddam Hussein in the events of 9/11. Hours after the horrible attacks, we searched for and located two Saddam Hussein ELSs in the Tanakh — not surprising with a seven-letter term. One of them sliced through Ezekiel 37. That was one of our first tip-offs that there was something significant going on in that portion of the Old Testament. The other appeared in 1 and 2 Samuel, a trail we have not yet explored.

Even more extensive than the Isaiah 53 cluster, the Ezekiel 37 cluster has become the most prodigious ever discovered. But that was not immediately apparent. For the first few hours after the terrorist attacks of September 11, 2001, we were in shock like everyone else in the free world. And like most other Americans, our concentration was interrupted all day long by the chilling news reports we were hearing on radio and television. The horrific impact of what had happened was so unreal that it never even occurred to us to consider the possibility that the attacks might be encoded in the Bible. But within hours of the disaster, we began receiving queries from visitors to the web site wondering if Bible codes said anything about what had happened.

By next morning, the first of what would become thousands of people had registered on our site requesting more notification. We dropped everything and focused our attention on looking for what came to be called the 9/11 codes.

Our first move was to e-mail Dr. Nathan Jacobi asking for Hebrew spellings of key words related to the attack. As an investment manager, Nathan is not normally available to work with us in the morning hours. But because the stock market was closed due to the suspension of trading, he immediately turned to the Ha'aretz website for some of the obvious contemporary terms. Ha'aretz is an Israeli newspaper that publishes online editions in both Hebrew and English.

Codes Begin to Emerge

Before 10:00 a.m., he had e-mailed us the Hebrew spellings for "plane hijackers" and "New York." A short time later, he sent us the Ha'aretz spellings of "Osama bin Laden," "World Trade Center," "Pentagon," "9/11/01," "Twin Towers," "Intelligence Failure," and "Islamic Terror." We ran searches for all of these mostly lengthy terms early Wednesday. Except for "Pentagon," we found nothing at all.

One of our first attempts to create a term on our own for which to search created a mistake, a misspelled ELS. We had used the wrong Hebrew words for the term. We wanted to look for "terrorist attack," but we actually used a term that was more accurately translated "attack the bully." We interpreted this unintentional discovery as a possible attitude of terrorists justifying a strike on the U.S. It turned out to be our second code find in Ezekiel 37.

By late morning, we had also found the two Saddam Hussein ELSs — one with a skip of -10,142 in 1 and 2 Samuel, and the other with a very long skip that touched down in Ezekiel 37. These were the full, seven-letter names for the dictator. By afternoon, we were also getting results with "airliner," "King of Babylon," "terror," "jihad," "bin Laden," and "Al Qaeda." These findings gave us four possible areas in the Tanakh to pursue. They were centered in the books of Daniel, Nehemiah, 1 and 2 Samuel and Ezekiel. Even though we were still reeling from the terrible destruction that we were seeing on the news, it was exciting to be on the trail of a fascinating and immediately relevant new cluster of codes.

Ezekiel 37 Becomes the Cluster to Zero in On

There were seven or eight codes in each of the five books of the Bible we were researching. But as we charted them, it appeared that there were enough ELSs around Ezekiel 37 to make us think that this was the cluster to focus on. Not only was there an impressive number of potential 9/11 ELSs that seemed to be close together, but the surface theme of the chapter was dramatically related to the nation of Israel. It is the well-known prophecy about the dry bones that rise up, reattach themselves, and come back to life.

Most Bible scholars believe it is a prophecy that was fulfilled with the 1948 creation of the nation of Israel. There is little question that U.S. support for Israel is the main reason for the terrorist attacks, so the location of the cluster seemed astonishingly relevant. Here is how the focal passage reads in English:

> The hand of the Lord was upon me, and he brought me out by the Spirit of the Lord and set me in the middle of a valley; it was full of bones. He led me back and forth among them, and I saw a great many bones on the floor of the valley, bones that were very dry.
>
> He asked me, "Son of man, can these bones live?"
>
> I said, "O Sovereign Lord, you alone know."
>
> Then he said to me, "Prophesy to these bones and say to them, 'Dry bones, hear the word of the Lord! This is what the Sovereign Lord says to these bones: I will make breath enter you, and you will come to life. I will attach tendons to you and make flesh come upon you and cover you with skin; I will put breath in you, and you will come to life. Then you will know that I am the Lord.' "
>
> So I prophesied as I was commanded. And as I was prophesying, there was a noise, a rattling sound, and the bones came together, bone to bone. I looked, and tendons and flesh appeared on them and skin covered them, but there was no breath in them.
>
> Then he said to me, "Prophesy to the breath; prophesy, son of man, and say to it, 'This is what the Sovereign Lord says: Come from the four winds, O breath, and breathe into these slain, that they may live.' " So I prophesied as he commanded

me, and breath entered them; they came to life and stood up on their feet — a vast army.

Then he said to me: "Son of man, these bones are the whole house of Israel. They say, 'Our bones are dried up and our hope is gone; we are cut off.'

Therefore prophesy and say to them: 'This is what the Sovereign Lord says: O my people, I am going to open your graves and bring you up from them; I will bring you back to the land of Israel. Then you, my people, will know that I am the Lord, when I open your graves and bring you up from them. I will put my Spirit in you and you will live, and I will settle you in your own land. Then you will know that I the Lord have spoken, and I have done it, declares the Lord.' " (Ezekiel 37:1-14)

By early afternoon on Thursday, we were able to send ELSs from this portion of text for "terror," "bin Laden," "airliner," and the one-word term "Saddam" to Nathan, along with a string of letters leading into and out of each code. By the next morning, he had extended some of the short ELSs running through Ezekiel 37 by translating the Hebrew and determining the best English expressions for the longer codes. Others he was not able to extend.

One of the "bin Laden" ELSs he was able to lengthen from its original six letters to a 19-letter code that read, "Bin Laden, the innocent is moaning, he is gross with the blood of the poor." This seemed to be a sad but appropriate fit with the emerging cluster. It appeared to be addressed to the terrorist, telling him that his victims were moaning and that he, bin Laden, was gross with their blood. Of course, there is always the possibility that the code is saying that bin Laden is bloody because of other victims, such as those at the embassy bombings in Africa. Perhaps some day we will know which of these meanings was intended, or it is possible that this code refers generally to all of bin Laden's planned acts of terrorism.

Enough Evidence

By 9:00 a.m. Friday morning, a little more than 72 hours after the attack, we decided that we had enough evidence to show that there was definitely a statistically significant cluster in Ezekiel 37 about the events, and that it was worth posting on our site. We began by compiling all of the information into a table. Normally, we would first enter all of our findings into an Excel spreadsheet so that we would be able to evaluate them individually and collectively according to the probabilities of their appearing by chance. In this case, however, our experience told us that the precise computations could wait until later. Even without analysis, this was obviously a statistically significant cluster of codes.

It was evident that the connection between the code cluster and the surface text was that of the terrorist acts of 9/11 and the nation of Israel. Two major symbols of U.S. power, the World Trade Center and the Pentagon, were successfully hit by Islamic forces because of American support of Israel. This was a monumental discovery of an insight given by God through an astonishing orchestration of events across 2,600 years of time. Of course, since God exists outside of time it is not a big deal for Him. As for us, we felt like Galileo might have upon his first view of Saturn through a telescope.

At about 1:00 p.m., we met for lunch with Nathan to take one more look for long ELSs before we posted our findings on the web site. In those days, we did our "snooping," or checking of shorter ELSs for possible extensions, over lunch a couple of times a week. During the summer, it is usually hot in southern Oregon, and it became a standing joke among us that when we wore shorts to our lunch meetings we would find more long codes. This day, two of us wore shorts and one of us had on long pants.

Our work that day focused on the word terror, which in Hebrew is a transliteration of the English word (טרור). The first extension we found was "Terror hot in me." Over the next hour or so, we eliminated quite a few possibilities as not extendable, but we also found "Terror of the sea is in them," "Place the gift of terror," and last but not least, "Where are they? And let God not strike terror." This one later emerged as a likely focal code of the cluster with its 21 letters and very short skip of −37.

A Major Cluster

After an hour, with the new long ELSs and the codes we had discovered earlier, we felt we had sufficient information on a major cluster to make a report to subscribers about our findings. We headed back to the office and plugged the new findings into our report. By 5:30 p.m., we had it up on the web site and had sent out an e-mail to subscribers about the posting.

The next day, we again met with Nathan over lunch and worked on a new group of World Trade Center and Saddam Hussein ELSs. We went through a dozen of them without finding any extension possibilities, and we were beginning to think that the day was going to be a disappointment. Some days we found a lot of new, long ELSs, some days we found very few.

But then, we suddenly came across the "Imagine a picture of terminal illness. The days of Saddam are over" code. That discovery woke us up. A few minutes later came "The rest of my severe illness is spreading, Saddam, like a missile to you, Esau. Where is he? Or, who is the tyrant?" (The next day, Nathan revised his translation of this to "The rest of my severe illness is spreading, Saddam, as if from a missile made for you. Where is he? Or, who is the tyrant?"). Fifteen minutes later we found the "Saddam, terminal illness from everything" ELS. Finding all three was like having panned unsuccessfully for gold all day, and then suddenly looking down into our pan to see three golf-ball-sized nuggets.

What is unusual about these three ELSs is that they all use the same word for terminal illness, the Hebrew "da'vai" (דוי). To find three ELSs on one subject in one session, all using the same word, is unheard of. We were nearly dumbstruck by it. Later that day, when we ran the full ELSs through the search software and found that they all appeared within 54 letters of each other, and that the seven-letter ELS with Saddam Hussein's full name touched down in the same area, we suspected that this was almost certainly the result of intentional encoding.

Two days later, on the ninth day after the attacks, we posted the news of our latest discoveries on the site. Over the next weeks and months, as the war on terror was announced and got underway, we continued our research into this amazing cluster. It eventually yielded a stunning code that accurately foretold the outcome of the war in Iraq some 15 months before it began.

> You will crush the guilty Saddam
> and the month of Iyar will be restful.

(סאדם אשם תהממי ואייר נח)

We found this code in December of 2001 and posted it on our web site within days — long before there was serious discussion about an incursion into Iraq. But its message made perfect sense to us when grouped with all of the Saddam Hussein codes we had found along with so many terrorism ELSs in the cluster. As it turned out, coalition forces did crush the Saddam Hussein government, and the month of Iyar (within the month of May in 2003) was restful. In June, of course, insurgent sneak attacks began to undo the restful atmosphere for occupying forces in Iraq. This code is not the only case we have seen of an ELS issuing a declaration about the outcome of a future event that was borne out by subsequent actions.

One such code is legendary among code researchers. Jeffrey Satinover's book, *Cracking the Bible Code*, told an unverified story about the use of Bible codes by the Mossad, Israel's intelligence agency, to foretell future events. This instance also involved Saddam Hussein. During the first Gulf War in 1991, the Mossad knew that Iraq planned to fire Scud missiles at Israel. But the Israeli government couldn't very well order citizens and tourists into bomb shelters for days on end. Such an action would cripple the nation's economy. The Mossad needed to know *exactly* when the Scud attacks would come.

Satinover states that he has seen a document noting that the date that the first scuds were launched and fell on Israel was found before the war started. He further notes that the contents were confirmed in an audiotaped interview with one of the principal individuals involved.[1]

The Mossad is not talking and probably never will, but rumors persist that they had the help of Israeli Bible code researchers in determining the date. They may be keeping this intelligence under wraps in case they have to use it again. We may never know for sure.

We will cover the question of whether the future can be accurately foretold with codes in topic A.

61-Letter Code

This awesome cluster also yielded a 61-letter code that was based on the name of an al Qaeda leader, Abu Zubaydah, captured in Pakistan on April 1, 2002.

There is quarrel in his speeches. A living brother uttered words to them and to me. And Zubaydah turned to his sea, without then lying for a whole week. Oh, the mountain of her interior will bear a testimonial to her name.

ריב מדבוריו לם לי מלל אח שחי ולימו זובידה בלי אז בד
זה שבוע אה הר תוכה יעיד שמה

The odds against ending up with an extended ELS as long as this one are less than 1 in 4,415 trillion each time an initial ELS is examined for extensions.

Very long codes came of age in our research during the weeks following the 9/11 disaster. As pressure increased to find out whether longer codes carried important messages, it became necessary to discontinue our casual code extension lunches and work out a more efficient way of attempting to extend one or two word codes. So we began working by e-mail, exchanging word processed attachments with a basic ELS. Each ELS had a dozen or more Hebrew letters before and after it for Nathan to check for extensions.

A few days after Abu Zubaydah was captured, we e-mailed Nathan for a Hebrew spelling of the terrorist's name. When he sent it back, we ran a search on the word in the Old Testament and found one occurrence running through the Ezekiel cluster with a skip of

-4,008. Using a matrix report on the find, we copied the letters before and after it to an extension sheet and e-mailed it to Nathan. The
basic information on the sheet looked like this:

למלימללאחשחיולימו
-- זובידה --
בליאזבדזהשבועאההר

That evening, Nathan found that there were indeed meaningful
words in front of the word Zubaydah. He sent the following information to us:

A live brother uttered words to them and to me, and
Zubaydah turned to his sea (23 letters). More letters at the start?

למ לי מלל אח שחי ולימו
-- זובידה
בליאזבדזהשבועאההר

Over the next week, we went back and forth several times, send-
ing more letters as Nathan requested them, and getting clarification
on the terms where necessary, until we received a final translation of
the stunning 61-letter code. Our last step was to check the whole
term by using our search software to make sure that it was correct.
This meant that we had to run three separate searches, because the
program we use can only search for one 30-letter term at a time. (Its
manufacturer surely thought at the time that no one would ever be
finding codes in the Bible more than 30 letters long.)

As we began to refine our research techniques, more long codes
resulted. The messages some of these ELSs contained were enigmatic in the extreme, while others were easily understood. Some
were apparently conversations between multiple voices. Others
seemed to be questions that went unanswered. Or, we wondered,
could there be ELSs crossing these questions, or otherwise con-
nected to them, that might contain the answers? It was at times like

these that we wished for the resources to be able to have 20 dedicated researchers working with us.

These are the longest codes in the cluster, with the English translation followed by the Hebrew:

There is quarrel in his speeches. A living brother uttered words to them and to me. And Zubaydah turned to his sea, without then lying for a whole week. Oh, the mountain of her interior will bear a testimonial to her name. *Skip 4,008*

ריב מדבוריו לם לי מלל אח שחי ולימו
זובידה בלי אז בד זה שבוע אה הר
חורה זעזד זזוזה

The trouble of the newborn one is vigilant and honest because of the ruin. Get out as if Iraq had been sent out. The majority is aware that, rest in peace, you will come — the villainy with light. You will understand the heart of granite. *Skip 194*

תמ מכת ער ולד בתל צא כשוגר עירק
רוב מודע עה תבוא הנכל לנר תבן לב שכם

The island was restful, elevated, and it happened. Where is Libya? And you have disrupted the nation. She changed a word, he answered them with combat. Why the navy and the smell of the bottom of the sea? *Skip 1,151*

האי נח רמ וקרה לוב אי וג וי תפר המירה
תבה יענן לחימה למה צי ותוהו ריח

For where has God consumed from you? And in it are stones of substantial sickness for us. You will indeed delay their diagnosis, because of his own reflection in the one who solves. *Skip 237*

כי יי אי עכל מכם ובו לן אבני חלי אמת
הרי אמדנם תשהי בשלו דמות בפותר

The Ezekiel 37 cluster continues to grow, but by six months after 9/11, we had compiled most of the terms you see in table 5A. Because of their length, they are the most significant of the 450 or so terms in the cluster.

Table 5A

Main ELSs in Ezekiel 37 Cluster		
ELS in English	**ELS in Hebrew**	**Skip Between Ltrs.**
There is quarrel in his speeches. A living brother uttered words to them and to me. And Zubaydah turned to his sea, without then lying for a whole week. Oh, the mountain of her interior will bear a testimonial to her name.	ריב מדבוריו לם לי מלל אח שחי ולימו זובידה בלי אז בד זה שבוע אה הר תוכה יעיד שמה	4,008
The trouble of the newborn one is vigilant and honest because of the ruin. Get out as if Iraq had been sent out. The majority is aware that, rest in peace, you will come — the villainy with light. You will understand the heart of granite.	תמ מכת ער ולד בתל צא כשוגר עירק רוב מודע עה תבוא הנכל לנר תבן לב שכם	194
The island was restful, elevated, and it happened. Where is Libya? And you have disrupted the nation. She changed a word, he answered them with combat. Why the navy and the smell of the bottom of the sea?	האי נח רם וקרה לוב אי וג וי תפר המירה תבה יענן לחימה למה צי ותוהו ריח	1,151
For where has God consumed from you? And in it are stones of substantial sickness for us. You will indeed delay their diagnosis, because of his own reflection in the one who solves.	כי יי אי עכל מכם ובו לן אבני חלי אמת הרי אמדנם תשהי בשלו דמות בפותר	237

Let the oppressed be congratulated, saturated from him at 2001. And let them be guarded by the echo of the father's son, supported by the U.S. I will see but he has the knowledge.	יבושר רש רווה תשסא ממנו וישמרן הד בן אב תמכה ארהב ארא ולו ידע	1,804
Imprison your burden there, to immerse her distinct feature, and in my waters to anthrax, king of all. Embrace it in the sea.	עולך כלא שם שבלתה לטבל ובמימי לגחלית מלך כל החבקו בו בים	1,524
Rabbi, behold! The Temple Mount is dormant. And he will deliver the fallen, as well as my mother, as she will see. She will lead a dried out enemy with her guilt offering.	רבי הן נם הר הבית ונופל יתיש ואמי ורא תה תנהג אויב יבש ואשמה	321
Hussein is a vapor. Like a guarded lamb, God is keeping Jews and Levites whole. And the cell inside your dwelling will become a torture chamber.	חוסין אד כשה יי משמר יהוד ולוי וממלונכ בכ תאכ יצא סד	1,620
From the salt of betrayal and from fire, a sand dune provided the foundation for a peace treaty. Yahweh — indeed God — came to the heights of the mountain.	ממלח המעל ואש הר חול שתת הסכם שלום יה כנ אל בא לרמי הר	23,429
God delivers the joyous. I will indeed inflict pain upon the rock. I am the God who strikes. They wiped out the nakedness.	לשש יה חולצ כי הן צור אכאיב אני יהוה מכה הם עריה מחו	11,355
The rest of my severe illness is spreading, Saddam, as if from a missile made for you. Where is he? Or, who is the tyrant?	יתר דויי נד סאדם מך טיל לך עשו איו או מי רדן	87

The joyful God is ruling. What is in it for me? And the red heifer is crying from the fire and the guilt offering.	אל רן שר מה לי והפרה אדומה מבכיה זו אש ואשמתו	25,854
The major dryness of hand in her is in your image. While setting the stage, become Russia.	אב יובש כף בה בן למכם בתורו במה היו רוסיה	487
He will suffer pain and restlessness, but the halo is his, and for her the monument will be Baghdad.	לו וכאוב ודיצה ולו ההילה לה העי יהיה באגדד	9,855
Hussein, his shoulder is dead. And it is appropriate that he prevented home-building everywhere, and is echoing in me.	חוסין שכמו מת ויאה שהניא את קן בכל והד בי	3,254
We will get the foreigner, Tom Brokaw. Something smells. Consider the flag valuable.	זרה נשיג ריח בה טום ברוקו שוי קח לדגל	18,613
You were harnessed. Contemplate my might. Let Zubaydah be kept in the limelight. Will they strike the sea?	היית רתם אוני הגי מואר יהא זובידה היבו ים	7,724
She has her army cells, which will be prepared and precise. The inside of Haman is water.	לה תאי צבאה יהה נכון דיוק תוך המ	58
N. Korea, exalt, rejoice, see that my creed is the truth. Here, their congregation is in her.	צקוריאה רם רני ראי כתי אמת הכא בה קהלם	32,548

Carry the mountain. Zubaydah will tell something of value as a gift as the monument of the sect is finished.	שא הר זובידה יגד ערך כשי כתל הכת תם	1,265
The Temple Mount is poor in my faith. God and father as a friend of the mountain. And he stopped from giving birth.	הר הבית דל דתי אל ואב כאח הר ונח מלדת	1,543
An idol to reflect his lot, Taliban. I will thus rise eastward.	אליל לשקף מנתו טליבן כן אעל קדמי	1,558
Armageddon, relieving my heart, will waste away a quarter dead. And God is my refuge.	הר מגדו לבי מקל ידלל רבע שמת מ לט יי	4,246
Bear the end of the fool's gift, 2001-2; show the substance of the contemplation.	שא את תום ללץ שי התשסב תוך שיח הראו	5,417
His people have been easily established, and the Iran you loved has died by me.	בנקל מכון עמו ומאתי מת אירן אהבת	38
And from Armageddon God has screamed to us. And who has ambushed whose shadow?	ומל הר מגדו ילל לן האלוה ומי ארב מי צל	13,460

To her and to the secret he rendered at the nose of the beast, anti-Semitism is dead.	לה ולרז עשה לאף חיה מת אנטישמיות	40,054
He was saved in the sea of Hamburg, without any commandment in them for the rabbi's lamb.	בים חמברג נצל ולא צו במו לשהרבי	2,413
He loves me that much. Watch in me the rehabilitation since Sept. 11, when his sea was rendered bitter.	כה אהבני ראי בי שקם בכג אלול ימו מרר שת	3,975
If she is a whore to the six, N. Korea is God's gift in proliferation.	אלו קדשה לשש צקוריאה שי יי בפרו	37,044
The farmer of Rome came. Bin Laden is dead. The deep throat burned everything.	איכר רומא בא מת בן לאדן לע בער כל	42,529
The perversion in me, Hussein, is the one in them, making them high. And the fugitive is tall.	התבל בי חסיני שבמ ורמו ונד תמיר	1,735
Know that the heart of bin Laden is snow, and silence the killed.	הלב בן לאדן שלג כי דע ומומת הסו	1,149

From a daughter of his. Where are they from? It is my season of the third temple — please.	מאת לו בת מאין הם בית שלישי עתי נא	22,004
She is as noble as my God, and I have suffered burns from the terrorism.	מיוחסה כאלי ואכוה משטר אימים	10,763
Conquer the axis of evil in the island, or an elephant that I raise will fly.	באי רדו ציר עול או עף פיל אעל	1,370
Give what is left to you. The Everlasting Father will be led by God.	תן את שאר לך אב לנצח ינהל אל	371
Or pay the devil of Afghan — a purchase is pending — bringing me the end.	או שלמו שד אפגן רכש בא תם לי	751
Where are they? And let God not strike terror.	איה הנם ואל אם ביה יכה טרור	37
The newborn one is a father with no yesterday. His name will melt as bait.	הולד אב בלי תמול לשלל	118
He warmed her. And where is the wanderer going to come? To the Temple Mount, where he will kiss the mother.	חממה ונד בא אפה הר הבית ישק אם	527

Command his echo and I will refute, destroying the innocent till they are finished.	הדו צו ואפרך להחריב תם והתמו	4,887
Provide a picture of terminal illness. The days of Saddam are over.	תן לצלם לדווי אבד עת סדם	139
Bin Laden, the innocent is moaning; he is gross with the blood of the poor.	בן לאדן מילל תם גך לרש דם	93
Woe, N. Korea, my protection has drowned and died.	צקוריאה צלי אבוי טבע ומת	34,089
Your total level of protection of N. Korea is that of a brother.	צלכא סך רמה צקוריאה אחא	62,873
Such a desert for the light to the one who rests from the claw of Kandahar.	או שלמו שד אפגן רכש בא תם לי	1,975
The high official will answer the anti-Semite. My joy will be pure.	אנטישמי שר יען רני צח יהי	49,552
The fasting oil in the Taliban will strike you badly.	שמן הצום בטליבן יכך רע	1,471

Antichrist of the people; where is the belief in his coming?	צר המשיח עמ אנה דת ביאה	7,094
You will crush the guilty Saddam and the month of Iyar will be restful.	סאדם אשם תהממי ואייר נח	6,387
The beauty in me was quite destroyed by Binalshibh.	נוי בי שבר די בן אל שיב	309
Hussein is making gestures to me due to the pressure.	חוסין ללחצ מביע לי	2,486
The wall of Armageddon is there for her a bed.	הר מגדו לה מחצל שמ או אינ	16,156
God will ignite the airliner fire from the heart.	יי אש מטוש יכית מלב	267
The pin serves them as name of the culprit.	היתד להמ כמו שמ הפושע	16,035
Who is for her, or the night of the newborn one?	מי עבורה או ליל הולד	34
The giving is finished. I will give them from Armageddon.	תמ מתנ אתנמ מהר מגדו	3,135

Yesterday evening they whispered, bin Laden is dead.	אנזש רחשו מת בן לדן	17,232
This is the king of Babylon, and to the vomit you will be imprisoned.	המלך בבל ולקיא תכלא	5,564
More than an easy description of N. Korea	מן תאר קל צקוריאה	55,013
You will spit at tradition, al Qaeda.	תרקי הוי אל קאעדה	1,430
Tower destroyed toward the mountain, oh, God!	מגדל חרב אה אל	904
We have thus been destroyed by suicide.	שממנו התאבדות כך	5,114
The gift will be delayed, 110 floors.	מתן ישהה קי קומות	7,893
Bin Laden is dead. Where is the monument for the oppressed?	מת בן לדן אי לדכ עי	33,908
My heart, Hussein, has elevated again.	לבי חסין שב מורם	1,735
The beauty of moving September 11.	נוי הובלה כג אלול	14,543
I will praise the monument of the Temple Mount.	אהלל התל הר הבית תתמ	2,048

The science of Moses is conspiring evil.	מדע משה חורש רעה	31,184
Death wish and the imprisonment	לשאוף מות והשבי	3,538
What is the postmaster for the poor?	מה מנהל דואר	30,070
Silence communism!	הסו קומוניזם	14,439
And with me 110 floors	קי קומות	51,032
Poverty of prisoners of war	שבויי לחמה עני	87,206
If to a mountain, the Temple Mount	אם להר הר הבית	2,423
Place the gift of terror (spoken to a group)	שימו שי טרור	369
Terror of the sea is there in them.	טרור ים שם בם	448
World War (2)	מלחמת עלם	18,036; 105,201
Anti-Semitism	אנטישמיות	40,054

Philippines	פיליפינים	20,040
Mystery Babylon	תעלום הבבל	60,855
Saddam, terminal illness, from everything	סדם דוי מהך	141
Bin Laden, his hand	בן לאדן ידו	9,501
Complete peace	שלום כולל	86,695
Tora Bora	טורה בורה	14,368
Third temple (2)	בית שלישי	22,004; 83,970
Ahmad Chalabi	אחמד חלבי	6,518
Pennsylvania	פנסלואני	8,587
Red Heifer (2)	פרה אדומה	16,013; 132,441
Giuliani (2)	גיוליאני	80,056; 97,261

When the tower fell	בנפל מגדל	124,203
Terror hot in me	טרור חם בי	430
Palestinians	פלשתיאים	6,957
Attack the "bully." (*terrorist point of view?*)	הכה בריון	57,235
States the Lord	נאם יהוה	405
N. Korea (3)	צקוריאה	2,941; 17,753; 59,652
Saddam is guilty.	סדם אשם	23,297
Muhammed Omar (6)	מחמד עמר	3,995; 4,785; 7,143; 29,683; 35,869; 37,162
Al Qaeda (3)	אל קאעדה	48,983; 53,205; 69,069
Terrorism	טרוריזם	2,534
Saddam Hussein	סדם חסין	150,684
Armageddon (8)	הר מגדו	10,001; 11,664; 12,634; 16,156; 16,721; 16,809; 19,115; 19,988
Hijackers (5)	חוטפים	4,467; 21,015; 23,472; 28,080; 29,268

Terrorism (2)	טרוריזם	58,566; 71,937
Pentagon	פנטגון	65,626
Jihad	ג׳יהאד	210
Extremist (3)	קיצוני	2,751; 3,100; 3,481
Taliban (2)	תליבן	81; 8,361
Manhattan (2)	מנהטן	698; 955

As we discovered these incredible codes, we posted them on our
web site to keep curious visitors abreast of our findings. Most of
these postings were made in late 2001 and early 2002. In the re-
mainder of this chapter, groups of these findings are presented and
discussed. The first group consists of codes about key al Qaeda operatives.

- Carry the mountain. Zubaydah will tell something of value
as a gift as the monument of the sect is finished.
- You were harnessed. Contemplate my might. Let Zubaydah
be kept in the limelight. Will they strike the sea? *("The
sea" in Hebrew typology refers to Gentiles, especially
Semitic Gentiles. Could this be referring to the attacks in
Riyadh and Morocco?)*
- There is quarrel in his speeches. A living brother uttered
words to them and to me. And Zubaydah turned to his sea,
without then lying for a whole week. Oh, the mountain of
her interior will bear a testimonial to her name.
- The beauty in me was quite destroyed by Binalshibh.

With officials in Saudi Arabia jolted from their apathy by the bloody bombings in Riyadh, al Qaeda terrorists were again on the run following the arrests of nine suspects in the holy Muslim city of Medina. One highly placed U.S. official described cooperation from Saudi authorities as "superb."

Earlier arrests of key al Qaeda operatives Abu Zubaydah and Ramzi Binalshibh inspired searches for ELSs that resulted in fascinating extensions. Khalid Sheikh Mohammed, the highest ranking terrorist yet netted, has not produced codes worthy of researching further. He is said to be giving a great deal of good information to his interrogators, however.

As war in Iraq loomed, we thought it might be valuable to bring together key findings on Saddam Hussein.

- Hussein is a vapor. Like a guarded lamb, God is keeping Jews and Levites whole. And the cell inside your dwelling will become a torture chamber.
- Hussein, his shoulder is dead. And it is appropriate that he prevented homebuilding everywhere, and is echoing in me.
- Hussein is making gestures to me due to the pressure.

These code discoveries in the Ezekiel 37 and Ezekiel 40 clusters seemed to join other ELSs found earlier in expressing bad news for Saddam Hussein. Unfortunately, they didn't include time frames.

A key word in the first code is "shoulder." The meaning tied to it is power, according to Wilson's Dictionary of Bible Types. For instance, Isaiah 9:6 predicts about the messiah, "and the government will be on his shoulders." In other words, if Hussein's shoulder is dead, his power is dead.

The word "vapor" in the Bible expresses the transitory nature of life, also according to Wilson's. In the second new code, Hussein's temporary standing is compared with the guarded wholeness of "Jews and Levites" under the care of God, their Shepherd. But there is a chilling warning in the last part of the code, which may be about the small, sealed rooms that some Israeli's prepared in their homes against the threatened chemical and biological attacks of Iraqi missiles during the Gulf War.

Research of codes that began soon after 9/11 has consistently turned up ELSs that seemed to say Hussein's rule was in trouble:

- Provide a picture of terminal illness. The days of Saddam are over.
- You will crush the guilty Saddam and the month of Iyar will be restful.
- And when Hussein will recognize the checkmate, there will be wine in them.

The second code is unique in that it provides a time of the year for its message, but the year remains unclear. The Jewish month of Iyar ran from May 3 to May 31 in 2003. President Bush declared victory in Iraq on May 3, 2003, and May was a peaceful month — in comparison with the preceding month and subsequent months.

In the third code above, "there shall be wine in them" seems to refer to a celebration at an inferred surrender when Iraq is checkmated.

There were several other codes that mention the Iraqi dictator in the same breath with terminal illness. However, it isn't clear whether the terminal illness is his, or something caused to others by his weapons.

- The rest of my terminal illness is spreading, Saddam, as if from a missile made for you. Where is he? Or who is the tyrant?
- Saddam, terminal illness from everything.
- This is the king of Babylon, and by the vomit you will be imprisoned.

However, we did locate references in the legitimate western media to Hussein's possible serious illness in early 2001.

It is quite astonishing to find three lengthy codes that all closely tie Saddam and terminal illness, and that all cross text within 53 letters of one another. Furthermore, the longest and third longest codes come within one letter of exactly overlapping one another.

The full name, "Saddam Hussein," appears as an ELS only twice in the Tanakh. One of them slices right through the main portion of the 9/11 cluster. It is seven letters long and appears spreading across most of the books of the Old Testament and touching down in Ezekiel 37:2 at letter number 780,935 with a huge skip of 150,684. Sharing this letter number is the code, "God will ignite the airliner fire from the heart." The ominous 33-letter term "The rest of my terminal illness is spreading, Saddam, as if from a missile made for you. Where is he? Or, who is the tyrant?" crosses the cluster at letter number 780,931. Another, "Saddam, terminal illness from everything," crosses the cluster at letter 780,930. In other words, all of these codes cross a tiny section of text that is only six letters long. Just 11 letters away, the code "Terror hot in me" crosses the cluster. "Place the gift of terror" is only 50 letters away, and the Hebrew construction indicates that these are words spoken to a group, as if the words are being spoken as an order.

Among newer additions to the cluster are:

• The Temple Mount is poor in my faith. God and Father as a friend of the mountain. And he stopped from giving birth.
• And from Armageddon God has screamed to us. And who has ambushed whose shadow?
• Antichrist of the people; where is the belief in his coming?
• The newborn one is a father with no yesterday. His name will melt as bait.
• The beauty in me was quite destroyed by Binalshibh.
• Who is for her, or the night of the newborn one?
• The giving is finished. I will give them from Armageddon.
• More than an easy description of N. Korea.

Several new long ELSs were added to the cluster, including the first long term mentioning Armageddon, the much-discussed final battle on Planet Earth, which prophecy experts say is to take place in northern Israel and to be climaxed by the second coming of Jesus Christ.

The code, which reads, "Armageddon, relieving my heart, will waste away a quarter dead. And God is my refuge," also runs through the Ezekiel 40 cluster.

Also adding to the cluster is a 41-letter code, "From the salt of betrayal and from fire, a sand dune provided the foundation for a peace treaty. Yah (or Yahweh) — indeed God — came to the heights of the mountain," which also runs through the newly emerging Daniel 2-3 cluster.

While we have purposely avoided interpreting codes as predicting future events, this 27-letter ELS seems to be doing just that: "Carry the mountain. Zubaydah will tell something of value as a gift as the monument of the sect is finished."

Hebrew has quite a bit of flexibility, but we would have to bend over backward to interpret this sequence of letters in any other way. We do not know what "carry the mountain" means, but intelligence specialists from the U.S. and other nations continue to question Zubaydah at an undisclosed location. This ELS seems to be saying that he will be yielding up significant information, and that the al Qaeda terrorist network could become history. Zubaydah is credited by some sources with providing the tip that led to the arrest of Jose Padilla aka Abdullah al Muhajir, the American citizen who was allegedly plotting with al Qaeda operatives to explode a dirty bomb somewhere in the U.S. That is certainly "something of value."

Saddam Hussein's Fingerprints on Turmoil in Israel

Secretary of Defense Donald Rumsfeld revealed Saddam Hussein's support of terrorist suicide bombers who forced Israel to take reprisals in the West Bank. The former Iraqi leader increased payments to terrorist's surviving families from $10,000 to $25,000. Since the increase, many suicide bombers have blown up themselves and dozens of Israeli citizens. The payments were acknowledged by a Palestinian pro-Iraqi group, the Arab Liberation Front.

Saddam Hussein has repeatedly appeared in codes about terrorist attacks we have discovered since the 9/11 attacks, both in this cluster and in the Ezekiel 7 cluster. Hussein and Iraq continue to appear in new finds in these clusters.

Two other discoveries added to the element of mystery surrounding this cluster — ELSs involving the Temple Mount and North Korea. This nation was singled out by President Bush as a key member of the "axis of evil."

Following are more long discoveries in this key cluster:

- From the salt of betrayal and from fire, a sand dune provided the foundation for a peace treaty. Yah (or Yahweh) — indeed God — came to the heights of the mountain.
- The joyful God is ruling. What is in it for me? And the red heifer is crying from the fire and the guilt offering.
- Armageddon, relieving my heart, will waste away a quarter dead. And God is my refuge.
- The trouble of the newborn one is vigilant and honest because of the ruin. Get out as if Iraq had been sent out. The majority is aware that, rest in peace, You will come — the villainy with light. You will understand the heart of granite.
- You were harnessed. Contemplate my might. Let Zubaydah be kept in the limelight. Will they strike the sea?
- Rabbi, behold! The Temple Mount is dormant. And he will deliver the fallen, as well as my mother, as she will see. She will lead a dried out enemy with her guilt offering.
- He warmed her. And where is the wanderer going to come? To the Temple Mount, where he will kiss the mother.
- I will praise the monument of the Temple Mount.

The Temple Mount codes are not the first in this cluster about the controversial real estate within the Old City of Jerusalem. "From a daughter of his. Where are they from? It is my season of the third temple — please" is a fascinating ELS. According to biblical prophecy experts, the third temple must be built in Jerusalem to satisfy many prophecies of the end times, making this an intriguing code.

Prophecy experts also believe that Russia and her allies will play a significant part in the final days, tying the nation to the Gog and Magog mentioned in Ezekiel 38–39, so the ELS, "The major dryness of hand in her is in your image. While setting the stage, become Russia." adds an interesting element to the cluster.

Another code, "Conquer the axis of evil in the island, or an elephant that I raise will fly," is interesting, to say the least. We wondered if perhaps it had something to do with the terrorists in the Philippines and the Republican Party. Or, it could refer to Republican success in the November 2002 U.S. election, which may have been due in part to Democratic resistance to Homeland Security legislation.

Other interesting discoveries include:

- Give what is left to you. The Everlasting Father will be led by God.
- Silence communism!
- The island was restful, elevated, and it happened. Where is Libya? And you have disrupted the nation. She changed a word, he answered them with combat. Why the navy and the smell of the bottom of the sea?
- Let the oppressed be congratulated, saturated from him at 2001. And let them be guarded by the echo of the father's son, supported by the U.S. I will see but he has the knowledge.
- An idol to reflect his lot, Taliban. I will thus rise eastward.
- The fasting oil in the Taliban will strike you badly.
- My heart, Hussein, has elevated again.
- To her and to the secret he rendered at the nose of the beast, anti-Semitism is dead.
- She is as noble as my God, and I have suffered burns from the terrorism.
- Bear the end of the fool's gift, 2001-2; show the substance of the contemplation.
- Command his echo and I will refute, destroying the innocent 'til they are finished.
- The high official will answer the anti-Semite. My joy will be pure.

The Literal Text — A Prophecy About Israel Coming to Life

We continue to be struck by the fact that the Ezekiel 37 cluster is located in a chapter well known for its prophecy about the coming back to life of Israel, a nation that did not exist in its own land for nearly two millennia. The prophet Ezekiel, writing approximately six centuries before the birth of Christ, has a vision. He is writing at a time when the nation of Judah was in decline and would eventually be conquered by Babylon and its citizens marched east in defeat. He begins the chapter, "The hand of the Lord was upon me, and he brought me out by the Spirit of the Lord and set me in the middle of a valley; it was full of bones . . . this is what the Sovereign Lord says to these bones: I will make you come to life."

The attacks upon the U.S. have, at least in significant part, been due to the terrorists' intense opposition to U.S. support for Israel, according to declarations from nearly all of the major terrorist groups. They have claimed that the attacks would cease when U.S. support for Israel ended. The location of this cluster of codes again suggests that Israel is a key issue in the attacks. Another Old Testament prophet said, "Behold I will make Jerusalem a cup of reeling to all the people around . . . on that day I will make Jerusalem a burdensome stone for all the peoples; all who burden themselves with it shall be grievously hurt." (Zechariah 12:2–3a) Why all of this trouble over a tiny little nation in the eastern Mediterranean? Because many radical Muslims hate Israel — and the U.S. as its foremost defender.

Bin Laden Codes

In addition to the discovery concerning a "tall fugitive," there are several codes involving bin Laden. Not to be found anywhere in the Tanakh was an ELS for the entire name of Osama bin Laden, partly because the term we searched for is long (10 letters). But there were some bin Laden codes discovered nearby. The closest, "bin Laden, his hand," is 128 letters from the center of the Ezekiel 37 cluster. The longest "bin Laden" code, with 23 letters, "Know that the heart of bin Laden is snow, and silence the killed," is 223 letters away from the core. The 19-letter code, "bin Laden, the innocent is moaning, he is gross with the blood of the poor," is 669 letters away, and the "You will spit at tradition, al Qaeda" code is 772 letters away from the center of the cluster.

These codes seem to form the heart of what may be a different focal point of the cluster — located in the range of Ezekiel 37:12 to 37:19. (Note: In the *Sunday Telegraph* of London, November 11,

2001, nearly two months after we found the latter "bin Laden" code, a story quotes Osama bin Laden as saying, "We kill their innocents." The statement was included in a videotaped message that circulated among bin Laden's supporters, according to the newspaper.)

When Afghan and alliance forces were unable to find bin Laden after routing opposition in Afghanistan, there was a good deal of discussion about what had happened to him. One strong opinion that made the rounds was that he died from chronic kidney disease. Two extremely interesting codes about the death of bin Laden were found in this cluster. The first is "Yesterday evening they whispered, bin Laden is dead," which appears with a skip of 17,232 and touches down in the cluster at Ezekiel 37:5. The second has a much larger skip of 33,908 and reads, "Bin Laden is dead. Where is the monument for the oppressed?" It crosses the cluster at Ezekiel 36:35. Could it have a relationship to a newly discovered 34-letter code that reads, "He will suffer pain and restlessness, but the halo is his, and for her the monument will be Baghdad?" If so, this may be still another connection between bin Laden and Iraq. (Note: In November 2001, an audiotape with a message spoken by bin Laden was received by the Arabic satellite news channel, al Jazeera. It was authenticated by U.S. intelligence experts a few days later. These codes about bin Laden's death evidently refer to a later date.) The problem with codes such as these is that they are not date stamped.

Other Interesting Codes

The enigmatic code "The pin serves them as name of the culprit" may be of interest to members of the intelligence community. The Hebrew word for "pin" could also mean "wedge," "chisel," or "nail." Could it also stand for Personal Identification Number (PIN)? Time will tell.

The primary candidate for a focal code for this cluster so far is "Where are they? And let God not strike terror." It qualifies in a number of ways. It is long, with 21 letters, and it has a nice, short skip of 37. Best of all, its content seems to work very well for this cluster, based on our knowledge so far. "Where are they" could refer to the fact that even though war has been declared on the terrorists by most of the world, their location is essentially unknown. "And let God not strike terror" could be the prayer of many world citizens in the wake of the attacks.

Two other lengthy codes are worth noting as being related to the attacks on the Twin Towers. Both are 14 letters long. The first reads, "Tower destroyed toward the mountain. Oh, God!" while the second says, "We have thus been destroyed by suicide." These two codes round out a very remarkable collection of a dozen codes that have 14 or more letters that are tightly clustered through the text of Ezekiel 37.

Another cluster we discovered at about the same time was located in Ezekiel 7 and seemed to be specific to the City of New York and the World Trade Center attacks.

These and other long codes, along with more clusters associated with the Ezekiel 37 cluster, are updated regularly on our web site at www.biblecodedigest.com.

On the Sundays following 9/11, people seemed to recognize the hand of God in the horrific events and rushed to churches *en masse*. Thousands turned to Christ during those days. We received dozens of e-mails from people acknowledging their belief that God was involved in the events, which some saw as a warning that the end of all things was indeed near. And yet on the second anniversary of 9/11, the Barna Research Group reported that the event had no lasting impact on church attendance in the U.S.[2]

R. Edwin Sherman

Chapter Six

Why the Ezekiel 37 Cluster
Cannot Be the Product of Chance

Is it possible for a cluster as extensive as the one in Ezekiel 37 to be the result of chance? Because of an experiment that we conducted comparing ELSs discovered in the Bible with those discovered in a text other than the Bible, the Leo Tolstoy novel *War and Peace*, we can answer with a definite "No." (A description of this experiment appears in appendix 5.) The sheer number of lengthy ELSs in the Ezekiel 37 terrorism cluster far exceeds what chance could produce.

In this chapter, we will describe how we used one of the key results of that experiment — that in an ordinary text there is a 19.4% chance per search opportunity that a Hebrew expert would find an extension to an initial ELS — to specifically answer this question.

To date, we have only examined 295 initial ELSs located in Ezekiel 37. And yet, from that review 33 ELSs emerged that are 25+ letters long. If we had been working with *War and Peace*, we would have expected to only find seven (7.36 to be exact) ELSs 25+ letters long. That is an enormous difference, and the improbability of finding 33 such long ELSs by chance is essentially zero, by any reasonable probability estimation process. We estimate that the odds of chance occurrence of a cluster as extensive as Ezekiel 37 emerging from 295 initial ELSs are 1 out of 6 followed by 131 zeroes. In other words, the Ezekiel 37 cluster is an impossibility.

In the experiment, it was noted that Dr. Jacobi found an extension to an existing ELS from *War and Peace* 19.4% of the time. The average extension he found was 6.95 letters long (rounded up to 7 letters). Figure 6A presents a formula for the expected number of ELSs with k extensions to emerge from an examination of an initial group of n ELSs found in a text.

Figure 6A

Number of Initial ELSs Examined (n)		Number of Extensions (k), Plus One		Discovery Rate, Raised to the kth Power		(1.0 Minus the Discovery Rate), Squared
	X		X		X	

The above formula was derived in appendix 7. We examined 295 initial ELSs in Ezekiel 37 to determine whether or not a longer ELS could be found among the letters appearing on either side of the initial ELS at the same skip intervals. Each extended ELS must consist of grammatically correct Hebrew and be reasonably intelligible.

On the basis of the above formula and assumptions (i.e., $n = 295$, discovery rate = .194), the expected number of extended ELSs of various lengths is displayed in table 6A, alongside the actual number of extended ELSs that have been discovered to date in Ezekiel 37. The actual number of extended ELSs of different lengths in Ezekiel 37 was reasonably close to expected for only two categories — those with zero and two extensions. For all other categories (shaded), there were statistically significant differences between actual and expected. If the frequency of extended ELSs in Ezekiel 37 had conformed to that from *War and Peace*, we would expect to find 7.36 ELSs consisting of three or more extensions (and having 25 or more total letters). That is a significant number of long ELSs — an indication of the fact that the terseness of Hebrew and the absence of vowels can result in the "discovery" of some longer ELSs — even in Tolstoy's writings.

In reality, we found 33 ELSs in Ezekiel 37 that consisted of 25 or more letters — approximately 348% more than the 7.36 expected by chance. This is an extremely significant difference statistically, no matter how one estimates the probability of its occurrence by chance. Stated simply, table 6B demonstrates three very important findings:

Table 6A

Number of Extensions (k)	Average Number of Letters	Range of Number of Letters	Number of ELSs	
Expected vs. Actual Long ELSs in Ezekiel 37 Cluster (Assuming 19.4% Discovery Rate)				
			Expected	Actual
0	7	4 - 10	191.6	214
1	14	11 - 17	74.4	28
2	21	18 - 24	21.6	20
3	28	25 - 31	5.60	16
4	35	32 - 38	1.36	6
5	42	39 - 45	0.32	5
6	49	46 - 52	0.072	4
7	56	53 - 59	0.0169	1
8+	- -	60+	0.0044	1
ALL			295.0	295

1. Longer ELSs can be discovered, even in ordinary texts, with some degree of frequency. This affirms the claim of code skeptics that codes can be found in any book.

2. The actual number of longer ELSs in Ezekiel 37 far exceeds that explainable by chance, conclusively affirming the claim that some real Bible codes do exist. The odds of a cluster of long ELSs as extensive as that in Ezekiel 37 being the result of chance is 1 out of 6 followed by 131 zeroes. This is based on a chi-square probability

Table 6B

Codes 46+ Letters Long From Ezekiel 37 Cluster
Expected: 0.092
Actual: 6

(61) There is quarrel in his speeches. A living brother uttered words to them and to me. And Zubaydah turned to his sea, without then lying for a whole week. Oh, the mountain of her interior will bear a testimonial to her name.

(53) The island was restful, elevated, and it happened. Where is Libya? And you have disrupted the nation. She changed a word. He answered them with combat. Why the navy and the smell of the bottom of the sea?

(52) For where has God consumed from you? And in it are stones of substantial sickness for us. You will indeed delay their diagnosis, because of His own reflection in the one who solves.

(52) The trouble of the newborn one is vigilant and honest because of the ruin. Get out as if Iraq had been sent out. The majority is aware that, rest in peace, you will come — the villainy with light. You will understand the heart of granite.

(48) Let the oppressed be congratulated, saturated from Him at 2001. And let them be guarded by the echo of the Father's Son, supported by the U.S. I will see but he has the knowledge.

(calculated by Excel's CHITEST function) applied to all extension categories. This probability does not change much if it is only applied to the longer extension categories since it is the dramatic contrast between actual and expected findings in those categories that is the predominant source of improbability.

To gain a greater appreciation for this, we will compare actual findings with expectations from a non-encoded text for the longest extension categories shown in table 6A. First, consider ELSs that are 46 or more letters long. Given that we examined 295 initial ELSs for extensions, we would have expected to find only 0.092 ELSs that were 46+ letters long from a non-encoded text. That means that nine times out of ten, after examining 295 initial ELSs, we would not have found any final ELSs that long. In actuality, we found six such ELSs — which is 65 times the expected number. Those final ELSs (number of Hebrew letters in parentheses) are in table 6B

Next, consider ELSs that are 39 to 45 letters long. Given that we examined 295 initial ELSs for extensions, we would have expected to find only 0.32 ELSs that were 39-45 letters long from a non-encoded text. That means that two times out of three, after examining 295 initial ELSs, we would not have found any final ELSs that were that long. In actuality, we found five such ELSs — which is 15.6 times the expected number. In table 6C are these final ELSs.

Now look at the ELSs that are 32 to 38 letters long. We examined 295 initial ELSs for extensions, so we would have expected to find only 1.36 ELSs that were 32-38 letters long from a non-encoded text. After examining 295 initial ELSs, we would only expect to have found one or perhaps two final ELSs that long. But we found six such ELSs — or 4.4 times the expected number. See table 6D.

Table 6C

Codes 39-45 Letters Long From Ezekiel 37 Cluster
Expected: 0.32
Actual: 5

(45) Imprison your burden there, to immerse her distinct feature, and in my waters to anthrax, king of all. Embrace it in the sea.

(41) From the salt of betrayal and from fire, a sand dune provided the foundation for a peace treaty. Yah — indeed God — came to the heights of the mountain.

(41) Hussein is a vapor. Like a guarded lamb, God is keeping Jews and Levites whole. And the cell inside your dwelling will become a torture chamber.

(40) God delivers the joyous. I will indeed inflict pain upon the rock. I am the God who strikes. They wiped out the nakedness.

(40) Third temple, the fullness of the illness will take place. And a land will emerge from a tight place. God is lofty, and it is time for a prince.

Table 6D

Codes 32-38 Letters Long From Ezekiel 37 Cluster Expected: 1.36 Actual: 6
(34) He will suffer pain and restlessness. But the halo is his, and for her the monument will be Baghdad.
(34) The joyful God is ruling. What is in it for me? And the red heifer is crying from the fire and the guilt offering.
(33) The rest of my terminal illness is spreading, Saddam, as if from a missile made for you. Where is he? Or who is the tyrant?
(33) You were harnessed. Contemplate my might. Let Zubaydah be kept in the limelight. Will they strike the sea?
(32) Hussein, his shoulder is dead. And it is appropriate that he prevented home-building everywhere, and is echoing in me.
(32) The major dryness of hand in her is in your image. While setting the stage, become Russia.

Then note ELSs 25 to 31 letters long. We would have expected to find 5.6 ELSs that were 25-31 letters long from a non-encoded text, in that we examined 295 initial ELSs for extensions. That means that after examining 295 initial ELSs, we would only expect to have found four or five or six or perhaps seven final ELSs that long. However, we found 16 such ELSs — seen in table 6E — which is 2.9 times the expected number.

Table 6E

Codes 25-31 Letters Long From Ezekiel 37 Cluster Expected: 5.6 Actual: 16
(30) He loves me that much. Watch in me the rehabilitation since Sept. 11, when his sea was rendered bitter.
(30) N. Korea, exalt, rejoice, see that my creed is the truth. Here, their congregation is in her.
(29) And from Armageddon God has screamed to us. And who has ambushed whose shadow?
(29) She has her army cells, which will be prepared and precise. The inside of Haman is water.
(29) We will get the foreigner, Tom Brokaw. Something smells. Consider the flag valuable.
(28) The Temple Mount is poor in my faith. God and Father as a friend of the mountain. And he stopped from giving birth.
(27) Armageddon, relieving my heart, will waste away a quarter dead. And God is my refuge.

(27) Bear the end of the fool's gift, 2001-2; show the substance of the contemplation.
(27) Carry the mountain. Zubaydah will tell something of value as a gift as the monument of the sect is finished.
(26) An idol to reflect his lot, Taliban. I will thus rise eastward.
(26) From a daughter of his. Where are they from? It is my season of the third temple – please.
(26) His people have been easily established, and the Iran you loved has died by me.
(26) To her and to the secret he rendered at the nose of the beast, anti-Semitism is dead.
(25) He was saved in the sea of Hamburg, without any commandment in them for the rabbi's lamb.
(25) If she is a whore to the six, N. Korea is God's gift in proliferation.
(25) The farmer of Rome came. Bin Laden is dead. The deep throat burned everything.

Finding as many lengthy final ELSs as we did, given how few would have been expected if Ezekiel were not an encoded text, led to my firm conviction that some Bible codes must be real. There simply is no other explanation that can be offered for what was discovered.

What is critical in answering the question of whether or not some Bible codes are intentional are differences in the discovery rate of extensions. As discovered in the Islamic Nations Experiment, the discovery rate was 19.4% in *War and Peace* and 27.0% in Ezekiel. The discovery rate for the first extension in Ezekiel was only 14.8%.

However, once at least one extension had been found, there was a 49.7% chance that an additional extension would be found — each time there was an opportunity to search for one. A discovery rate of virtually 50% is unimaginable — unless numerous very lengthy ELSs were *intentionally* placed in Ezekiel 37.

It is not our expectation that such a high discovery rate would persist within any given section of the Bible and any topically related collection of initial ELSs. Lengthy ELSs tend to be topically related to the surface text as well as to one another. Consequently, we would not expect that a collection of initial ELSs about the Hawaiian Islands would result in a high discovery rate in Ezekiel 37. On the other hand, the topic of recent terrorist related events is very heavily represented by long ELSs in Ezekiel 37, as is demonstrated in the tables shown.

But what if we used the 27.0% discovery rate for Ezekiel from the experiment in calculating the odds? First, we get the comparison seen in table 6F.

What does all of this mean?

It says that the odds of a cluster of long ELSs as extensive as that in Ezekiel 37 being the result of chance is 1 out of 114,300,000,000,000,000,000,000.

As sensitive as the odds are to the assumed discovery rate, those odds are essentially zero for any realistic discovery rate.

Another key finding is that the odds of a given long ELS being intentional increase dramatically for longer ELSs. If one assumes that all long ELSs in excess of the number expected by chance are intentional, the odds of a given long ELS being intentional can be easily calculated, and are shown in table 6G.

This analysis is oversimplified, if only because it is possible for a long ELS to be partly intentional and partly coincidental.

Table 6F

Expected vs. Actual Long ELSs in Ezekiel 37 Cluster (Assuming a 27% Discovery Rate)				
Number of Extensions (k)	Average Number of Letters	Range of Number of Letters	Number of ELSs	
			Expected	Actual
0	7	4 - 10	157.2	214
1	14	11 - 17	84.9	28
2	21	18 - 24	34.5	20
3	28	25 - 31	12.4	16
4	35	32 - 38	4.2	6
5	42	39 - 45	1.35	5
6	49	46 - 52	0.43	4
7	56	53 - 59	0.132	1
8+	- -	60+	0.057	1
ALL			295.0	295

Nevertheless, table 6G is indicative of the fact that increasing length does tip the odds in favor of a long ELS being intentional.

Bottom line, though, this is one of the most powerful pieces of evidence that we have discovered showing that the Bible had to have been written by an intelligence far, far beyond the capabilities of mankind. The only intelligent conclusion is that it was designed and orchestrated by God.

Table 6G

Odds of Given Long ELSs Being Intentional (Assuming a 19.4% Discovery Rate)				
Number of Letters	(A) Total Actual Number of ELSs	(B) ELSs Expected by Chance	(C) Number of Intentional ELSs [(A) – (B)]	(D) Probability of ELS Being Intentional [(C)/(A)]
25 - 31	16	5.60	10.40	65.0%
32 - 38	6	1.36	4.64	77.3%
39 - 45	5	0.32	4.68	93.6%
46 - 52	4	0.072	3.928	98.2%
53 - 59	1	0.0159	0.9841	98.4%
60+	1	0.00441	0.9956	99.6%

In Conclusion

As our investigation of code phenomena has expanded and deepened, every one of the stock opinions of most code skeptics, as well as those of most code proponents, has been contradicted by new evidence. It shouldn't be surprising that reality can stubbornly disagree with preconceptions, yet it is often true.

The saga of Bible codes has been characterized by attempts to rush to judgment. To advance above this primitive state we must bravely confront and listen to the realities of hard data — impartially gathered and analyzed.

The various findings of our experiments and related investigations, as set forth here, are upsetting to code critics and proponents alike.

- Longer ELSs in grammatically reasonable Hebrew can be found in books other than the Bible.
- The rate at which such longer ELSs appear in non-biblical texts is dramatically less than in the Bible. Consequently, there is strong support for the claim that real Bible codes do exist in abundance.
- The primary claim of code critics that "codes can be found in any book" is a primitive assertion that greatly oversimplifies and distorts the real situation. Much more relevant would be the question, "Is the discovery rate of longer ELSs in the Bible decidedly greater than that from a control text?"
- Any long ELS in the Bible could be a coincidence, or it could be partly intentional and partly coincidence. The longer it is, the less likely it is to be coincidental. For example, as shown in table 6G, an ELS from our Ezekiel 37 cluster that is 25 to 31 letters long is about 65.0% likely to be intentional as opposed to appearing by chance. If it is 39 to 45 letters long, it is about 93.6% likely to be intentional; if 46 to 59 letters long, 98.3%; and if 60 or more letters long, it is 99.6% likely to be intentional.
- To date, there is no reliable way of objectively distinguishing real from coincidental ELSs, although subjective reviews may indicate that a particular ELS is unusually "appropriate" or "descriptively accurate."
- Because of the many uncertainties inherent in the message of any single ELS, Bible codes cannot reliably be used to make predictions or to attempt to support doctrinal positions or

opinions. Furthermore, even if we could be certain a code is real, we do not know for certain who is speaking, and the source could be an untruthful one.

With our Isaiah 53 cluster vs. Hanukah cluster in *War and Peace* study, we compared the extensive cluster about the last days of Christ with the Hanukah codes in *War and Peace* to show that while it may be possible to find codes like the ones presented by Michael Drosnin in his two books, the skeptic's counter-example does nothing to call into question the reality of many of the codes in clusters like those in Isaiah 53 and Ezekiel 37.

While Drosnin did much to introduce the public to Bible codes, he simultaneously did code researchers a great disservice by giving skeptics an entire book of trivial examples that they could easily discredit.

Although code research has come a long way since the publication of his first book in 1997, there has been a lingering question mark over the whole phenomenon because of skeptical opinions that continue to appear on the Internet even though they are long out of date.

So while code research has moved on dramatically, it is also fighting a rear-guard action against these old, outdated statements from critics of the codes. It is a rare week when we don't get at least one e-mail asking us about the codes in *Moby Dick* or *War and Peace*.

Most likely, code skeptics would take exception to our comparison of the Hanukah cluster from *War and Peace* with the Ezekiel 37 cluster. It is not a fair comparison, they would say, because we searched for many more ELSs in Ezekiel 37 than they did in *War and Peace*. And they are right. However, our purpose in making such a comparison was to show that the Hanukah cluster is no longer a relevant counter-example. It has been hopelessly outclassed.

Given the utter improbability of the Isaiah 53 and Ezekiel 37 clusters, the appropriate conclusion is that the Bible was intentionally encoded. This begs the questions of who encoded it and for what purpose.

Drosnin proposed that super-intelligent aliens with knowledge of the future encoded the Bible for the purpose of warning mankind of possible catastrophic future events. The Alien hypothesis fails because of the many inherent weaknesses in codes (see topic A, page 185) that make them fundamentally unreliable for such a purpose.

If God encoded the Bible, what characteristics would such codes likely have, and what purpose would they serve? There is a wealth of material from the literal text of the Bible itself from which to formulate a God hypothesis. Here is what I believe it indicates:

1) *Codes by definition are hidden, but this would not be inconsistent with the nature of God.* "It is the glory of God to conceal a matter . . . " (Proverbs 25:2).

2) *Divine codes would probably relate generally to the subject matter of the surface text.* The Bible clearly sets forth the principle of confirmation — that is, a matter must be established by the testimony of two or three witnesses. This principle is clearly stated twice in the Hebrew Old Testament (Deuteronomy 17:6, 19:5), and three times in the New Testament (Matthew 18:16, 2 Corinthians 13:1, and 1 Timothy 5:19). So codes that served as another witness to the message of the literal text would seem quite natural.

3) *Divine codes would often relate to future events.* God claims that one of His unique abilities is His full knowledge of the future. "To whom will you compare me or count me equal? . . . I am God, and there is no other; I am God, and there is none like me. I make known the end from the beginning, from ancient times, what is still to come. I say: My purpose will stand, and I will do all that I please" (Isaiah 46:5, 9-10). About 25% of all Bible verses are prophecies of future events.

4) *The reliability of Divine codes should be clearly inferior to that of the literal text.* If Bible codes were truly reliable, the content of the literal text would be open to challenge on the basis of newly discovered codes. Such discoveries, or the proclamation of prophecies based on codes, would give glory to the researchers who discovered them, rather than giving

glory to God. Yet we know that God will not share His glory with others (Isaiah 42:8, 11).

5) *Divine codes should be inherently unreliable as the basis for accurately predicting the future.* Otherwise, God would be openly tempting us to do evil. Yet God does not tempt anyone (James 1:13). Using Bible codes to attempt to predict the future is akin to practicing divination, sorcery, and/or the reading of omens. Such practices are strongly condemned in the Bible (e.g., Leviticus 19:26, Deuteronomy 18:10-13).

6) *Divine codes may well be foolish, lowly, and despised, and yet they would still confound the wise.* "God chose the foolish things of the world to shame the wise . . . . He chose the lowly things of this world and the despised things — and the things that are not — to nullify the things that are, so that no one may boast before him" (1 Corinthians 1:27-29).

While the first three aspects of Divine codes are common sense, the last three may be surprising to many. Yet, "As the heavens are higher than the earth, so are my ways higher than your ways and my thoughts than your thoughts" (Isaiah 55:9).

Why would God intentionally encode unreliable messages within a sacred text? This would make sense if God wanted to provide implicit evidence within the text that He composed it, while at the same time discouraging attempts to derive new truths or predictions from such messages. It appears that the only real purpose of Bible codes is like that of the embedded strip in $20 bills. The strip adds nothing except proof that the bill is the real thing.

When Moses and Aaron brought on the first two plagues (i.e., turning water into blood, and then swarms of frogs), Pharaoh's magicians were able to duplicate these miracles (Exodus 7). Yet the magicians were unable to duplicate the third plague (gnats or lice, depending on the translation). Then "the magicians said to Pharaoh, 'This is the finger of God' " (Exodus 8:19). The Bible is filled with instances of God using weak, flawed people (and things) to accomplish His purposes and to bring glory to Him alone and not to others. Bible codes are the gnats (lice) of God that code skeptics cannot mimic adequately from non-encoded texts.

Chapter Seven

Three Hundred Jesus Codes:
An Astonishing Collection of Affirmations

For many people, the validity of Bible codes depends on the quality and content of specific code findings. Are they convincing? Do they make sense? The Jesus codes presented in chapters 3 and 4 fare much better in this regard than do the terrorism codes in chapters 5 and 6 — even though many of the latter codes are longer. This is also true of other clusters of Jesus codes, as compared with Ezekiel 37 codes as well as other terrorism clusters. So, it is fitting that the concluding chapter of this book is devoted to a review of the content of over 300 Jesus codes from Isaiah 53 as well as three other major clusters.

In chapters 3 through 6, we took a scientific approach to testing the claimed reality of the phenomenon, and its validity was affirmed. In this chapter, that validity will be underscored dramatically by the sheer breadth and depth of the content of over ten different topical collections of Jesus codes.

The content of any given Bible code is subject to many uncertainties, as detailed in topic A and appendix 8. Nevertheless, it is astonishing how readily our research unearthed hundreds of affirmations of the New Testament's literal content about Jesus Christ. To have found as many highly pertinent codes as we did, with relatively little searching, would have been totally impossible from a non-encoded text. If the Bible were not encoded, this would be a very short chapter. And it would be filled with findings like "The disciples ate Korn Nuts in the Louvre while bailing marshy reeds," or a wide range of other ridiculous things, even though they might be in good Hebrew.

What follows is a collection of the most cogent Jesus codes, drawn from only four locations in the Old Testament: (1) Isaiah 53, (2) Psalm 22, (3) the Ten Commandments (Exodus 20), and (4) Proverbs 15. The forcefulness and forthrightness of many of these codes is breathtaking. Within each topic, codes are presented in their descending order of: (1) relevance and appropriateness of content, and (2) length. Twice as much weight was given to relevance as to length in determining each ranking.

Table 7A

Text	Top Crucifixion Codes (Codes in Descending Order of Relevance and Length)
Ps. 22	You will cry out for the blood of the Messiah.
Ps. 22	The guilt offering, the son of man, humbled himself.
Ps. 22	Golgotha, where his reputation came from.
Isa. 53	And where are they? The Sanhedrin is finished.
Isa. 53	Dreadful day for Mary.
Ps. 22	And chief cornerstone found guilty.
Isa. 53	Piercers of my feet
Isa. 53	Deer of the Dawn
Ps. 22	Let him be crucified.
Ps. 22	Who crucified Jesus?
Pr. 15	Deer of the Dawn
Ps. 22	Who is Jesus? The guilt offering.
Isa. 53	Those who hated me without cause.
Ex. 20	Three holidays, Mount of Olives is a witness.
Pr. 15	Extinguish the light. A living sacrifice
Ps. 22	Final guilt offering.
Isa. 53	She weeps much.
Ps. 22	Living offering

Ps. 22	She weeps much.
Ps. 22	Mt. Moriah
Ps. 22	My God why?
Ps. 22	Jerusalem
Ex. 20	He was oppressed.
Pr. 15	Jerusalem
Ps. 22	Crucified
Ps. 22	And he will teach about the humble Kidron, as if bearing my robe.
Isa. 53	It is finished.
Isa. 53	The evil Roman city
Isa. 53	Yeshu — be judged.
Ps. 22	Struck by God.
Pr. 15	It is finished.
Pr. 15	Cross
Isa. 53	His spirit on a tree
Ex. 20	Pierced
Pr. 15	You will see that they will bear arms.
Ps. 22	The damp Kidron is singing for her.

For those desiring the Hebrew of any of the codes in this chapter, they can be found at www.biblecodedigest.com/page.php/14 for Isaiah 53 codes; . . . /page.php/282 for Psalm 22 codes; /page.php/194 and 45-49 for Exodus 20 codes; and /page.php/20 for Proverbs 15 codes. Appendix 3 contains a discussion of the possible meaning of some of the Isaiah 53 codes that are less obvious in content.

The above codes were discovered in the same way as those mentioned in chapter 4. For example, we first looked for occurrences of "messiah" as an ELS in each of the four clusters. When we did that in Psalm 22, a lengthy code was found that sounds like a description of a scene from the movie, *The Passion of the Christ*: "You will cry out for the blood of the Messiah." Finding a messiah ELS was not impressive, but discovering this entire, dramatic sentence, and many like it, changed me from a skeptic about Bible codes into a believer in the reality of this phenomenon. It is as simple as that. Just locating a Golgotha ELS in Psalm 22 did not convince me, but seeing that it was only part of the pithy code, "Golgotha, where his reputation came from," helped to change my mind.

As long as many of the crucifixion codes in table 7A were, the resurrection codes in table 7B are generally longer and just as pertinent.

Table 7B

Text	Top Resurrection Codes
Isa. 53	He offended. The resurrection of Jesus. He is risen indeed.
Isa. 53	And command fleets of resurrection from above to flee with raging excitement.
Pr. 15	Rejoice, he said, with fire from his soul, and he arose.
Pr. 15	And bless her people as in the resurrection.
Ps. 22	It is enough for us. And the resurrection is lofty. And God (Jehovah) died. And God (Elohim), the prophet of the temple is afraid.
Ps. 22	He will know the turmoil of resurrection. I will carry this declaration, my mother.
Isa. 53	The value of resurrection is thus dear.
Ps. 22	Long live the risen God of action. It is finished. And where is the resurrection of Jesus of blessed memory? For whom are the twelve?
Pr. 15	The ascension of Jesus, and light persevered for them.
Pr. 15	Resurrection, his end will be built up into a humble messenger.
Pr. 15	His word was defeated. The people have turned and nourished the shoot of my womb in the resurrection of last evening.
Pr. 15	The sea in the island of promises, and the head of resurrection, are repeated with me here.
Isa. 53	From my fear of resurrection he made a monument, or the power of the mouth.

Pr. 15	I will be asleep. Take bread and water. I will console the living by the resurrection of my cedar, the lamb of everybody's daughter.
Ps. 22	Keep resurrection for heaven. You were a man.
Ps. 22	The memory of resurrection is in me.
Ps. 22	Resurrection, but let it be obscure.
Ps. 22	God — which God? — is resurrection.
Ps. 22	Resurrection

There are not as many ascension codes in table 7C as there were crucifixion or resurrection codes. This is most likely due to the fact that we have not yet looked for as many codes on this topic. Nevertheless, several long, interesting codes appear in table 7C.

Table 7C

Text	Top Ascension Codes
Isa. 53	And command that we skip everything but the gem of ascension.
Isa. 53	Long live the ascension coming from God.
Isa. 53	The ascension of Jesus: for the sleeping one will shout. Listen!
Isa. 53	Father, the ascension of Jesus is heavenly.
Isa. 53	Ascension, considering God's hands under me.
Ps. 22	The ascension of Jesus, the lofty one, to him.
Pr. 15	The ascension of Jesus, and light persevered for them.
Ps. 22	He disguised the might. And God is there in the gift of dwellings of ascension. Her daughter will rule the sea.
Isa. 53	Ascension, we will thank God, and they will be near my shelter. Recognize her blood.
Isa. 53	Ascension, be a cause for my heart, and render my father transformed. I will be ashamed, and will divide the temple of the messenger.
Isa. 53	Ascension, monument of the saturated. And the hand of the monument is the daughter of the cedar supporter.
Isa. 53	The ascension of Jesus is the death of the witness.

Are there any Bible codes that support claims for the divinity of Jesus Christ? Not only are there short codes that do that, but in table 7D there are long, highly improbable ones with appropriate surrounding phraseology.

Table 7D

Text	Top Divinity of Jesus Codes
Ps. 22 Pr. 15	Please be merciful, miracle of God. Rule gently, the son soars from on high.
Pr. 15	They are for him — God and Jesus are one — and for you.
Isa. 53	God is for them, and long live the exalted flame. God is Jesus.
Ex. 20	Jesus has laid the foundation for existence. Where is the I AM?
Ps. 22	And the son of God loved you.
Isa. 53	Mary is the mother of God.
Pr. 15	Jesus is God almighty.
Ps. 22	God's Son will count for them.
Ps. 22	Jesus (Yeshu) is the living God.
Pr. 15	Jesus (Yeshu) is the living God.
Isa. 53	It will be understood. Jesus created.
Pr. 15	Jesus (Yeshu) is man and God.
Pr. 15	Yeshu is son of the name.
Isa. 53	Jesus created to the father
Isa. 53	Jesus created a high gift
Pr. 15	Son of the name
Pr. 15	Son of the highest
Pr. 15	Your God is Jesus.
Ps. 22	God and man
Ps. 22	King of Kings
Pr. 15	Man and God
Pr. 15	Son of God
Isa. 53	Son of Elohim

Ex. 20	Son of Elohim
Pr. 15	Living Yahweh
Pr. 15	The Trinity
Pr. 15	Immanuel
Ex. 20	Immanuel

We looked for "true messiah" and "false messiah" in each of the four clusters of Jesus codes. "True messiah" appeared twice as a code in Exodus 20 and once in Isaiah 53. The two Exodus 20 occurrences included additional adjacent wording. "False messiah" only appeared once, as part of the sentence, "What is the false messiah?" in Exodus 20. The powerful title, "Yeshua HaMashiach," or "Jesus the messiah," was found in Proverbs 15. And in Psalm 22, the code "only messiah" appears, followed by an incisive command: "Dwell in those words that he taught on high as our prince." It would be challenging enough to "dwell on" his words, but to "dwell in" them, or to live them out, is what this code states.

Table 7E

Text	Top Messiah Codes
Ps. 22	And only messiah: Dwell in those words that he taught on high as our prince.
Ps. 22	You will cry out for the blood of the messiah.
Isa. 53	Give them a Jewish messiah who will become a priest.
Ex. 20	For the weak ones, the prophesied messiah is a prevention.
Pr. 15	Jesus the messiah
Ex. 20	True messiah, lift up God almighty.
Ex. 20	Every eye is looking for a true messiah.
Ps. 22	Hello, the one mentioned above! Where is the rib (i.e., the basis) founded by the convert of Jesus my messiah?
Pr. 15	Wonderful counselor
Pr. 15	Newborn infant is a king.
Pr. 15	Your God Jesus is putting on a crown.
Ex. 20	What is the false messiah?

Ex. 20	Prince of peace
Isa. 53	Jesus reigns.
Pr. 15	Ruler in Israel
Pr. 15	Prince who is light.
Pr. 15	And father of root of Jesse
Isa. 53	True messiah
Ps. 22	My messiah is Jesus.
Ps. 22	Only messiah
Ps. 22	King Jesus
Pr. 15	Jesus is a messiah.
Ex. 20	Son of David
Ex. 20	Everlasting father
Pr. 15	The promised one
Pr. 15	He will be great.
Ps. 22	The king
Ps. 22	Messianic

Our research also uncovered a large number of codes about salvation (table 7F). Even though the extent of our research was quite limited, what has been found to date includes statements that cover a very broad number of aspects of this subject.

Table 7F

Text	Top Salvation Codes
Pr. 15	Raise the weak. He provided a Godly portion of guilt offering, a complete peace.
Ex. 20	Or come down, for the father of destiny will make you rejoice. Who is Yeshua? Our master over death.
Ps. 22	He wove the light to be my might, a living sacrifice for him to put on.
Isa. 53	God's miracle to us is appropriate for them in the temple.
Isa. 53	Who will it be that God's miracle will save?
Ps. 22	God's Son will count for them.

Pr. 15	The guilt offering, the son of man, humbled himself.
Isa. 53 Pr. 15	Her struggle is for them; God has graced them; Lord of Hosts.
Ps. 22	Who is Jesus? The guilt offering.
Ps. 22	Bear a rich jewel, eternal life.
Ps. 22	Those who dwell in God's miracle have lived.
Ps. 22	Her struggle is for them; God has graced them; Lord of Hosts.
Ex. 20	Please join to the one who returns, where God heals.
Ps. 22	Jesus is the guilt offering.
Ex. 20	Jesus is the guilt offering.
Isa. 53	Shiloh is a guilt offering.
Isa. 53	And brother of the Gospel, where has the manna spread?
Ps. 22	Final guilt offering
Ex. 20	Final guilt offering
Pr. 15	All of us in the glory of the Lord.
Ex. 20	Jesus our righteousness
Pr. 15	Have mercy on me, arm of the Lord.
Isa. 53	God has atoned.
Pr. 15	Atonement lamb
Ps. 22	Atonement
Pr. 15	Salvation
Pr. 15	Savior
Pr. 15	Redeemer
Ps. 22	Jehovah who sanctifies.
Ps. 22	Bread of life was fit for a prince.
Ps. 22	Jesus is my banner.
Ps. 22	Only savior
Ps. 22	Everlasting life
Ex. 20	Jehovah who sanctifies.
Pr. 15	Lamb of God
Ps. 22	Bread of life was plenty.
Ps. 22	And God will provide.
Ps. 22	Savior
Ps. 22	Blood of God
Ps. 22	Redemption

We looked for many short codes that, if they were part of longer codes, might provide clues as to who Jesus was and/or is. We were definitely not disappointed by what we found. Codes discovered in one of the three clusters beside Isaiah 53 are shown in table 7G.

Table 7G

Text	Top "Who is Jesus?" Codes
Ex. 20	Jesus is my name as any ignorant person from among them would have realized.
Ex. 20	Or come down, for the father of destiny will make you rejoice. Who is Yeshua? Our master over death. Prevent my fever for him. And who is God, who, like their nation, has crushed you?
Ps. 22	He attracts a man with the lion of Judah.
Ex. 20	They wished evil to Jesus the king.
Ex. 20	King Jesus, the heart of the nation
Ps. 22	Who is Jesus? The guilt offering.
Ex. 20	His name is Yeshua. Recognize thus.
Pr. 15	What is he? The gift. Yeshua . . .
Ex. 20	His name is Jesus (Yeshua).
Ps. 22	His name is Jesus.
Ps. 22	Jesus is the shepherd.
Pr. 15	Jesus the Nazarene
Ex. 20	The last Adam
Ex. 20	He is the word.
Pr. 15	Newborn king
Pr. 15	King is a child.
Pr. 15	Descendant of David
Pr. 15	Second Adam
Ps. 22	Second Adam
Pr. 15	Came in the flesh.
Ps. 22	The Nazarene
Pr. 15	Nazareth
Pr. 15	The Galilee

Pr. 15	Son of man
Pr. 15	Carpenter
Pr. 15	Galilean
Ps. 22	Nazareth

The question of who the "suffering servant" is who is portrayed in Isaiah 53 has been the subject of heated debate for two millennia. Codes found in Isaiah 53 that seemed pertinent to this question appear in table 7H.

Table 7H

Text	Top "Who is the Suffering Servant?" Codes
Isa. 53	Gushing from above, Jesus is my strong name, and the clouds rejoiced.
Isa. 53	And thirst for all of him is the faith of Mary the mother.
Isa. 53	Jesus the gift is master and my lord.
Isa. 53	Bemoan the prince, Jesus the king.
Isa. 53	The Rabbi from the glory of God
Isa. 53	My shepherds are among the disciples.
Isa. 53	Who is Jesus? Master.
Isa. 53	True messiah
Isa. 53	Second Adam

One of the more controversial verses in the New Testament is John 14:6: "Jesus answered, 'I am the way and the truth and the life. No one comes to the Father except through me.' " After looking for each of the shorter statements, "Jesus is the . . . ," we put together table 7I to display our findings.

Table 7I

Text	Top "The Way, the Truth and the Life" Codes
Isa. 53	And in his name, as he commanded, Jesus is the way.
Ex. 20	Only Jesus is the life, the memorial stone.
Isa. 53	Wonder! Jesus is the truth.
Ps. 22	Jesus is the life.
Ex. 20	Jesus is the life.

Finding the names of some of the disciples in the various passages was not unexpected, but the sheer length of the entire codes found around the names of these disciples was quite startling, as shown in table 7J.

Table 7J

Text	Top Disciples Codes
Isa. 53	If the friend of evil will thirst for the end of my innocence, his home is an urn. Let Judas have his day. To me, the exalted one, they fasted. Where are you? Its content will be written from my mouth. Father, indeed you will raise the dead over there.
Isa. 53	The cloud water is like a brother. What is measured? Where is God, Matthias? Who is a nail to his night? They are a nail to the emerging one that is not there.
Isa. 53	Greed, according to Matthew, was the rule.
Isa. 53	If indeed all the detail of this one is a string, does Peter detest the burden of the extra ships? And does my throne rest? So spoke God's poor.
Isa. 53	My people are in them. The sign of threshold of the weight of the tree is circular. Now, Andrew, violate (the law). Why this nail?
Isa. 53	As a poor man, Judas's heart is soft and light. Know that I will wait till the tooth in the jaw rejoices.

Isa. 53	Being naïve and indirect, James (Jacob) weakened. Or will it render him a truly comic actor to her voice with me?
Isa. 53	And to Andrew the light turn, my hand, and entertain . . . .
Pr. 15	According to Matthew

Six of the codes in table 7J are not mentioned in chapters 3 and 4 — because they were discovered after these chapters were written, and just prior to publication of this book. They are the codes about Matthias, Peter, James, and Andrew, as well as the second Judas code. If these recent findings had been included in the earlier chapters, the odds of the Isaiah 53 cluster emerging by chance would be even more remote than what is stated in those chapters.

Mary was the subject of several intriguing Jesus codes found in the four passages we examined. Curiously, the longest one in table 7K seems to refer to the Immaculate Conception.

Table 7K

Text	Top Mary Codes
Ex. 20	You are happiness to us, said the Lord. She became pregnant unto/by the Father.
Pr. 15	The Holiday of the Nativity (i.e., Christmas) is a gift to him and to the mother.
Isa. 53	And thirst for all of him is the faith of Mary the mother.
Isa. 53	Mary is the mother of God.
Pr. 15	Holy newborn Child
Ex. 20	Jesus (Yeshu) is her seed.
Pr. 15	Mother of Jesus of Nazareth
Isa. 53	Dreadful day for Mary
Isa. 53	She weeps much.
Pr. 15	The root of Jesse
Pr. 15	Son of Mary
Pr. 15	Elizabeth
Pr. 15	Betrothed
Pr. 15	Virgin

As mentioned before in chapter 3, the ELS for Mary appears 16 times with skips of 1-50 in Isaiah 52:12-54:3, even though it would only be expected to appear 4.76 times by chance in these verses. When we scrambled the Hebrew letters for Mary, and looked for them as ELSs, none of these jumbled spellings of Mary appeared an unusual number of times in this text.

We started looking for "God's miracle" as a code because it was one of the codes that appeared in the skeptic's Hanukah cluster. To our surprise, we found the five long codes shown in table 7L. After reviewing the content of these codes, they seemed to imply that "God's miracle" was Jesus Christ. When we started searching, we had no idea who or what "God's miracle" would turn out to be. We were surprised to find that these codes provided a consistent answer to that question.

Table 7L

Text	Top "God's Miracle" Codes
Ex. 20	When does God's miracle become our fire, motivation for his work?
Isa. 53	God's miracle to us is appropriate for them in the temple.
Isa. 53	Who will it be that God's miracle will save?
Ps. 22	Those who dwell in God's miracle have lived.
Ex. 20	God's miracle is alive as well as plentiful.

We believe that "God's miracle" refers to Jesus because the second code refers to that miracle being an appropriate sacrifice, the third code implies that this miracle brings salvation, and the last code states that this miracle is alive and abundant.

In Israel, Christmas is referred to as the "Holiday of the Nativity." The place where this ELS appears in the entire Old Testament with the shortest skip is in Proverbs 15, and because of this we began a search for other terms related to the Nativity in that chapter. Table 7M displays our findings.

Table 7M

Text	Top Nativity Codes
Pr. 15	The Holiday of the Nativity (i.e., Christmas) is a gift to him and to the mother.
Pr. 15	Newborn infant is a king.
Pr. 15	Holy, newborn child
Pr. 15	Cradle of hay
Pr. 15	Cradle of straw
Pr. 15	Gift of frankincense
Pr. 15	In the king of light is a gift.
Pr. 15	Gift of gold
Pr. 15	Gift of myrrh
Pr. 15	Gift of myrrh
Pr. 15	City of David
Pr. 15	At the inn
Pr. 15	Two Word Codes: Cow shed, From Nazareth, Holy child, No room, Roman tax, The Magi, To Egypt
Pr. 15	One Word Codes: Adoration, Angelic, Angels, Anna, Astrologer, Bethlehem, Caesar, Camel, Camels, Childbirth, Eastern, Egyptian, Ephratah, Gabriel, Gifts, Herod, Homage, Joseph, Manger, Persian, Pilgrim, Quirinius, Registration, Shepherds, Simeon, Stable

Most of the Nativity codes are short — for the simple reason that very few of them have been examined for possible extensions.

The final collection (table 7N) is truly miscellaneous, covering a wide range of topics. Nevertheless, many of them are quite interesting, and sometimes quite compelling.

Table 7N

Text	Top Miscellaneous Codes
Isa. 53	Know who the chosen people are or God will be angry.

Isa. 53	Hurry to pay heed about giving, for in it hearing will be given to you.
Ex. 20	What are they? But come and use Bible codes.
Ps. 22	God the healer, their joy, exists.
Ex. 20	God's word is enlightenment to me.
Ps. 22	Bread of life was fit for a prince.
Pr. 15	He will cut down evil in Jesus' name.
Isa. 53	Shed light on ark of the covenant and fade away. (about John the Baptist?)
Ps. 23	Bread of life was plenty.
Isa. 53	Captain of the army of the Lord, carry the ark of sight.
Isa. 53	From the joy of God my friend
Ps. 22	The presence of God (Shekinah)
Ex. 20	For the multitude there is the ark of the covenant and the sea.
Ps. 22	Please forgive the shrinking coast line. To me (Mel?) Gibson appears joyous.
Isa. 53	God will have his own day.
Ex. 20	The chosen people were circumcised by fire.
Pr. 15	Bread of life and for instruction
Ex. 20	For Jesus be glad
Ps. 22	The Jews of Jesus' joy to his bosom
Ps. 22	And God provides (Jehovah Jireh).
Isa. 53	And treasure in it
Ex. 20	Will make intercession
Ex. 20	Glory of the Lord
Isa. 53	Lamp of the Lord
Ps. 22	Made intercession
Ex. 20	The everlasting father
Ex. 20	He was oppressed.
Isa. 53	King of light
Ex. 20	Mighty God
Various	One Word Codes: Cleopas, Covenant, Hebrew, Immanuel, Intercessor, Isaiah, Jew, Joseph, Mediator, Rome, Salome

The Mel Gibson code is intriguing because the "coast line" is a nickname for Hollywood, whose general movie sales languished during 2004 while Gibson's *The Passion of the Christ* and three other movies (*Shrek 2*, *Spider-Man 2*, and *The Incredibles)* garnered far greater sales.

In this chapter, we have surveyed over 300 Jesus codes that have been grouped topically. What makes most of these codes different from those in previously published books is their length and the clear appropriateness of their content. On a subjective level, there could not be stronger proof of the reality of Bible codes than the substantive nature of most of these codes. While most of the terrorist codes are mysterious, most of the Jesus codes are cogent and to the point.

What is more astonishing is the process by which these codes were discovered. We began with the Hebrew Old Testament only. We used software produced in Israel. We retained the translation services of an agnostic Jew who was entirely educated in Israel in both biblical and contemporary Hebrew. Through all of this, the picture of Jesus that emerges is sheer gospel.

Yes, we admit there are enough uncertainties about any one code that it should not be relied upon for its content. Nevertheless, the collective force of all of the Jesus codes in this chapter is astonishing. One might wonder if we are hiding a number of strange Jesus codes that were found. While some of these exist as alternative translations, the codes presented in this chapter were chosen because they were in the best Hebrew, and not because they conformed more closely to Christian beliefs. And the translator is an agnostic Jew.

There is a bottom line. The phenomenon of Bible codes has been verified. It tells us that the Hebrew Old Testament was authored by God. Thus, we can do no better than to believe the Bible's literal message and to look to it as our guide for understanding who God is, how we should relate to Him, and how we should live.

Bible codes are not an end in themselves, but only a means to the end of appreciating the divine origin of the Bible. Just as we should not worship angels (Revelation 19:10), so we should not get hung up with Bible codes. Just as there are fallen angels, so there are codes from a terrorist's point of view (appendix 8). We would do well to heed the words of the angel before whom John bowed:

At this I fell at his feet to worship him. But he said to me, "Do not do it! I am a fellow servant with you and with your brothers who hold to the testimony of Jesus. Worship God!"
– Revelation 19:10

Topic A

Can Bible Codes Be Used to Predict the Future?

If one accepts the hypothesis that there truly are Bible codes about twentieth century people and events, then it is natural to wonder whether or not Bible codes could be used to accurately predict the future. Is it possible?

What follows is a summary of some of the key problems that confront anyone attempting to use Bible codes to predict the future.

- *It Appears That Real Codes Only Express a Viewpoint.* If the viewpoint is that of an untruthful person, the content of the code is not reliable. This would also be true of some verses in the Bible if attribution were eliminated (e.g., the serpent's statements in Genesis 3:4-5). With very few exceptions, codes lack attribution as well as sufficient context to determine who is speaking *(see appendix 8).*
- *Any Given Code Could Be Coincidental.* There is always the possibility that a particular code could only be a chance appearance. For most ELSs, especially those of six letters or less, there is a fair chance that they could be a pure coincidence. In other words, any particular ELS or code may not have any meaning at all. For this reason, it is often helpful to have some idea of the odds of each given ELS appearing coincidentally.
- *Adjacent Codes Could Be about Different Events.* Just because a particular code appears in close proximity to other codes about a particular event doesn't mean that it also is about the same event. It could well be about some other event. For example, suppose there is a cluster of 15 codes that two years from now we will clearly know are about Event A. Further suppose that there might be a cluster of 20 codes about some difficult period of history that won't occur for another 50 years (Event B). It is certainly possible that two or more such clusters about totally distinct events could appear in virtually the same place. If that were the case, how would we decide, before both events transpire, which codes refer to

Event A and which to Event B? Another possibility is that a particular cluster of ELSs could refer to a period of time that only begins in a given year. That period of time could be a month, a year, a decade, a century, or a millennium.

• *Adjacent Codes Could Be about Events That Occur around the Same Time but in Very Different Places.* While two codes could relate to things that happen on the same day (or some other time period), they could occur in places as far from one another as Timbuktu and New York City, or Jerusalem and New Delhi. For example, suppose we find codes for "terrorist attack" and "February 23, 2008." This raises the possibility that such attacks could occur at different places around the world.

• *Reasonable Alternative Translations May Mean Something Entirely Different.* The source data of Hebrew letters does not include vowels or syntax markings. It does not even specify where spaces between successive Hebrew words are. Because of all of these factors, it is quite frequently impossible to come up with a unique reasonable translation.

• *How Can We Be Sure We Have the Whole Message?* Even if we could somehow conclusively show that a certain code was "about Event A," we are still left with some major uncertainties until that event actually transpires or fails to take place. For example, one of the codes that appears in the Ezekiel 37 cluster is "Yesterday evening they whispered, bin Laden is dead." Without a more complete context, who is to say whether the appearance of that code could mean that bin Laden is dead now or will be dead later? When is "yesterday evening?" Until we are dealing with a past event, there is no definitive way to know what such a code could be referring to.

• *The Very Process of Selecting Possible Words to Search for Is Inherently Subjective.* Given our focus of looking for logically related words appearing as codes that are in close proximity, someone has to pick potential words for computer searches. (While this obviously injects a regrettable element of non-objectivity into our analysis, we have not as yet come up with a way to avoid this subjective element. We have, however, taken the approach of recording not only those codes we found, but also those we did not find. This makes all of the elements of our research potentially accessible to a critical reviewer.)

- **Some Intended Encoded Words May Now Be Extinct.** That is, they may not be part of the vocabulary of either biblical or contemporary Hebrew. The total vocabulary of the Hebrew Bible is only about 8,000 distinct words. It is quite likely that the total vocabulary of ancient Hebrew was considerably larger than this.

Because of these considerations, it should be evident that it will probably never be possible to use Bible codes to make accurate predictions about the future. This dovetails with scriptural warnings not to dabble in trying to read the future, to use "divination." God reserves for himself and for a few prophets the knowledge of events to come. The law He gave clearly prohibits it.

Do not practice divination or sorcery (Leviticus 19:26).

A man or woman who is a medium or spiritist among you must be put to death. You are to stone them; their blood will be on their own heads (Leviticus 20:27).

And other passages of the law equate fortunetelling or attempting to seek out future events with wicked practices of the nations that would surround them.

Let no one be found among you who sacrifices his son or daughter in (or who makes his son or daughter pass through) the fire, who practices divination or sorcery, interprets omens, engages in witchcraft . . . (Deuteronomy 18:10).

The nations you will dispossess listen to those who practice sorcery or divination. But as for you, the LORD your God has not permitted you to do so (Deuteronomy 18:14).

Nevertheless, our natural human curiosity compels us to attempt to catch glimpses of the future, even if they are, at best, only unreliable, haphazard glances that could be totally misleading!

Michael Drosnin's hysterical, if altruistic, attempts at using Bible codes to warn the world of imminent disaster in his book *Bible Code II: The Countdown* are a potent mixture of bad science and end-time prophecy. He has demanded audiences with world leaders — and in some cases gotten them — to warn that the violence between the Palestinians and Israel is going to develop into a catastrophic war, possibly involving nuclear weapons. Anyone who is at all familiar with the prophecies in the surface text of the Bible would consider these as probabilities, not possibilities.

In his earlier book, he predicted time frames for cataclysmic earthquakes, atomic holocaust and financial collapse. What he is basing most of his warnings on are truly insignificant codes. And what else? Divination?

For example, the chances of his cluster predicting a great earthquake for Los Angeles in 2010 appearing coincidentally are breathtakingly close to 100% (99.45%, by my calculation). Displaying such nearly inevitable examples is a disservice to serious codes analysis.

Topic B

Can You Find Anything
If You Look Long Enough?

Critics of Bible code proponents often present the argument that
the whole thing has simply been conjured up by ardent searchers
with powerful computers. If you sleuth long enough, in their opinion, you are bound to find just about anything you are looking for.
Or at least, you'll probably find some related words that support
your case.

There is a great deal of truth to this argument. In this chapter, we
will try to make explicit the nature of that truth. And we will also
raise issues about limits to the applicability of that truth to the question of the potential validity of the whole phenomenon of Bible
codes.

Critics point to the notion that there are an infinite number of
ways that the text of the Torah can be rearranged. If this is true, then
it might follow that if you did look long enough, you could find almost anything — or at least enough to support your original point of
view.

While intuitive consideration of the question of whether there
really are an infinite number of possible ELSs that can be found in
the Torah might lead to the emotional conclusion that this is true, the
reality is that it is not. What is true is that an enormous number of
ELSs can be lifted from the text of the Torah — or from any text, for
that matter. The number is so large that it feels like it must be infinite. Yet it is not. If we start to think of ways to get our arms around
how many ELSs could be formed, our minds boggle.

On the other hand, if we tackle the whole question in a slow and
methodical way, defining some algebraic terms and building up a
series of equations, it is not that difficult to determine precisely how
many ELSs can be formed from the Torah. In appendix 1, we have
provided a mathematical derivation of the number of possible ELSs
that can be formed from the Hebrew text of the Torah. Table 9A
shows the results.

Table 9A

Number of Letters in the ELS	Number of Possible ELSs in the Torah
2	92.9 billion
3	46.5 billion
4	31.0 billion
5	23.2 billion
6	18.6 billion
7	15.5 billion
8	13.3 billion
9	11.6 billion
10	10.3 billion
15	6.2 billion
20	4.6 billion

As table 9A shows, the number of possible ELSs is dependent on how many letters are in the proposed code. The more letters there are, the fewer possible ELSs. This makes intuitive sense because the bigger something is, the less of it one can expect to fit into a given space.

By the way, the numbers of possible ELSs in table 9A include both "forward" and "backward" ELSs. In other words, the ELS "anaid" is treated the same as "diana."

At this point, another argument might be raised to support the idea that the total possible number of ELSs that can be found in the Torah is infinite. Table 9A only shows the total number of possible ELSs for any given number of skips. To find the total possible number of ELSs, regardless of the number of letters, it would be necessary to add up the numbers in the above table and to extend the table to include all possible numbers of letters. Now the largest possible number of letters is the total number of letters in the Torah (304,805). This ELS would consist of the entire text of the Torah, all in exactly its current sequence of letters.

What happens if we expand the above table so that the number of letters goes all the way up to 304,805? Surely then the number of ELSs would become infinite? Again, our intuition fails to give us the correct answer. Using a derivation included at the end of appendix 1, we find that the total possible number of ELSs that can be formed with the Hebrew letters of the Torah, regardless of the number of letters, is less than 1,185,000,000,000, or a little less than 1.2 trillion. This is much smaller than the national debt, and is certainly a very finite number. So we see that there is a limit to the number of ELSs and that at some point you will have exhausted your search. You won't be able to come up with something simply by doggedly continuing to search — no matter how long you try — if that something isn't in this very large, but nevertheless finite, collection of possible ELSs.

Certain Words

Here is another twist for fledgling searchers. Certain words are much more likely to appear in that finite collection of ELSs than are others. The most important characteristic of such words is that they have only a few letters. The longer a word is, the less likely it is to occur at all as an ELS within the Torah.

There are only 22 letters in the Hebrew alphabet. If an ELS is only two letters long, then it could be any one of 484, or 22 times 22, combinations of letters. This is because the first letter can be any one of 22 possible letters, and the second letter can be any one of the same 22 possible letters.

If an ELS is three letters long, it could be any one of 10,648 (22 x 22 x 22) combinations of letters, and so forth. Table 9B dramatically shows how rapidly the number of possible letter combinations increases as the number of letters increases.

Table 9B

Number of Letters	Number of Different "Words" That Can Be Made With the Given Number of Letters
2	484
3	10,648
4	234,256
5	5,153,632
6	113,379,904
7	2,494,357,888
8	54,875,873,536
9	1,207,269,217,792
10	26,559,922,791,424
11	584,318,301,411,328
12	12,855,002,631,049,200
13	282,810,057,883,083,000
14	6,221,821,273,427,820,000
15	136,880,068,015,412,000,000
16	3,011,361,496,339,060,000,000
17	66,249,952,919,459,400,000,000
18	1,457,498,964,228,110,000,000,000
19	32,064,977,213,018,400,000,000,000
20	705,429,498,686,404,000,000,000,000

It shouldn't be surprising that the number of possible letter combinations increases so rapidly. After all, each number is 22 times greater than the previous one.

How can we find out how many times a given ELS might appear in the Torah, or any other text? Suppose that all Hebrew letters are equally likely to occur. (They aren't, but for the sake of simplicity let's say they are.)

Further suppose that the given ELS has seven letters. From the earlier table we see that there are 15.5 billion possible ELSs that can be formed from the letters of the Hebrew Torah. On the other hand, there are 2.5 billion possible combinations of letters that can be seven letters long. That means that the particular ELS we have chosen is only one of 2.5 billion possible letter combinations. Therefore, the typical ELS may be expected to occur 6.2 times (15.5 billion divided by 2.5 billion) within the Torah.

From this example, we can see that the expected number of times a given ELS might appear is going to be the total possible number of ELSs divided by the total possible number of different letter combinations that can be formed with those letters.

Table 9C

Number of Letters	Expected Number of Occurrences of a Given ELS in the Torah
2	191,954,098
3	4,362,579
4	132,199
5	4,507
6	164
7	6.208
8	0.242
9	0.00962
10	0.000389
11	0.0000159
12	0.000000657
13	0.0000000274
14	0.00000000115
15	0.0000000000485
16	0.00000000000206
17	0.0000000000000876
18	0.00000000000000375
19	0.000000000000000161
20	0.00000000000000000693

This clearly shows the enormous impact that the number of letters in a selected ELS has on the likelihood that it will appear within the Torah.

So if we see an example in a book on Bible codes that includes an ELS with only four letters in it, for example the name of Jesus (ישוע), we should probably yawn. This is because we can expect that ELS to appear 132,200 times within the Torah.

On the other hand, there is more to this question than what we have just covered. Suppose that of these 132,200 occurrences of the example ELS, the one in the book has the shortest skip. Suppose there is only one ELS with such a small skip. That is a much better cause for being impressed.

Drosnin's book is full of ELSs that are quite short. Unless these ELSs have very short skips, it is likely that they are nothing more than chance events. Two other authors who have written about Bible codes have also presented a number of short codes and discussed their appearance as being remarkable. They are Grant Jeffrey and Yacov Rambsel.

These authors have attached great significance to the appearance of the four-letter ELS for Jesus in the same text that describes prophecies that the authors claim were fulfilled by Jesus. The basic problem is that Yeshua is only four letters long, and furthermore, three of its letters are unusually common ones in the Hebrew alphabet.

Because of this, the ELS for Jesus is expected to occur more than 550,000 times in the Torah merely by chance. This means that Jesus ELSs are everywhere in great abundance in the first five books of the Bible, as are ELSs of random permutations of the Hebrew letters of the name of Jesus. Consequently, claims of significance regarding Yeshua ELSs being near something cannot be based on it being an unusual event. Likewise, the claims of certain Jewish people regarding the fact that the ELS for Jesus is close to the Hebrew word for false messiah are meaningless. In both cases, there is an absence of evidence that such occurrences are anything more than coincidence.

Longer ELSs

If we are dealing with an ELS that has eight or more letters, we may not have to look into the question of whether or not the given appearance of an ELS has the smallest skip. If there are eight letters, for example, the expected number of occurrences is only 0.242, so the chances are good that any appearance may be the only appearance of the ELS within the entire Torah. Clearly, as the number of letters in the ELS increases further, a chance occurrence becomes even more unlikely.

If a particular "code" is simply an original word in the Hebrew Torah, it doesn't make sense to talk about the chances it might appear accidentally. Specific words that appear in the text were all intentionally placed there as part of the literal text.

Significance Standards, or "What Would It Take to Convince You That Something Did Not Take Place by Chance?"

"What a coincidence!"

How many times have you heard that about some seemingly chance event? You are thousands of miles away from home, and you run into a friend from back home. Or you find out that someone else was born on the same day you were. Same day, and even the same year. Highly improbable things happen to most people.

Suppose you really wanted to get a good idea about whether or not such serendipitous events were just that. Or that they really were things that someone or "God" intended and caused to take place. How would you distinguish between coincidence and fate?

What if you had an R2D2 droid following you around that would instantly calculate the odds that any unusual event in your life was just happenstance? What kind of unlikely odds would impress you?

There are many philosophical types of people in the world. At the one extreme are those who see the hand of God in every event, no matter how trivial or commonplace. At the other are hard-core skeptics who would turn away and scoff at the possibility that something was predestined, no matter how small the chances were that it could have taken place by coincidence.

Making a Personal Choice

The minds of both the true believer and the invincibly skeptical have been made up, and there is no point in creating belief confusion by presenting contrary evidence to them. Most of us are somewhere in between these two extremes. Call us open-minded, broad-minded, or whatever you will. We've made a personal choice everyone is entitled to make.

On the one hand, the true believer would be convinced that God was directly intervening in his life whether or not unlikely things had taken place. If the R2D2 droid indicated odds of one in ten whenever something good happened, he would be reverently grateful for the divine blessings he had received.

In contrast, the committed skeptic might refuse to believe that any highly unusual event was "divinely appointed" unless the odds were less than a billion to one or a trillion to one. Winning the Publishers' Clearinghouse Sweepstakes once wouldn't be enough. After all, that could happen by sheer luck. The hard-core skeptic would need to win it two or three times before being open to the possibility that fate had pre-ordained his good fortune.

The Rest of Us

What about the rest of us? We don't fit into either of these extremes. A viable option for us would be the guidelines that those steeped in science and statistics have been trained to apply.

Statisticians speak of "hypothesis testing." A particular idea is translated into specific things that should occur if that idea is true. A scientific experiment is conducted. Based on the results, the hypothesis is either accepted as true or rejected as false based on a certain selected standard of significance.

If it can be shown that the odds are less than 1 in 20, or 5%, that something could happen, and it did occur, then that would be viewed as being "significant." If the experiment is repeated with comparable results even more confidence can be placed in the findings.

Were a revolutionary hypothesis tested, there would probably be a need to require that the odds be even smaller, such as 1 in 1,000 or 1 in 1 million. A severe test like this might be reserved for an idea that would severely challenge, or perhaps utterly overturn, the current consensus of theories that make up our view of reality.

For example, suppose that radio astronomers began receiving nonrandom signals from the same location in a nearby galaxy. How improbable would it have to be that those signals were truly non-random before the scientists had to acknowledge that they must be due to some form of intelligent life? For such a momentous conclusion, most of us would demand very rigorous standards — and that we should.

Contact?

In his book, *The Bible Code*, Michael Drosnin makes the claim that we have been receiving such non-random signals, not from a nearby galaxy, but from a book written at least 2,100 years ago. These "non-random" messages are about people and events in the twentieth century. They consist of ELSs, or equidistant letter sequences, extracted from the Hebrew letters of the Bible.

An example code highlighted in Drosnin's book is the name of a recent Prime Minister of Israel, Yitzhak Rabin. One of the letters of Rabin's name intersects with the word, "murdered," which appears in the original text of the Bible.

Drosnin makes reference to statistical standards regarding the chances that a particular code or clustering of codes could happen coincidentally. He then proceeds to claim that all of the examples shown in his book are "beyond chance" according to the ordinary standards of statistics and scientific testing. Based on his comments on page 28, it is his view that if the odds that a particular occurrence of codes has a chance of random occurrence of 1% or less, it is then "beyond chance." He then goes on to say the most rigorous test ever used is 1 in 1,000.

Unfortunately, not all is scientific in Drosnin's book. A true scientific experiment requires recording all the results obtained from every experiment conducted. And those results must be reckoned with in applying any significance test. Applying significance tests to the kinds of phenomena presented in Drosnin's book is quite possible. However, it would require careful documentation, not only of every finding, but of everything not found.

Bill and Monica

As an example of what such an experiment might look like, consider the following. A researcher picks two potentially related codes, such as "Bill Clinton" and "Monica Lewinsky."

He enters each into his code search program and notes the occurrences, if any, of each code and its location. He also uses a program that calculates the expected number of occurrences of each code within the search text. Each search is made and then it is noted whether or not each code was found.

If both of these codes are found and they are "near" one another, he would use his odds calculator to determine how improbable such an occurrence was. The results of each experiment would be recorded. A log of the results might look something like the data in table 9D.

Table 9D

First Code			Second Code		
Name of Code	No. of Occurrences		Name of Code	No. of Occurrences	
	Exp'd	Act.		Exp'd	Act.
William Clinton	0.002	0	Monica Lewinsky	0.005	0
Bill Clinton	0.119	0	Ms Lewinsky	0.344	0
President Clinton	0.001	0	Lewinsky	34.564	27
Wm Clinton	0.276	0	M Lewinsky	1.452	0
Clinton	1.971	4			
TOTAL OF ABOVE	2.369	4	TOTAL OF ABOVE	36.365	27

After completing this portion of the study, our hypothetical researcher also notes that there was one instance where one of the four ELSs for Clinton was "close" to one of the 27 ELSs for Lewinsky. In fact, it was so close that the L of Clinton is the same L as the first letter of Lewinsky. He also notes that the odds of this happening by chance are about 1 in 100.

Now, if he were a Republican, he might be satisfied with this level of significance. If he were a Democrat, it is likely that a higher standard would be desired. In either case, however, an objective researcher would log his failures as well as his successes. How might this be done?

Suppose that the researcher has tried 12 different possible spellings of Lewinsky in Hebrew. For each spelling, he calculates and records the expected number of incidents where the Clinton ELS and the Lewinsky ELS are "close," according to whatever criteria of closeness he chooses. He then searches for a close occurrence of both codes and also records how many, if any, such occurrences he finds. The results might be recorded as in table 9E.

Using Drosnin's method, we would most likely have been presented with a crossword illustrating the one incident where these codes are "close," and we would have been told that this incident was "beyond chance" because the odds were 100 to 1 against it happening.

But our researcher would have had a different story to tell. He would have presented the above results and noted that the probability of one of the spellings of Lewinsky being near the Clinton ELS was about 1 in 8. With odds at that level, he would have stated that his research was inconclusive and that it was quite possible that such a close occurrence could simply happen by chance.

Now, suppose that our researcher had conducted the same kind of search relative to all of the various possible ways that Clinton could be spelled in Hebrew. Suppose he came up with 12 different, plausible ways that Clinton could be spelled. Then, for each one of these different spellings, he compiled a table just like the one shown above. However, only one combination of a possible spelling of Lewinsky and a possible spelling of Clinton resulted in locating two codes that were sufficiently close to one another to be considered as possibly significant.

If the expected number of instances of these two codes being close was always 0.01, then we would have 144 (or 12 times 12) possible combinations of codes and the total number of expected occurrences of close crossings would be 1.44. Would this mean that it was certain, by chance, that some code for Clinton would be close to some code for Lewinsky? Actually, not.

Table 9E

Spelling of Lewinsky	Number of Incidents Where Clinton ELS & Lewinsky ELS Are "Close"	
	Expected	Actual
לונסקי	0.008	0
לונשקי	0.014	1
לוינסקי	0.007	0
לוינשקי	0.009	0
לונסקיי	0.013	0
לונשקיי	0.016	0
לבנסקי	0.006	0
לבנשקי	0.008	0
לבינסקי	0.012	0
לבינשקי	0.011	0
לבנסקיי	0.009	0
לבנשקיי	0.012	0
TOTAL	**0.125**	**1**

Statisticians use a probability distribution called the Poisson distribution that provides estimates of the chances of a given number of occurrences of some event, given that we know what the expected number of occurrences is. Based on that distribution, table 9F tells us the probability that a given number of occurrences will actually take place.

As table 9F shows, if there are 1.44 expected times that some code, which is a possible spelling of Clinton, is "close" to another code, which is a possible spelling of Lewinsky, there is still a 23.7% chance that none of these codes will be close. The chances of this event occurring once is about 1 in 3; of it occurring twice is about 1 in 4; of it occurring three times is about 1 in 9, and so forth.

Table 9F

Number of Occurrences	Probability
0	23.7%
1	34.1%
2	24.6%
3	11.8%
4	4.2%
5	1.2%
6	0.3%
7	0.1%
8	0.011%
9	0.002%
10	0.0003%
More Than 10	0.00004%
Total	**100.0%**

In contrast to the scientific experiment approach, Drosnin only tells us about his successful finds and says nothing about how many different things he or others attempted to find and could not. This adds a certain open-ended nature to Drosnin's quest that renders his efforts decidedly unscientific.

Some have argued that given fast enough computers and enough time any researcher can find anything as a code in the Hebrew text of the Bible — or in the English text of any book, for that matter. But there are only so many Hebrew letters in the Bible, and there are only so many possible codes that may be found by locating equidistant letter sequences within its text. As appendix 2 shows, there are many possible codes that simply cannot be found anywhere within the 1,000 pages of Hebrew letters that make up the Hebrew Bible, no matter how long you might look or how fast or powerful your computer's search engine may be. This fact, however, does not rescue Drosnin from the valid criticism that he has not been engaging in a true scientific experiment where the ordinary significance standards of statistics can be applied.

There are two other major problems with Michael Drosnin's view of his own findings. First, he discovers an intriguing word as a code. Then, he searches for other related words as codes. Again, he only reports his successes. Suppose there are 100 possible related words to the key word he has found as a code. He begins searching and only finds one of these that is close to his original key word. He reports his success. Suppose the odds of finding any one of these codes close to the original word was one in a thousand. Then you might suppose that if he could only find one such code out of 100 possible words that are "related," then the odds of that happening might be something like one in ten. Clearly, that is not very impressive.

Multiple Spellings Problem

Finally, we have the problem of multiple possible spellings for any given word. If the word was one that exists within the original Hebrew text, then it would be reasonable to take the position that there is only one acceptable spelling. But what if it is a modern word? We have a few choices. We could limit possible spellings to those in current use in Israel today. That would seem simple enough. However, if we didn't apply such a restriction, then there might be a dozen or so possible ways to spell a given word.

Given such problems, it might appear to make sense to simply dismiss the whole Bible code phenomenon as sheer nonsense. But what if some combination of codes "near" to one another had ridiculously small odds of occurring? Say a trillion to one? Such an improbable find is quite unlikely to be the result of the long hours put in by Drosnin, or by having a large bevy of possible related words or possible spellings of each possible related word.

And so it is that we need to raise the bar much higher than Drosnin proposes. Nevertheless, we can reasonably come up with standards of significance that are much higher than normal to deal with the hidden or not-so-hidden agendas of the various code searchers. And we can see if any of Drosnin's examples, or those of other researchers, can pass the test.

Let's say that we pick "Kennedy" as the key word and that there are 100 possible words that people would normally and readily associate with the word "Kennedy." Let us further assume that the chances of any one of those possible words being near "Kennedy" is 1 in 1,000, or 0.1%.

What, then, is the probability that at least one related word will be near? In this case, for any given possible related word, the odds are 99.9% that it won't be "near" the code for "Kennedy." This is true because the laws of probability state that the probability of the given related word being "near" and the probability of it not being "near" must total up to 100%. Now if there are two related words, say "Jacqueline" and "President," the probability that neither will be "near" to the ELS for "Kennedy" will be

$$99.9\% \times 99.9\%, \text{ or } 99.9\%^2.$$

Because the event of the "Jacqueline" ELS being close to the "Kennedy" ELS and the "President" ELS being close are independent, it follows that the chances of neither of them being close is the product of the individual probabilities. This is also true of the chances that the "Jacqueline" and "President" ELSs will be close to the "Kennedy" ELS.

It follows that for any N given possible related words, the probability is 99.9% times itself N times, or $(99.9\%)^N$, that none of the key words will be near the primary key word. It is important that the occurrence of each of these possible related words is unrelated to whether or not the other word appears near the "Kennedy" ELS. In the language of statistics, we would say that these events are independent of one another. Consequently, the key words can't be some variation of one another.

What happens as the number of possible related words (N) increases? Table 9G shows what odds would be equivalent to a significance standard of 99.9% for different values of N. If there are numerous possible ways to spell a given word in Hebrew, then each of these should be counted as a distinct, related ELS.

Table 9G

Number of Possible Related ELSs	Odds Equivalent to a Significance Standard of 99.9%
1	1,000
10	9,995
100	99,950
1,000	999,500
10,000	9,995,000
100,000	99,949,992
1,000,000	999,499,901

If there is only one possible related ELS to a given code, then a significance standard of 99.9% is the same as odds of 1 in 1,000. If there are 10 possible ELSs, this same 99.9% significance standard would be identical to the odds being 1 in 9,995 that any given related ELS would cross the original ELS. If there are 1,000 possible related ELSs, then the equivalent odds would be 1 in 999,500, or 1 in 1 million.

We can quickly approximate any of these odds by starting with the original significance standard, expressed in odds of 1 out of X, and multiplying the X by the value of N, the number of possible related ELSs, to get the approximate odds equivalent to that significance standard. For example, if we start with an original significance standard of 1 in 1,000 and there are 100 possible related ELSs, then the equivalent significance standard would be about 1 in 1,000 times 100, or 1 in 100,000. According to the above table, the actual equivalent standard would be 1 in 99,950.

The next table shows how different probabilities of a given related ELS not being near change as we increase the number of possible ELSs that could be associated. The data in table 9H was computed using the formula $1/(1-X)^N$, where X is the significance standard.

Table 9H

Number of Possible Related ELSs	Significance Standard Required for Any One Given ELS				
	Significance Standard				
	99.9%	99%	98%	95%	90%
1	1,000	100	50	20	10
10	9,995	995	495	195	95
100	99,950	9,950	4,950	1,950	950
1,000	999,500	99,500	49,499	19,496	9,492
10,000	9,995,000	994,992	494,984	194,958	94,913
100,000	99,949,992	9,949,917	4,949,832	1,949,573	949,123
1,000,000	999,499,901	99,499,163	49,498,317	19,495,726	9,491,222

Remember now that Drosnin stated that the most rigorous significance standard ever used was 1 in 1000, or 99.9%. If there are 1,000 possible related ELSs, then we should apply a significance standard of 1 in 1 million. In many of Drosnin's examples, we are dealing with this kind of situation, and we would do well to dismiss any of his examples unless the odds are less than 1 in 100,000 or 1 in 1 million. Otherwise, we are in danger of attaching importance to what is probably coincidental.

R. Edwin Sherman

Frequently Asked Questions and Answers

What Should We Make of the Bible Codes?
Key Questions and Answers

Are Bible codes real?

Some ELS phenomena must be real because they are far too improbable to be due to chance.

Isn't the Bible just a collection of old myths and fables?

The existence of real code phenomena provides compelling evidence that when the text was written 2,500+ years ago, the Author of the Hebrew Bible had knowledge of modern day events. Given the prescience and super-human intelligence of the Author, the view that the Bible is merely a collection of ancient myths should be rejected.

Has any relationship been discovered between the content of the literal text and its underlying codes?

Yes. There is a very strong relationship. In just one example, the Isaiah 53 cluster, where the prophet describes the sufferings of a coming messiah, there are more than 50 ELSs that are each long enough to be quite unlikely to appear by chance and that all ostensibly relate to the topic of Jesus Christ.

Who wrote the Bible?

Because of the answers to the above three questions, considered together, and the clear message of the literal text regarding its authorship, the evident author of the Bible is God, not human beings or aliens.

Why would the author of the Bible go to the trouble of encoding it?

Of the two likely purposes for encoding (a) authentication of the super-human authorship of the literal text and (b) extraction of reliable new information/predictions by decoders), only the first is potentially valid. The primary reason that (b) is not a valid purpose is that real codes only express a viewpoint. If the viewpoint is that of an untruthful person, the content of the code is not reliable.

This would also be true of some verses in the Bible if attribution were eliminated (e.g., the serpent's statements in Genesis 3:4). With very few exceptions, codes lack attribution as well as sufficient context to determine who was speaking. For this reason, it is unlikely that codes could ever be used to conclusively support or refute any specific doctrine of an established religion — other than providing an answer to the question of who wrote the Bible.

What are some of the problems in deciding which ELSs are real and which aren't?

The relative improbability of the appearance of different ELSs can be accurately gauged. However, even the messages of the most improbable ELSs are inherently not reliable, for one or more of the following reasons:

a. Codes only express a viewpoint (see answer to the previous question), which could be that of God, terrorists, or any person, notable or otherwise.

b. Spaces selected between words may differ from those originally intended.

c. Interpretations of Hebrew experts may differ.

d. Copying errors in manuscripts of the Hebrew Bible can create unintended ELSs and eliminate intended ELSs. However, the possibility that codes were designed to appear in one or more of today's faulty Hebrew manuscripts, should not be ruled out.

e. Some intended encoded words may now be extinct (i.e., not part of the vocabulary of either biblical or contemporary Hebrew).

f. Any individual word or phrase in an ELS may be coincidental, in part or in whole, or its translation may differ from its original content and/or meaning.

g. A long ELS could represent a conversation where the viewpoint shifts.

Why would God encode unreliable messages?

If individual Bible codes were truly reliable, their messages would compete with the literal text and Bible code researchers would become prophets on whom many people would rely. Neither of these would be positive situations, so it is best that the content of Bible codes should always be subject to question.

What about the millions of short ELSs in the Bible?

Short (three to six-letter) ELSs are everywhere, and their individual appearance, either alone or close to other short individual ELSs, should not be construed as having any intended existence or relationship.

What is your opinion of the codes presented in Michael Drosnin's two books on codes?

Nearly all of the examples in his books are trivial (i.e., they are not remarkable in comparison with those extractable from a non-encoded Hebrew text).

How do you respond to the Mathematicians' Statement against Bible codes?

The Mathematicians' Statement is severely outdated and should be retracted (see www.math.caltech.edu/code/petition.html). At www.biblecodedigest.com/page.php/57 you may see a full response to the petition.

Why do you place so much emphasis on longer codes?

The longer an intelligible ELS is, the less likely it is to be a coincidence.

Is it possible to find longer ELSs in non-encoded texts?

Yes. The extension discovery rate (d) to an existing ELS is 16% to 20% in a widely accepted non-encoded Hebrew control text (a Hebrew translation of *War and Peace*). A realistic benchmark for the total number of final ELSs in a cluster that consists of k extensions expected to emerge from a search around n initial ELSs, is

$$n(k+1)d^k(1-d)^2.$$

None of the cluster examples in published books significantly exceed this benchmark.

Why are clusters of codes important?

Some extensive clusters of lengthy codes, such as the Ezekiel 37 cluster and the Isaiah 53 cluster, must be real, at least in part, because the total number of lengthy ELSs in them decisively exceeds the benchmark in the previous answer. For example, the Isaac Newton Bible Code Research Society examined 295 initial ELSs about post-9/11 events in Ezekiel 37. According to the formula presented in the answer to the previous question, they *should* have found only seven ELSs with three or more extensions if the text was not encoded. In actuality, they found 33 such ELSs — far more than the seven that were expected. This is very compelling evidence of the extreme improbability of their appearance by chance. The indicated discovery rate in these clusters is significantly higher (31% and 48%, respectively) than in the non-encoded control text.

Do Bible codes show up only in the Old Testament?

Highly improbable ELS groupings have been discovered in preliminary research of the Aramaic New Testament. Since Aramaic uses Hebrew letters, available code search software can be used to research the Peshitta, as the Aramaic New Testament is known. More work needs to be done in the Peshitta before conclusive results can be presented.

Are the codes you find in both ancient and modern Hebrew?

Nearly all ELSs discovered to date (by BCD) are expressed in biblical Hebrew phrasing, in some cases using modern Hebrew words.

Can codes predict the future? Why can't we use them to avert disasters like the September 11 attacks?

Some intended prophecies may have been preserved intact. But although many codes appear to be prescient, none are completely reliable as predictions (see the answer to the question, "What are some of the problems in deciding which ELSs are real and which aren't?" earlier in this chapter).

What is the connection between Bible codes and the Kabbalah?

The scientific exploration of improbable Bible code phenomena has no connection to the mystical practices of the Kabbalah, an ancient offshoot of Judaism. A rumored relationship grew out of the fact that Kabbalah practitioners developed a method of encoding and decoding any language with a system of early probability computation. This system developed into the one many intelligence units use today to create codes and crack enemy codes.

What about the claim that aliens wrote the Bible?

Though some have claimed that real codes are evidence that aliens wrote the Bible, to our knowledge no one has formulated a substantive hypothesis that can be examined (or tested statistically) in support such a belief.

What is a "code?"

Suppose we start with the sentence, "All of our avenues are wide." We eliminate the spaces and look for words that could be formed from letters that are equally spaced within the letter string. If we start with the second letter (L) and then skip 3 letters to pick up the next letter of the code (O), and so forth, we will find the word, LOVE within the string: a **L** l o f **O** u r a **V** e n u **E** s. LOVE is an equidistant letter sequence (ELS). Such codes can have a skip of any length and can either be forward or backward.

Can you find anything as a code?

Yes and no. What makes the difference is how long the code is. If the code consists of six or fewer letters, it is almost certain that it will appear somewhere in the Bible by chance. If the code has eight or more letters it is very unlikely that anyone will be able to find it as a code. And the longer it is, the more unlikely it is that it will be found.

Are codes with odds of 1 in 1000 beyond chance?

Generally not. The odds need to be much smaller than that. First of all, to date, the most popular authors have been very unscientific in their research. They have only reported their successes and not their failures. If you look for 1,000 different things, each of which has a 1 in 1,000 chance of occurring, you will probably find one or more such things. Second, there are no real vowels in Hebrew, so this makes it possible for a few given strings of letters to represent several possible words. Third, if the word is a contemporary person or thing, there may be many possible ways to spell it.

How small should the odds be before we should conclude that some group of codes is beyond chance?

At least 1 in 100,000 or 1 in 1 million. If the odds are less than 1 in 1,000 or 10,000, then the code may be viewed as "intriguing," but not beyond chance.

Isn't it true that there is no limit to the number of ELSs that can be found in the Bible?

Though very large, the total number of ELSs in the Hebrew Bible is actually quite limited. In fact, it is a bit less than 20.2 trillion. That's in the same ballpark with the Gross National Product of the United States.

Couldn't you find relevant ELSs about any topic if you looked long enough in any text?

It heavily depends on how long the ELSs are. If the ELS is six or less letters long, it is almost certain we will find it somewhere within the Hebrew Bible at some skip. If it is ten or more letters long, it is unlikely we will find it anywhere. And the longer it is, the more unlikely it is that we will find it anywhere. For example, if it is 15 letters long, the odds are 1 in 1.3 billion against finding it anywhere in the Hebrew Bible. If it is 20 letters long, the odds are 1 in 9,621 trillion against finding it anywhere. This is why we attach such significance to the many lengthy ELSs presented in this book.

So what makes the difference between a coincidental and a highly improbable cluster?

The coincidental one will only have ELSs that are eight or fewer letters long. The highly improbable cluster will have a number of ELSs that are ten or more letters long. The longer the ELSs, the better, and the more long ELSs in the cluster, the better. How close together or spread out the ELSs are is also a factor.

Can you give examples of coincidental and highly improbable clusters?

The Hanukah cluster only consists of seven ELSs and the longest one is seven letters long. As table 4C documents, the Isaiah 53 cluster includes 50 ELSs that are each longer than the longest ELS in the Hanukah cluster. Furthermore, ten of the Isaiah 53 ELSs are more than three times longer than the longest Hanukah ELS. And 27 of the Isaiah 53 ELSs are more than twice the length of the longest Hanukah ELS.

Couldn't codes about Jesus have been embedded in the text after he lived?

No. The Dead Sea Scrolls include a nearly complete copy of the book of Isaiah that is dated at 100 B.C.

How can you know for certain whether or not a particular code is intentional?

You can't. There's always some chance, however small, that the code could be coincidental. Like other code breakers, Bible code analysts use statistics to help them evaluate codes. We can know "beyond a shadow of a doubt" that a given code was intentional if statistical analysis shows that the odds of its chance occurrence are extremely small (e.g., less than 1 in a trillion).

Can you know for certain that a code cluster is predominantly real?

Yes. If the odds of the combined cluster appearing by chance are extremely small (say, less than 1 in a trillion times a trillion), then chance should be ruled out.

Wouldn't changes in the Hebrew text down through the centuries destroy codes?

The fact that some clusters cannot be coincidental is evidence that much encoding has survived the effects of whatever copying errors were made. It is possible that the same God who dictated the earliest texts of the Hebrew Bible also guided the medieval rabbis who finalized the copies of the Masoretic text that today are used for code searches.

Why would God give us codes we can't understand?

That is an excellent question. Some of the codes we turn up are easily understood, but some of them — especially the longer ones — are difficult to interpret. In fact, we believe that some of them are imparting several unconnected thoughts.

After giving this a great deal of consideration, we have decided that since we are on the cutting edge of this research, we will simply not be able to comprehend a lot of what we find. Eventually, we (or other researchers) will be able to put it all together. The longer codes may be combined with numerics, three-dimensional ELSs, parallel codes, or other disciplines that have not yet been applied to them. In truth, the sky is the limit when it comes to discovering and trying to understand the mysteries of the Bible.

A fair comparison is the surface text of the Bible itself. To someone unfamiliar with it, the text is strange and incomprehensible. Parts of the book of Revelation, for instance, are difficult to understand even for those who read the Bible daily. And yet down through the centuries, researchers have unlocked the great truths of the Bible and how they all fit together.

And if the message of a code is mysterious, perhaps God wants us to focus on the implications of the sheer fact that codes exist rather than the specific content of any handful of codes.

Our view is based at least in part on the Old Testament verse that reads, "It is the glory of God to conceal a matter . . . " (Proverbs 25:2).

What contributions have skeptics made to code research?

They have helped people to understand that if someone presents only a few short codes, all they have done is come up with something you could pull out of almost any book. That's clearly worth knowing, for otherwise people might jump from some simple code example to highly unwarranted conclusions. Such abuses should be avoided.

Are abuses of the codes a good reason to dismiss the whole thing?

The Bible has often been misused. Is that a reason to reject it? Of course not! Dubious code practices are analogous to the bad practice of quoting Bible verses out of context. The cure isn't to throw the whole thing out, but to approach it correctly. Much education is needed. Over time, the difference between proper, in-depth research and naïve or self-serving misuse will become evident.

What valid purpose could Bible codes serve?

I believe that they serve as a source of authentication of the Bible — that it was written by an intelligence far greater than that of any human being — who knew the future when it was written. To me that means God. Codes could also serve as evidence in clarifying the meaning of various literal passages. For example, if something had been prophesied in a given passage, and there is uncertainty as to whether or not some subsequent event was a fulfillment of that prophecy, the existence of an extremely improbable cluster of codes about that event (or person) might serve as supporting evidence of its realization.

Is it true that no codes have yet been found that are beyond chance?

Many clusters of codes have been discovered that have odds that are smaller than 1 in 1 billion — or beyond chance. In my opinion, such discoveries are statistically very significant and are "intentional" codes. They were not placed where they were by accident.

What characteristics make given codes less likely to appear by chance?

First, there are one or more lengthy codes (eight or more letters). Second, there needs to be a cluster — several codes of related words that are close together. Closeness is generally critical because it greatly shrinks down the span of text within which a code can appear. This significantly reduces the probability of a chance occurrence. Third, the shorter the skips between the successive letters of a code, the more unlikely each code is to occur.

What codes discovered to date are the most improbable?

The longest and most coherent codes from either the Isaiah 53 or the Ezekiel 37 clusters are the most improbable ones discovered to date.

How improbable are these clusters?

The odds of a cluster as extensive as that in Ezekiel 37 being coincidental are about 1 in 6.4 followed by 131 zeroes. The odds of a cluster as extensive as Isaiah 53, and that contains as many relevant long codes as this cluster does, are considerably more remote (less than 1 in 2.189 followed by 192 zeroes).

Is there validity to the claim that the codes prove Jesus is a false messiah?

No. These claims are based on an incident where the Hebrew word for Jesus, Yeshua, is close to the word for false messiah. However, Yeshua (ישוע) consists of four very common Hebrew letters and should be expected to appear as a code more than 550,000 times in the Torah (the first five books of the Old Testament) alone by chance. In other words, Yeshua is everywhere and so the fact that it is near a code for false messiah has no statistical significance.

Are there secret messages or esoteric knowledge in the codes?

Nothing of that kind has been discovered to date.

What of the claim that only the Torah contains significant codes?

Not true. As mentioned previously, the Ezekiel 37 cluster includes the most significant codes yet discovered.

If an author presents clearly coincidental codes as improbable ones, should we dismiss everything the author presents?

No. Codes either exist or they don't — in a cold, hard, factual way. Whether or not the person who discovers them has the math skills to distinguish between likely and unlikely codes has nothing to do with whether any codes they present are improbable or not.

Does the existence of some utterly improbable code clusters prove anything?

They scientifically substantiate that the author(s) of the Bible (or some source inspiring those authors) knew current events at the times the portions of the Hebrew Bible that contain the codes were written. This is a very revolutionary finding that should challenge every open-minded scientist and intellectual who does not believe in the miraculous. In addition, the extreme improbability of the Isaiah 53 cluster indicates that Jesus Christ is the "man of sorrows" described in that passage.

Should we only consider the occurrences of a code that are the ones with the smallest skips?

Some writers on the subject have advocated such a restriction, but it is not necessary. To be sure, if a code is the one in the entire text with the smallest skip, that makes it more improbable than just any appearance of the code. Since it is possible to calculate the odds in those cases where the code isn't the one with the smallest skip, consideration of such occurrences is acceptable.

Are there other mathematicians who believe the codes are real?

Yes. They include math professors at Harvard (Kazhdan and Bernstein), Yale (Piatetski-Shapiro), Hebrew University of Jerusalem (Rips and Furstenberg), and UCLA (Michelson).

Where could I get more information about the codes?

I suggest reading Dr. Jeffrey Satinover's book, *Cracking The Bible Code* (William & Morrow, New York). Dr. Satinover's scholarship is quite respectable and his book is an informative presentation of a Jewish perspective on the codes. Further information is available on our web site (www.biblecodedigest.com) or other sites that can be readily located by searching with the term, Bible codes.

What concerns do you have about common opinions people have today about the Bible codes?

On the one hand, some people are excited about meaningless noise. At the other extreme, some are dismissing the whole thing out of the incorrect belief that you can find anything as a code. Finally, because popular authors have taken an unscientific approach and generally lack the necessary math skills, their writings may lead many to dismiss the entire phenomenon as an illusion. In short, misconceptions are the norm and solid knowledge is in short supply.

What has been the main response of skeptics to the claims of code proponents?

Similar codes can be found in any book.

Are the skeptics right?

Definitely not. All the skeptics have shown is that very simple clusters of short codes can be found in any book. The examples they provided from *Moby Dick* and *War and Peace* were fairly comparable to many of the simpler published examples, but they are seriously out of date. Some proponents' recently discovered clusters of Bible codes are so complex and extensive that they really couldn't be a coincidence. The most extensive cluster of Bible codes found to date (the Isaiah 53 cluster) is vastly more complex and improbable than the most extensive cluster found in any book other than the Bible. There really is no comparison.

Since words or phrases expressing any viewpoint, whether positive or negative, about virtually any subject, can be found as Bible codes, doesn't that invalidate the entire phenomenon?

It does invalidate usage of Bible codes to prove the validity of any particular viewpoint or prediction. As stated above, all that real Bible codes do is express a viewpoint, which could be that of God, a terrorist, or advocate of a well-known group, or for that matter, someone with obscure views.

What other clusters of significance have been discovered?
Other significant clusters of codes about Jesus Christ have been discovered in Psalm 22 and Proverbs 15. Additional significant clusters of codes about the war on terrorism and end-time events have been found in Ezekiel 7, Ezekiel 40, Jeremiah 17, and Daniel 2. Details on these findings can be obtained from the www.biblecodedigest.com website.

Have any other kinds of Bible code phenomena been discovered that are highly improbable?
Yes. Mosaics and underscoring. A mosaic occurs when two or more occurrences of the same ELS form a visual image when laid out in a crossword matrix format. One such mosaic is described in the section, "The Third Non-Random Facet: Excess Occurrences of Prophecy/Guilt Offering ELS Crosses," in chapter 3. These consist of images of a cross formed by two intersecting ELSs of the Hebrew word for guilt offering. When this Hebrew word is spelled backwards, it is the Hebrew word for prophecy. Thus, these cross images emphasize that Isaiah 53 is a prophecy about a guilt offering.

Underscoring is the tendency for an ELS about a specific topic to appear much more often than expected by chance in passages about that topic. The most prominent example discovered to date is one where every one of the 35 letters of the five shortest occurrences of the King David ELS in the Hebrew Bible appear in verses about King David (see www.biblecodedigest.com/page.php/134).

Who did the Hebrew translations for this book and what are his qualifications?
Nathan Jacobi, Ph.D., is a retired college professor with more than 20 years of research, development and scientific computing in applied physics, aerospace and geophysics. Dr. Jacobi received a Ph.D. in physics from Weizman Institute of Science in Rehovot, Israel. He received an M.Sc. in physics and a B.Sc. in mathematics from Bar-Ilan University in Ramat-Gan, Israel. He has taught atomic and molecular physics, quantum mechanics, college algebra, trigonometry and analysis, analytic geometry, and calculus both in Israel and in the United States.

Dr. Jacobi is a Holocaust survivor. He was born in France in 1938 of Jewish parents. His parents fled France early during the Nazi occupation, leaving him to be raised by an anti-Nazi German family in the forests of southern France. After the war ended, his parents returned, and he moved with his family to Israel, where he was educated (1945-1969). There he received a thorough education in both biblical and contemporary Hebrew. Recently, he has taught numerous Hebrew classes at introductory and intermediate levels.

Who reviewed the formulae presented in this book?

Reider Peterson, Ph.D., is professor emeritus of statistics at Southern Oregon University. He has 22 years of experience as a college professor, specializing in mathematical probability and statistics, experimental design and multiple regression. Dr. Peterson received his B.S. at Northern Arizona University (1961), his M.S. from the University of Maine (1965), and his Ph.D. from Montana State University (1974).

Dr. Peterson reviewed all formulae in the book except for those recently derived for the Markov Chain ELS Extension Model presented in appendix 7. These formulae were reviewed by Dr. Jacobi and included in the paper, "Non-Random Equidistant Letter Sequence Extensions in Ezekiel." The paper was presented at the Fourteenth Conference of the Association of Christians in the Mathematical Sciences, in May 2003. The Association is primarily comprised of mathematics professors at Christian colleges and universities throughout the United States.

Who was the editor of the book?

Dave Swaney has many years of experience as an editor and writer. He has written for the Los Angeles Times, Entrepreneur, The Robb Report, Crawdaddy and many others. During his years in the record business, he wrote liner notes for several top-selling recordings, including "The Byrds Greatest Hits" and "The Chambers Brothers Greatest Hits." He also produced records for CBS Records, Maranatha Music, and Mercury Records. In the mid-90s, he was a senior copywriter and associate creative director for Focus on the Family in Colorado Springs. Since 1999, he has served as the editor and as a primary contributing author of the Bible Code Digest. He is currently pastoring a new home church in Nelson, New Zealand, and continues as a contributing editor for the Digest.

Appendix One

Estimating the Total Number of
Possible Equidistant Letter Sequences

Suppose we start with a given text, such as the first 25 letters of Lincoln's Gettysburg Address. Once we remove all the spaces between its words, we have the following body of text:

fourscoreandsevenyearsago

We will define a letter sequence (LS) from the above text as being a grouping of consecutive letters. For example, "foursc" is an LS with six letters which begins at the start of the text. When we describe a given LS, we could describe its length in terms of the number of letters of which it consists. Alternatively, we could measure its length in terms of the number of jumps or skips between consecutive letters. For the LS, "foursc," there are five skips. First there is the one between the "f" and the "o." Second, there is the skip between the "o" and the "u." And so forth. Clearly, the number of skips in an LS is equal to the number of letters in it, less one. This gives us

---

Definition 1A. The length (L) of an LS is the number of skips between its letters. It is one less than the number of letters in the LS.

Next, we will assign a number to each letter of the given text, which is its position in relation to the beginning of the text. Thus, the number 1 is assigned to the first letter in the text (f), 2 to the second (o) and so forth.

The first formula we will derive is that for the number of letter sequences (LS) of a given length (L) that can be found in the text. An LS must consist of consecutive letters. We will first look only at forward LSs — those that run in the direction from the earlier to the later section of the text. Later we will consider backward LSs as well. We will denote the number of the first letter of the LS as b (for beginning) and the number of the last letter of the LS as e (for ending). The position of a given LS may then be precisely described as (b, b+1, b+2, . . . , b+ L) or as (b, b+1, . . . , e).

How many forward LSs of length L may be found in a text of length T? We may count the number of possible LSs by using the number corresponding with their first letter. The last LS we can form is defined by its last letter having the number e = T. That LS is then (b, b+1, b+2, . . . , T). Since this LS is also described as (b, b+1, b+2, . . . , b+L), we can equate the formulas for the position of the last letter. This gives us T = b + L. Therefore, the number of forward LSs of length L in a text of length T is T - L. This becomes

---

Formula 1A. The number of forward LSs of length L in a text of T letters is

$$T - L.$$

Example One. How many forward LSs of length 2 can be found in a text of 10 letters? The possible LSs are (1, 2, 3), (2, 3, 4), (3, 4, 5), (4, 5, 6), (5, 6, 7), (6, 7, 8), (7, 8, 9) and (8, 9, 10). So there are 8 possible forward LSs. Formula 1A gives us the answer of 10 - 2 = 8.

It may seem inconsistent to measure the length of the text by the number of letters (T) and the length of an LS by the number of skips (L) between its letters. And it is. However, defining things this way significantly simplifies the various formulas derived in these appendices. That is why we have chosen the definitions we have presented.

Let us define an equidistant letter sequence (ELS) as a letter sequence where there is a skip, or interval (i), between the successive letters in the sequence. Such a sequence would be denoted by (b, b+i, b+2i, . . . , b+L*i). An LS is a special case of an ELS where the interval i is 1.

Let's take the example text above. An ELS of interval 2 beginning with the third letter in the text would be

fo u r s c o r e a n d s e v e n y e a r s a g o

In this example, the ELS is "usoen." As one might imagine, most ELSs formed from an intelligent text where the spaces have been eliminated will be nonsense sequences. One of our goals will be the derivation of formulas to begin to form an opinion about whether the occurrence of intelligent ELSs is a matter of coincidence or of intentional embedding within a given section of intelligent text. This will involve the deriving of formulas to determine the probability that a given ELS could appear by chance.

Now "usoen" is a forward ELS because its letters progress in the same direction as the surface text. If we reversed the order of the letters in the ELS, we would have a backward ELS. In this example, it would be "neosu."

How many forward ELSs of a given length L and interval i can be formed out of a text of length T? To determine this, we proceed much as we did to derive a formula for the number of possible LSs. We look at the representation of the last possible ELS:

$$(b, b+i, b+2i, \ldots, b+L*i).$$

We know that the number of the last letter is also T, so we have the formula

$$T = b+L*i.$$

As in the case of the number of possible LSs, the number of possible ELSs with a given interval is the b of the last possible LS. In other words, we may start counting the possible ELSs starting with the one that begins with the first letter in the text. Then, to solve for the number of possible forward ELSs, we only need to solve the above formula for b for the last, or rightmost ELS:

$$b = T - L*i.$$

This gives us

Formula 1B. The number of possible forward ELSs of a given length L and interval i that can be formed out of a text of T letters is

$$T - L*i.$$

Notice that when $i = 1$, the number of ELSs is $T - L$, which is Formula 1A.

Example Two. How many forward ELSs of length 2 (skips) and interval 2 can be formed out of a text of 10 letters? The possible forward ELSs are (1, 3, 5), (2, 4, 6), (3, 5, 7), (4, 6, 8), (5, 7, 9) and (6, 8, 10). This is six ELSs, as shown in the chart below. Our formula gives us $10 - (2*2) = 10 - 4 = 6$.

Table App1A

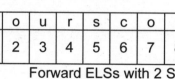

Text	f	o	u	r	s	c	o	r	e	a
Position	1	2	3	4	5	6	7	8	9	10
Count	Forward ELSs with 2 Skips of Interval 2									
1	f		u		s					
2		o		r		c				
3			u		s		o			
4				r		c		r		
5					s		o		e	
6						c		r		a

In table App1A, we can see that the possible forward ELSs with two skips of interval 2 which can be formed from the first ten letters in the Gettysburg Address are:

fus   orc   uso   rcr   soe   cra

Let us now go on to derive a formula for the total number of possible ELSs of a given length L that can be formed out of a text of T letters when the interval can be any number between 1 and N. Suppose we set up a table (table App1B) showing for each interval i the number of possible ELSs:

Table App1B

Interval (i)	Number of Possible Forward ELSs
1	T- L
2	T- 2L
3	T- 3L
N	T- N*L

There are N rows in table App1B and the number in the second column goes down by the same amount (L) from one row to the next. The average number in the second column will be the average of the first and the last numbers — since these numbers decline by the same amount from one row to the next. That average is

$$\frac{T - L + T - (N * L)}{2}$$

This reduces down to

$$(\tfrac{1}{2})(2T - L - N*L).$$

The sum of the numbers in the second column will simply be the number of rows (N) times the average of the numbers in the second column. To get the number of possible ELSs, either forward or backward, we only need to multiply the above result by 2. This eliminates the (1/2), giving us

---

Formula 1C. The total number of possible ELSs with L skips (including both forward and backward ELSs) that can fit within a text of T letters when the interval can be any number between 1 and N is

$$N* (2T - L - N*L).$$

Example Three: table App1C lists every possible ELS of two skips that can be formed within a text of 10 letters.

Table App1C

Interval	Possible Forward ELSs	Number of Forward ELSs
1	(1,2,3), (2,3,4), (3,4,5), (4,5,6), (5,6,7), (6,7,8), (7,8,9), (8,9,10)	8
2	(1,3,5), (2,4,6), (3,5,7), (4,6,8), (5,7,9), (6,8,10)	6
3	(1,4,7), (2,5,8), (3,6,9), (4,7,10)	4
4	(1,5,9), (2,6,10)	2
All		20

Since there are 20 forward ELSs, there are also 20 backward ELSs, giving us a total of 40 possible ELSs. Formula Three also gives us 40 as a result (4 * [20 - 2 - 4*2] = 4 * 10).

Suppose we want to determine the maximum number of ELSs possible from the given text, where the interval can be any possible number. To do this, we need to determine what the maximum interval M is and substitute it for N in the above formula. First, it will be helpful to develop a new concept, the span (S) of any given ELS. We will define it as the total number of spaces of text that are letters covered by or surrounded by letters in the ELS. For example, consider any of the ELSs in the last table with an interval of 1. The first one covers spaces 1, 2, and 3. Its span (S) is 3 because it occupies 3 spaces in the text.

Next, take one of the ELSs with an interval of two. For example, (3, 5, 7). This ELS covers three spaces (3, 5, and 7) with its three letters. However, it also surrounds spaces four and six. So it spans five spaces (3, 4, 5, 6, and 7). Finally, let's look at one of the ELSs with an interval of four (1, 5, 9). Obviously its span is nine (1, 2, 3, 4, 5, 6, 7, 8, and 9). Its span is again made up of the three spaces occupied by the three letters of the ELS (1, 5, and 9) and two groups of "surrounded" spaces ((2, 3, 4) and (6, 7, 8)). The number of groups of surrounded spaces will always be the same as the length of the ELS (in skips). This may be seen from table App1D.

Table App1D

Length (in skips)	Example ELS	Groups of Surrounded Spaces	Number of Groups
1	(4, 8)	(5, 6, 7)	1
2	(3, 6, 9)	(4, 5) (7, 8)	2
3	(2, 4, 6, 8)	(3) (5) (7) (9)	3
4	(1, 4, 7, 10, 13)	(2, 3) (5, 6) (8, 9) (11, 12)	4

This becomes apparent from examining table App1E.

Table App1E

Interval	Example ELS	First Surrounded Space	Spaces Covered
1	(1, 2, 3)	none exist	0
2	(1, 3, 5)	(2)	1
3	(1, 4, 7)	(2, 3)	2
4	(1, 5, 9)	(2, 3, 4)	3
5	(1, 6, 11)	(2, 3, 4, 5)	4

In short, we have that the number of surrounded spaces spanned by a given ELS is

(the # of groups of surrounded spaces) *
(the # of surrounded spaces in each group of surrounded spaces) =

$$L * (i - 1).$$

Putting these two components together, we conclude that the total span (S) of an ELS of L letters and interval i is

(the # of letters in the ELS) + (the # of surrounded spaces) =

$$L + 1 \;\; + L * (i - 1) =$$

$$L + 1 \;\; + (L * i) - L =$$

$$i * L + 1.$$

This gives us

Formula 1D. The total span (S) of any ELS of L letters and interval i is

$$S = i * L + 1.$$

Obviously, the maximum span (S) of any ELS is T. Therefore, the maximum interval (M) can be found by solving the equation

$$T = M * L + 1.$$

This gives us

$$M = (T - 1)/L.$$

228

However, an interval can only be a whole number. Therefore,

Formula 1E. The maximum interval (M) for a given ELS of L letters is

$$M = integer[(T - 1)/L].$$

In the above formula, the function "integer" means that we have deleted any numbers to the right of the decimal point. For example, integer (7.3496) = 7, and integer (3.99998) = 3, rather than 4.

Since we now know what is the maximum interval possible for any ELS with L skips, we can use formula 1C and formula 1E to determine the total number of possible ELSs that can be formed with L skips. To do this, we only need to substitute the formula for M from formula 1E for the variable N in formula 1C. This gives us

---

Formula 1F. The total number of possible ELSs (forward or backward) with L skips that could fit within a text of T letters when the interval can be any possible number is

$$M* (2T - L - M*L)$$

where

$$M = integer([T - 1]/L).$$

Using this formula, we can quickly see what the total possible number of ELSs would be for L = 4 and different values of T — where both forward and backward ELSs are allowed. The last two values of T represent the length of the Torah (304,805) and the length of the entire Hebrew Bible (1,196,921). These are displayed in table App1F.

Table App1F

L	T	Number of Possible ELSs
4	10	16
4	100	2,400
4	1,000	249,000
4	10,000	24,990,000
4	100,000	2,499,900,000
4	304,805	23,226,217,202
4	1,196,921	358,153,773,140

We may note that as T increases by a factor of 10 in the above table, the number of possible ELSs generally increases by a factor of 100, or 10 squared. If we were to take formula 1F and boil it down to the terms that contribute the most to its magnitude, we would find that the total number of possible ELSs is approximately

$$(1/L)* T^2 - T.$$

As T becomes larger, the T^2 term is the primary contributor to the total possible number of ELSs. So, by and large, it varies largely as the square of the number of letters in the total text (T). It is also interesting to look at how the total number of possible ELSs within the Torah varies as L changes (table App1G).

Table App1G

L	Number of Possible ELSs in the Torah
1	92.9 billion
2	46.5 billion
3	31.0 billion
4	23.2 billion
5	18.6 billion
6	15.5 billion
7	13.3 billion
8	11.6 billion
9	10.3 billion
10	9.3 billion
15	6.2 billion
20	4.6 billion

Why does the number go down? In simple terms, the bigger something is, the fewer examples of it will fit into a given space. If we go back and look at the approximation we derived for the rough magnitude of the total number of possible ELSs, we found that it was

$$(1/L) * T^2 - T.$$

Since the T^2 term becomes the dominant contributor, as T becomes larger, the total number of possible ELSs will tend more and more to go down by the ratio of the successive coefficients of T^2, or by the ratio of $1/L$.

For example, suppose we want to approximate how much the number of possible ELSs in the Torah will decrease as L increases from 4 to 5. How much less is 1/5 than 1/4? It is 20% less, because 0.2 is only 80% of 0.25. How much less is 18.6 billion than 23.2 billion? It is 19.83%, which is very close to 20%.

The title of this appendix is, "Estimating the Total Number of Possible Equidistant Letter Sequences." Formula 1F provides that total number, once we have specified how many letters or skips are in a possible ELS. Suppose, however, that what we want to determine is the total number of possible ELSs, regardless of how short or long they are. This could be accomplished by extending the above table for skips all the way up to the maximum possible. Since the maximum skip for an ELS in the Torah is 304,804 letters, this would mean generating a table with that many rows. If there were 50 rows per page for this table, this would take nearly 6,100 pages! Intuitively, it might seem that such a number could be so large as to be infinite. However, some quick reasoning will prove otherwise. First, we note that in the above table the number of possible ELSs for a given L is always less than it was for the next smaller L. This tells us two things. The largest number of ELSs for any L is 92.9 billion. Since all of the other numbers are less than this, then the total of all of the numbers in this huge table must be less than

304,804 x 92.9 billion = 28,316,291,600,000.

Although 28.3 trillion is a very large number, it is far from being "infinite." In actuality, the total number of possible ELSs that can be extracted from the Torah is only about 1.13 trillion, which is even less "infinite."

How can we better estimate what the total number of possible ELSs would be? Formula 1F tells us what the number of possible ELSs is for any given L. So all we need to do is to total up those amounts for all L values from 1 to T, which is 304,805 in the case of the Torah. Mathematically, this gives us

$$\sum_{L=1}^{T} M * (2T - L - M*L)$$

where

$$M = \text{integer}([T - 1]/L).$$

First, we will use (T-1)/L as the value for M in the above formula in order to simplify the algebra. Then we will look at how much this distorts our final answer. Making that substitution, we have

$$\sum_{L=1}^{T} \{(T-1)/L\}*[2T-L-M*L] =$$

$$\sum_{L=1}^{T} \{(T-1)/L\}*[2T-L-(T) =$$

$$\sum_{L=1}^{T} \{(T-1)/L\}*[T-L+1] =$$

$$\sum_{L=1}^{T} (T^2 - L*T + T - T + L - 1)/L =$$

$$T^2\sum_{L=1}^{T}(1/L) - \sum_{L=1}^{T}T + \sum_{L=1}^{T}1 - \sum_{L=1}^{T}(1/L) =$$

$$T^2\sum_{L=1}^{T}(1/L) - T^2 + T - \sum_{L=1}^{T}(1/L) =$$

$$T - T^2 + (T^2 - 1) * \sum_{L=1}^{T}(1/L).$$

For T = 304,805, the summation of values of (1/L) is equal to 13.20464, based on a full calculation of all values by a spreadsheet. If we substitute 304,805 for T in the above equation, the total number of ELSs possible from the Torah is

1,133,878,222,886, or

1.13 trillion.

In making the above calculation, we simplified the algebra by using (T-1)/L instead of the integer part of (T-1)/L. How much did that simplification distort the above answer? Table App1H provides a comparison of the total number of possible ELSs derived using the correct integer part of (T-1)/L and the total number obtained when the actual value of (T-1)/L is used.

Table App1H

L	Integer M # of ELSs	Fractional M # of ELSs	Integer M	Fractional M	Difference
1	92,905,783,220	92,905,783,220	304,804	304,804.00000	0
2	46,452,739,208	46,452,739,208	152,402	152,402.00000	0
3	30,968,391,204	30,968,391,204	101,601	101,601.33333	0
4	23,226,217,202	23,226,217,202	76,201	76,201.00000	0
5	18,580,912,800	18,580,912,801	60,960	60,960.80000	-1
6	15,484,043,200	15,484,043,200	50,800	50,800.66667	0
7	13,271,993,486	13,271,993,485	43,543	43,543.42857	1
8	11,612,956,200	11,612,956,199	38,100	38,100.50000	1
9	10,322,593,866	10,322,593,865	33,867	33,867.11111	1
10	9,290,304,000	9,290,303,998	30,480	30,480.40000	2
11	8,445,703,200	8,445,703, 198	27,709	27,709.45455	2
12	7,741,869,200	7,741,869,198	25,400	25,400.33333	2
13	7,146,317,354	7,146,317,352	23,446	23,446.46154	2
14	6,635,844,342	6,635,844,341	21,771	21,771.71429	1
15	6,193,434,400	6,193,434,398	20,320	20,320.26667	2
16	5,806,325,700	5,806,325,698	19,050	19,050.25000	3
17	5,464,759,200	5,464,759,197	17,929	17,929.64706	3
18	5,161,144,534	5,161,144,531	16,933	16,933.55556	3
19	4,889,489,306	4,889,489,303	16,042	16,042.31579	3
20	4,644,999,600	4,644,999,597	15,240	15,240.20000	3
21	4,423,794,630	4,423,794,626	14,514	14,514.47619	4
22	4,222,699,200	4,222,699,197	13,854	13,854.72727	3
23	4,039,090,332	4,039,090,327	13,252	13,252.34783	5

24	3,870,782,200	3,870,782,197	12,700	12,700.16667	3
25	3,715,938,720	3,715,938,717	12,192	12,192.16000	3
26	3,573,006,278	3,573,006,274	11,723	11,723.23077	4
27	3,440,661,420	3,440,661,419	11,289	11,289.03704	1
28	3,317,769,770	3,317,769,768	10,885	10,885.85714	2
29	3,203,353,410	3,203,353,404	10,510	10,510.48276	6
30	3,096,564,800	3,096,564,797	10,160	10,160.13333	3
	371,149,481,982	371,149,481,920			62

As can be seen from the above comparison, the total number of ELSs for L values between 1 and 30 only differs by 62 out of 371 billion. Unfortunately, our shortcut substitution results in a somewhat lower number than the actual one. If it had resulted in a somewhat higher number, we could use the simplified calculations above to obtain a fairly tight upper bound for the total number of possible ELSs within a text with T letters.

Table App1I

L	Integer M # of ELSs	Fractional M # of ELSs	Integer M	Fractional M	Difference
100	928,756,080	928,756,076	3,048	3,048.04000	4
1,000	92,601,440	92,601,284	304	304.80400	156
10,000	8,988,300	8,985,805	30	30.48040	2,495
25,000	3,415,320	3,411,440	12	12.19216	3,880
50,000	1,557,660	1,553,318	6	6.09608	4,342
75,000	938,440	933,944	4	4.06405	4,496
100,000	628,830	624,257	3	3.04804	4,573
125,000	469,220	438,445	2	2.43843	30,775
150,000	319,220	314,570	2	2.03203	4,650
175,000	259,610	226,088	1	1.74174	33,522
200,000	209,610	159,726	1	1.52402	49,884
225,000	159,610	108,112	1	1.35468	51,498
250,000	109,610	66,820	1	1.21922	42,790
275,000	59,610	33,036	1	1.10838	26,574
300,000	9,610	4,883	1	1.01601	4,727
304,805	0	1	0	1.00000	-1

In table App1I, we look at the kinds of differences that result from a very broad range of L values — all the way up to the L value of 304,804 which is the largest value possible for the Torah.

One pertinent observation is that the differences are always less than 25% of the given L value. If we assume that for every L value the differences are always less than L, we can obtain an inequality that will enable us to obtain a reasonable upper bound for the total number of possible ELSs

$$\sum_{L=1}^{T-1} L = \{[(T-1)/2] \times (T-1)\} = (1/2) \times [(T^2)-2T+1]$$

since the sum of a series of integers that increase by 1 will equal the average of those integers times the number of integers being totaled. This is clearly a finite number since it is less than $(1/2) \times T^2$.

So we have that the total number of ELSs possible in a text of length T is less than

$$T - T^2 + [T^2 - 1] \times \sum_{L=1}^{T} (1/L) + (1/2) \times [T^2 - 2T + 1].$$

This reduces down to the following inequality:

Formula 1G. The total number of ELSs possible in a text of length T is less than

$$[T^2 - 1] \times \sum_{L=1}^{T} (1/L) - \frac{T^2}{2} + 1.$$

This will be finite as long as the summation of values of $(1/L)$ from L=1 to T is finite.

From the book, *Summation of Series*, collected by L.B.W. Jolley, and published by Dover in 1961, we have from formula (70) on page 14 (as compiled from *Smithsonian Mathematical Formulae* [1922]) that the sum of values of (1/L) from 1 to T is equal to

Euler's Constant + ln (T) + (1/(2*T)) +
a series of terms with negative values.

We can therefore conclude that the summation of values of (1/L) from L=1 to T is less than

0.5772156649 + ln (T) + (1/(2*T)).

This means that this sum of values of (1/L) is less than 13.20464 for the Torah (where T = 304,805) and less than 14.577248 for the entire Hebrew Bible (where T = 1,196,921). It is also less than 19.17765 for 100 books which are each as long as the Hebrew Bible, and it is less than 23.78282 for 10,000 books as long as the Hebrew Bible.

Using these inequalities for the values of different sums of (1/L) and different lengths of texts, we get that the total possible number of ELSs for each given text is as shown in table App1J.

Table App1J

Given Text	T	(1/L) Sum	Total Number of Possible ELSs
Torah	304,805	13.204645	1,180,338,849,232
Hebrew Bible	1,196,921	14.572479	20,160,513,275,175
100 books	119,692,100	19.177649	267,579,710,430,527,000
10,000 books	11,969,210,000	23.782819	3,335,542,939,746,760,000,000
1 million books	1,196,921,000,000	28.387989	39,952,887,757,748,000,000,000,000
1 billion books	1,196,921,000,000,000	35.295744	49,849,075,298,257,000,000,000,000,000,000

We have generously assumed above that every book is exactly the same length as the Hebrew Bible, which is about 800 pages long, and that these books have been placed in a fixed order, so that an ELS could be formed that would start with one or more letters in one book and finish with one or more letters from a subsequent book.

Since it is unlikely that a billion different books have ever been written by mankind, we may conclude that the total possible number of ELSs in all of the books that have ever been written is less than 50 followed by 30 zeros. All of these numbers, though quite large, are certainly quite finite. Therefore, it is simply not true that there are an infinite number of possible ELSs that can be discovered within either the Torah, or the Hebrew Bible or even a billion books that are each 800 pages long.

Appendix Two

Estimating the Expected Number of Occurrences
of a Given ELS within a Specific Text

Now that we have derived a formula for the total number of ELSs with L skips and various intervals within a text of T letters, we are in a position to derive the expected number of occurrences of a specific sequence of letters as an ELS. That number will be the product of the probability that a given ELS will consist of the given sequence of (L+1) letters, times the total number of ELSs that can be formed with L skips.

First, we will derive a formula for the probability part of the equation. Suppose that our text is the first 50 letters of Lincoln's Gettysburg Address. With spaces eliminated, it would look like this:

fourscoreandsevenyearsagoourfathersbroughtforthont

Then suppose we compile a table showing the total number of times that each letter of the alphabet appears. We can then divide the total number of appearances of each letter by the total number of letters (50) in this opening section of Lincoln's speech to obtain estimates of the probability of any letter turning out to be the given letter. We would then have table App2A:

Table App2A

Letter	Number of Occurrences	Probability of Occurrence	Letter	Number of Occurrences	Probability of Occurrence
a	4	8%	n	3	6%
b	1	2	o	7	14
c	1	2	p	0	0
d	1	2	q	0	0
e	5	10	r	7	14
f	3	6	s	4	8
g	2	4	t	4	8
h	3	6	u	3	6
i	0	0	v	1	2
j	0	0	w	0	0

k	0	0	x	0	0
l	0	0	y	1	2
m	0	0	z	0	0

Now suppose that we want to find out what the chances are that a randomly selected ELS of 10 letters (with some interval i and starting letter) taken from the above excerpt from Lincoln's speech were to spell out, "gettysburg." That would be estimated by taking the product of the probabilities in the above table. Suppose that we denoted the probability of a given letter being an m as P(m), then the chances we are estimating are:

P(g) * P(e) * P(t) * P(t) * P(y) * P(s) * P(b) * P(u) * P(r) * P(g), or

4% * 10% * 8% * 8% * 2% * 8% * 2% * 6% * 14% * 4% =

0.000000000000275 %.

This percentage is the same as the odds being

1 out of 3,633,045,014,881

or 1 out of 3.6 trillion.

This is such an incredibly small probability that we might jump to the conclusion that it would be virtually impossible to find any ELS that spelled "gettysburg." However, to determine the expected number of times that "gettysburg" might occur as an ELS, we need to multiply the above percentage odds by the total number of possible ELSs that can be formed using 10 letters out of a text of length 50, with any interval possible and with both forward and backward ELSs permitted. We can calculate that number by using Formula 1C. We get 230 possible ELSs, including both forward and backward sequences. This results in an expected number of occurrences of the ELS of "gettysburg" within the first 50 letters of Lincoln's address of

0.0000000000633.

This is about the same as the odds being 1 out of 15.8 billion that it would occur by chance. Obviously, this is extremely unlikely. If it were to occur, we would strongly suspect that Lincoln had deliberately constructed his speech to contain the ELS of "gettysburg" within it. If it is done deliberately, making one such insertion would not be that hard to do. It would be much like constructing part of a crossword puzzle.

What would the likelihood be of finding "gettysburg" as an ELS within a text the length of a typical book? Suppose that book contained 500,000 letters, which would be about average for a book of 250 pages in length. Again, if we take the product of the probability of any given ELS spelling "gettysburg" times the total possible number of ELSs with 10 letters (or nine skips) within the entire text of 500,000 letters, we obtain an expected number of occurrences of the ELS of "gettysburg" within the given text.

Using formula 1C from the previous appendix, we conclude that there are 27,777,277,780, or 27.8 billion possible ELSs of nine skips that could be formed. When we multiply this number times the probability that any given ELS will spell "gettysburg," we come up with an expected number of occurrences within the 250 pages of text of 0.00765:

$$(1 \text{ out of } 3.6 \text{ trillion}) * (27.8 \text{ billion}) = 0.00765.$$

This is about the same as saying that the odds of it occurring by chance are 1 out of 131 (=1/.00765), or somewhat less than 1 in 100, or 1%.

If we were to expand our search to include 12 books of 500,000 letters in length, we would have 3,999,994,000,002 (or 4 trillion) possible ELSs. When we multiply this number by the probability of any given ELS spelling "gettysburg," we come up with 1.1 expected occurrences. In other words, the chances are quite high that it would crop up by coincidence within the text of 12 books of typical length.

Now we all know that within the given 12 books, the ELS of "gettysburg" will either not appear at all, or will appear perhaps once or twice, or maybe even three times or more. So, how can we interpret this finding that there are 1.1 expected occurrences? Mathematicians use a probability distribution called the Poisson distribution to determine the probability of any given number (k) of occurrences of an event, given that its expected number of occurrences (E) is known. That probability is

$$\frac{(E \wedge k) * \exp(- E)}{k \text{ factorial}}$$

In the above expression, *k* factorial is the product of the number *k* itself times every whole number smaller than k. So 3 factorial is equal to 3 times 2 times 1, or 6. And 5 factorial is 5 times 4 times 3 times 2 times 1, or 120.

What is exp(-E)? Exp (E) is defined as Euler's constant (e), or 2.7182849, raised to the E-th power.

Using the Poisson distribution, we can estimate the probability of any number of actual occurrences of the ELS of "gettysburg" within 12 books of average length, given that the ELS has an expected number of occurrences of 1.1 (E). This is given to us by table App2B.

Table App2B

Occurrences	Probability	Odds of 1 out of
0	33.3%	3.00
1	36.6%	2.73
2	20.1%	4.97
3	7.4%	13.54
4	2.0%	49.25
5	0.4%	223.84
6	0.1%	1,221
7	0.013%	7,770
8	0.0018%	56,507
9	0.0002%	462,331
10	0.000024%	4,203,007

Now suppose we consider the ELS of "abe." The probability of any given ELS spelling "abe" is

$$P(a) * P(b) * P(e) = 8\% * 2\% * 10\% = 0.00016\%, \text{ or}$$

$$1 \text{ out of } 6,250.$$

There are 4,900 possible ELSs that can be formed using three letters within a text of 50 letters. Taking the product of the probability of any ELS being "abe" times the total number of possible ELSs gives us 0.784 expected occurrences. Using the Poisson distribution this gives us the following probabilities for the number of occurrences of the ELS of "abe" (table App2C):

Table App2C

Occurrences	Probability	Odds of 1 out of
0	45.7%	2.19
1	35.8%	2.79
2	14.0%	7.13
3	3.7%	27.27
4	0.7%	139.13
5	0.11%	887.34
6	0.01%	6,791
7	0.0016%	60,632
8	0.0002%	618,698
9	0.000014%	7,102,404
10	0.000001%	90,591,882

So this tells us that the odds are almost fifty-fifty that the ELS of "abe" won't appear at all, about 1 out of 3 that it will occur once and about 1 out of 7 that it will appear twice. If the ELS "abe" were to appear 10 times within the first 50 letters of the Gettysburg Address, we would suspect Lincoln had embedded his name as a code within his speeches. After all, the odds of that happening by chance are almost 1 in 100 million!

Some have argued that it is possible to find whatever you want as an ELS in the Torah. This question can be answered definitively on the basis of the types of formulas discussed in this appendix. Earlier we described a formula that mathematicians commonly use for determining the probability of a given number of occurrences of something — given that we know what the expected number of occurrences is. That formula is given by the Poisson distribution

$$\frac{(E \wedge k) * \exp(-E)}{k \text{ factorial}}.$$

What then is the probability that *k* will be zero, given E expected occurrences? By substituting k=0 in the above formula, we get

$$\exp(-E),$$

since $E^0 = 1$ and [0 factorial] also equals 1. So if we can somehow determine E, the expected number of occurrences of an ELS, we can then calculate exp(-E) to obtain the chances that the ELS will simply not occur at all within a given text.

The expected number of occurrences of an ELS in a given text can be derived as the product of the total possible number of ELSs times the probability that any single given ELS will have the exact sequence of letters that we have selected. For example, suppose there are 1 billion possible ELSs and that the chances that any given ELS is the one we are looking for are 1 in 100 million. Then we would expect that ELS to occur 10 times in the text since

$$\frac{1 \text{ billion}}{100 \text{ million}} = 10.$$

How can we determine what is the total possible number of ELSs? Formula 1F from appendix 1 provides the answer.

How can we determine the chances that any single given ELS will have the exact sequence of letters we have chosen? That has been the subject of this appendix. Now suppose that we take the simplifying assumption that all 22 Hebrew letters are equally likely to occur. This, of course, is not true, but we are assuming it for the sake of discussion. Then the number of letter combinations that can be formed when there are A letters is simply

$$22 \wedge A.$$

In other words, if there are 5 letters, there are 22^5 possible letter combinations, or 22 x 22 x 22 x 22 x 22 possible different strings of letters. Using this formula and the table from appendix 1 for the total possible number of ELSs, we arrive at the following expected number of occurrences of any ELS, given how many letters it has (table App2D).

Table App2D

Number of Letters	Number of Possible ELSs	Number of Different "Words" That Can Be Made With the Given Number of Letters	Expected Number of Occurrences of a Given ELS in the Torah
2	92,905,783,220	484	191,954,098
3	46,452,739,208	10,648	4,362,579
4	30,968,391,204	234,256	132,199
5	23,226,217,202	5,153,632	4,507
6	18,580,912,800	113,379,904	164
7	15,484,043,200	2,494,357,888	6.208
8	13,271,993,486	54,875,873,536	0.242
9	11,612,956,200	1,207,269,217,792	0.00962
10	10,322,593,866	26,559,922,791,424	0.000389
11	9,290,304,000	584,318,301,411,328	0.0000159
12	8,445,703,200	12,855,002,631,049,200	0.000000657
13	7,741,869,200	282,810,057,883,083,000	0.0000000274
14	7,146,317,354	6,221,821,273,427,820,000	0.00000000115
15	6,635,844,342	136,880,068,015,412,000,000	0.0000000000485

If we now use the expected number of occurrences in the last column of table App2D and apply the formula of exp(-E), we obtain the results shown in table App2E.

Table App2E

Number of Letters	Expected Number of Occurrences of a Given ELS in the Torah	Probability That the Given ELS Will Not Occur Anywhere in the Torah
2	191,954,098	0.00%
3	4,362,579	0.00%
4	132,199	0.00%
5	4,507	0.00%
6	164	0.00%
7	6.208	0.20%
8	0.242	78.5%
9	0.00962	99.0%
10	0.000389	99.96%
11	0.0000159	99.998%
12	0.000000657	99.999934%
13	0.0000000274	99.999997%
14	0.00000000115	99.999999885%
15	0.0000000000485	99.999999995%

These are highly conclusive — and intriguing — results. *In summary, if an ELS has six or fewer letters, then it is basically certain that that ELS will appear at least once in the Torah.* In other words, for such short ELSs it is true that you can find whatever you are looking for.

If the ELS has seven letters, then there is a 1 in 500 chance that the ELS will simply not appear anywhere in the Torah. If the ELS has eight letters, there is nearly an 80% chance that it will not appear anywhere in the Torah. If it has nine letters, chances are 99% that it won't appear anywhere. And the more letters the ELS has above nine, it becomes increasingly unlikely that it can be found anywhere in the Torah.

In conclusion, the assertion that you can find anything you want as an ELS in the Torah is true if the ELS has six or fewer letters, and is basically false if the ELS has eight or more letters.

If we can find any intelligible ELSs with 10 or more letters, then we have discovered something that is quite unlikely to occur by chance.

As any reader of Michael Drosnin's book may note, many of his codes have only three to five letters and so are basically certain to appear at least somewhere in the Torah. However, what is also typically a part of most of the examples in his book is that appearances of an ELS must also somehow be "near" other related ELSs or sections of text. In the next four appendices, we will be covering ways to estimate the probability that such occurrences could happen by chance.

Appendix Three

Possible Meanings of
Lengthy ELSs in the Isaiah 53 Cluster

Some words and phrases in the Isaiah 53 cluster are undeniably related to Christ. The connection of others is less obvious. What follows is a discussion of those about which we have some understanding. All quotations are from the *New International Version* of the Bible.

Gushing from above, my mighty name arose upon Jesus, and the clouds rejoiced.

This 22-letter long ELS reads like poetry taken from the Psalms. It can naturally be translated as we have shown it above, or as, "Gushing from above, Yeshua was my mighty name, and the clouds rejoiced." Obviously, the former translation is more acceptable from a Jewish perspective, whereas the latter is more acceptable from a Christian viewpoint. Either way, the entire ELS is grammatically acceptable biblical Hebrew (as contrasted with contemporary Hebrew).

The prophets spoke of God often as "the fountain of living waters." Jesus linked himself to this aspect of God when He told the Samaritan woman at Jacob's well, "If you knew the gift of God and who it is that asks you for a drink, you would have asked him and he would have given you living water . . . whoever drinks the water I give him will never thirst again" (John 4:10, 13).

In John 7:38, Jesus is quoted as saying, "Whoever believes in me, as the Scripture has said, streams of living water will flow from within him." By this He meant the Holy Spirit, whom those who believed in Him were later to receive. To which Scripture He was referring is not clear, but there are several in Isaiah that refer to "the pouring out" of the Holy Spirit, including Isaiah 32:14-15: "The fortress will be abandoned, the noisy city will be deserted; citadel and watchtower will become a wasteland forever, and delight of donkeys, a pasture for flocks, till the Spirit is poured upon us from on high, and the desert becomes a fertile field, and the fertile field seems like a forest."

In Ezekiel 43:1-2, the prophet tells of his encounter with someone he describes as "the glory of the God of Israel." Ezekiel states that the sound of this person's voice was "like the roar of rushing waters." John had a similar vision of "someone like a son of man" that he described in Revelation 1:14-15: "His head and hair were white like wool, as white as snow, and his eyes were like blazing fire. His feet were like bronze glowing in a furnace, and his voice was like the sound of rushing waters." The context makes it clear that this person was Jesus.

The word for "gushing" (שקק, or sh-KAHK) is translated as "to run about, bustle, be lively" or "to be hungry or thirsty." It becomes gushing when used to refer to the action of water, in which case it is also translated as "rushing" and "overflowing."

Clouds have long been a symbol of the presence of God (c.f., Psalm 18:9-12, 68:4; 104:3 and 148:8). In Exodus 13:21-22, the Lord guided the children of Israel by a pillar of cloud in the day.

In Daniel 7:13-14, the prophet tells of a vision of a messianic figure: "In my vision at night I looked, and there before me was one like a son of man, coming with the clouds of heaven. He approached the Ancient of Days and was led into his presence. He was given authority, glory and sovereign power; all peoples, nations and men of every language worshiped him. His dominion is an everlasting dominion that will not pass away, and his kingdom is one that will never be destroyed."

Luke 21:27 echoes this imagery: "At that time they will see the Son of Man coming in a cloud with power and great glory."

If the friend of evil will thirst for the end of my innocence, his home is an urn. Let Judas have his day. To me, the exalted one, they fasted. Where are you? Its content will be written from my mouth. Father, indeed you will raise the dead over there.

This enormous, 73-letter code seems to have several parts, and may even be a conversation. The beginning seems to be about Judas, who could certainly be labeled the "friend of evil." What "his home is an urn" may mean is unclear, unless it refers to a vessel for the ashes of the dead. We believe that "Father, indeed you will raise the dead over there" is a reference to the afterlife for Christians, as 1 Thessalonians 4:16 promises: "For the Lord himself will come down from heaven, with a loud command, with the voice of the archangel and with the trumpet call of God, and the dead in Christ will rise first."

If indeed all the detail of this one is a string, does Peter detest the burden of the extra ships? And does my throne rest? So spoke God's poor.

Here is a classic case of a code that concerns a subject that is unclear. That Peter would be associated with ships seems natural, since he was a fisherman. This code implies that Peter was a leader, and so he was among the disciples while Jesus was on earth, and so he was as a leader of the early church.

Have obedience to God, even if for a day only — Peter.

Whether this is something said by Peter or spoken to him is difficult to determine. The Gospels describe a number of instances where the impulsive and strong-willed Peter had difficulty in following the leadership of Jesus. Examples may be found in Matthew 26:69-75 (Peter denies Christ three times); in Matthew 16:21-23 (Peter disputes Jesus' prophecy of His death); and in Matthew 26:40 (sleeping when he should have been keeping watch in the garden of Gethsemane).

Being naïve and indirect, James (Jacob) weakened. Or will it render him a truly comic actor to her voice with me?

The James or Jacob here certainly doesn't sound like the James who authored the New Testament epistle, which is anything but indirect. There is a legend that the name of the disciple Jacob was changed to James to please the sponsor of the King James Bible, first published in 1611.

I fought suffering in God's servant, and in God he slept.

This could be attributed to Peter, who vowed to protect Jesus, and then denied Him (Matthew 26:31-35).

There God will raise everything to the lion, God's witness being Matthew.

Revelation 5:5 calls Jesus the Lion of Judah: "Then one of the elders said to me, 'Do not weep! See, the Lion of the tribe of Judah, the Root of David, has triumphed. He is able to open the scroll and its seven seals.' "

Bemoan the prince, Jesus the king

This could describe the cry of Jesus' followers at His execution. In Matthew 27:37, it states, "Above his head they placed the written charge against him: 'This is Jesus, the King of the Jews.' "

And brother of the Gospel, where has the manna spread?

Here we have Christian "brother" being restated in an unusual way. Then, Jesus compared himself to manna in John 6:57-58: "Just as the living Father sent me and I live because of the Father, so the one who feeds on me will live because of me. This is the bread that came down from heaven. Your forefathers ate manna and died, but he who feeds on this bread will live forever."

Give them a Jewish messiah who will become a priest.

In Hebrews 7, the Apostle Paul discusses how Jesus became a priest: "The Lord has sworn and will not change his mind: 'You are a priest forever.' " Because of this oath, Jesus has become the guarantee of a better covenant.

Now there have been many of those priests, since death prevented them from continuing in office. But because Jesus lives forever, He has a permanent priesthood. Therefore, He is able to save completely those who come to God through Him, because He always lives to intercede for them. Such a High Priest meets our need — one who is holy, blameless, pure, set apart from sinners, exalted above the heavens. Unlike the other high priests, He does not need to offer sacrifices day after day, first for His own sins, and then for the sins of the people. He sacrificed for their sins once for all when He offered himself in the place of the animals and birds who, as it turned out, were only temporary replacements for Him. For the law appoints as high priests men who are weak; but the oath, which came after the law, appointed the Son, who has been made perfect forever.

Hurry to pay heed about giving, for in it hearing will be given to you.

Here is another situation where an ELS is not a scripture, but easily could be. There is a spiritual law about giving. Jesus touched on it in Matthew 6:3 4 when He said, "But when you give to the needy, do not let your left hand know what your right hand is doing, so that your giving may be in secret. Then your Father, who sees what is done in secret, will reward you." One reward can be hearing — a supernatural ability to hear God's voice, or to hear what someone is really saying to you, or to hear the music of heaven. Many times you may hear God telling you to give more.

The ascension of Jesus: for the sleeping one will shout. Listen!

Here the "sleeping one" may refer to Christ as He was in the tomb following his crucifixion. Or, it may be about one of the many who were converted to "the way" in the months following His ascension. Paul, for example, may not have literally raised his voice, but his message to a pagan Mediterranean region was most definitely a shout of redemption.

Her struggle is for them; God has graced them; Lord of Hosts.

This term seems vague and subject to a wide variety of interpretations. Who is "her?" Could it be the Church, which is referred to as the bride of Christ? And who is "them?" Could this be about non-believers? If "her" is the Church and "them" is non-believers, the term would begin to come into focus. The struggle of the Church has always been to work with the Holy Spirit to bring more of those who are without Christ into a relationship with Him. God has certainly "graced them." As the New Testament says, "In him (Jesus Christ) we have redemption through His blood, the forgiveness of sins, in accordance with the riches of God's grace that he lavished on us with all wisdom and understanding." (Ephesians 1:7). The final phrase of the term, appearing almost as a signature, is the Hebrew name of God whose English equivalent is Lord of Hosts, or Jehovah-Sabaoth. Not Lord of the Sabbath, but the Lord who is there when there is no other recourse.

And thirst for all of him was the faith of Mary the mother.

The poetry and the continuity of the water symbolism, so evident in the code "Gushing from above, my mighty name arose upon Jesus, and the clouds rejoiced," is seen again in this 18-letter code. It actually begins its backward journey into the cluster in Jeremiah 2, where the prophet repeats God's lament about the unfaithfulness of Israel. Its first two letters bracket a passage where God describes himself as "the spring of living water" in the 13th verse. The first letter of the ELS is in a familiar passage on idolatry, Jeremiah 2:27: "They say to wood, 'You are my father,' and to stone, 'You gave me birth.' They have turned their backs to me and not their faces; yet when they are in trouble, they say, 'Come and save us.' " Its second letter touches down in verse 6, whose message powerfully suggests thirst: "They did not ask, 'Where is the Lord, who brought us up out of Egypt and led us through the barren wilderness, through a land of deserts and rifts, a land of drought and darkness, a land where no one travels and no one lives?' "

God's miracle to us is appropriate to them in the temple.

"God's miracle" seems to refer to Jesus Christ in its many appearances in Bible codes. "Who will it be that God's miracle will save?" for example, also appears in this cluster. The Genesis-Exodus cluster includes the ELSs "God's miracle has the savor of a lamb" and "God's miracle is alive as well as plentiful." Perhaps the best-known scripture in the Bible, John 3:16, supports the phrase "God's miracle to us." ("For God so loved the world that he gave his one and only Son, that whoever believes in him shall not perish but have eternal life.") And clearly, this ELS is saying that Jesus Christ was given for Jews as well as Gentiles.

Shed light on ark of the covenant and fade away.

The ark of the covenant was located in the most profound area of the tabernacle, and later temple – the Holy of Holies. It was a small box of acacia wood overlaid with gold, and contained the original tablets that Moses brought down from the mountain, as well as a jar of manna and Aaron's rod that miraculously budded. Guarded by two winged angels, its top was the mercy seat, God's throne. While the ark spoke of judgment and wrath, the mercy seat intervened. Once a year the high priest would sprinkle it with the blood of a goat to atone for the sins of the people of Israel. Christians believe that Jesus took the place of the ark of the covenant under a new covenant based on the atoning of His death and resurrection. At the moment He died on the cross, the 18-inch thick woven curtain protecting the Holy of Holies was torn from top to bottom, representing free access to God for anyone. Perhaps this code is urging us to examine the lessons of the ark, but fade away, or don't continue to spotlight or dwell on the ark. There is also the possibility that the code may refer to the role of John the Baptist, the one who preceded and exalted Jesus Christ, and who said, "He must become greater, I must become less" (John 3:30).

Who will it be that God's miracle will save?

Here is one of the many question codes that have been popping up in our research. In some cases we have found answers to these questions in other ELSs that cross the questions at critical points. But in most cases we are still watching for the answers to reveal themselves, and this is one of them. It is a question that could have many valid answers, so it will be interesting to see what it will turn out to be. One of the verses that the ELS passes through may be instructive. Isaiah 25:9 reads, "In that day (of salvation of the nation of Israel) they shall say, 'Surely this is our God; we trusted in him, and he saved us. This is the Lord, we trusted in him; let us rejoice and be glad in his salvation.' "

Greed, according to Matthew, was the rule.

Historians are agreed on the wholesale corruption that reigned in Jerusalem at the time of the execution of Jesus. The payment to Judas for betraying His Lord is the most obvious example, but greed was certainly the rule in both the Jewish and Roman hierarchies of Jesus' day.

Jesus exposed religious greed when he drove the moneychangers out of the temple. Even in this holiest of places official fraud was ubiquitous. Not only did pilgrims have to buy "approved" animals and birds for sacrifice instead of being able to bring their own, but they could buy their sacrifices only with temple money, and had to pay a fee to exchange their own currency for it.

King of Light

In John 8:12, we read, "When Jesus spoke again to the people, he said, 'I am the light of the world. Whoever follows me will never walk in darkness, but will have the light of life.' "

Sponge

John 19:29 reads, "A jar of wine vinegar was there, so they soaked a sponge in it, put the sponge on a stalk of the hyssop plant, and lifted it to Jesus' lips. When he had received the drink, Jesus said, 'It is finished.' With that, he bowed his head and gave up his spirit." Similar references to a sponge appear in Matthew 27:48 and Mark 15:36.

Deer of the Dawn

Deer of the Dawn is a Hebrew term used even to this day for the morning star, the last star to shine at the break of day. Deer of the Dawn, which can be expressed "Doe of the Dawn" or "Hind of the Morning," as well, was also the title of a familiar song in King David's day. The introduction to another prophetic passage about the death of Jesus, Psalm 22, instructs that its words are to be sung to the tune of "Deer of the Dawn." Finding an ELS for the term in Isaiah 53 dramatically links the two scriptures.

Spitting

In Isaiah 50:6, it was prophesied, "I offered my back to those who beat me, my cheeks to those who pulled out my beard; I did not hide my face from mocking and spitting." Jesus alluded to this prophecy in Mark 10:32-34. Mark 15:19, states, "Again and again they struck him on the head with a staff and spit on him." Other references include Matthew 26:67, 27:30, and Luke 18:32.

Silver (Money)

This could be a reference to the 30 pieces of silver that Judas accepted as a bribe for betraying Christ, as described in Matthew 26:15-27:9. An ELS for silver with a skip of -40, and an ELS for thirty with a skip of +106, both cross the first word of Isaiah 52:14. The next word is crossed by an ELS for money with a skip of +13 and an ELS for blood with a skip of +6, perhaps referring to blood money.

Lamp of the Lord

In John 8:12, we read, "When Jesus spoke again to the people, he said, 'I am the light of the world. Whoever follows me will never walk in darkness, but will have the light of life.' "

Meal/Feast

Could refer to the Last Supper.

Glorify

This could refer to a use of this word in John 17:1-5: "After Jesus said this, he looked toward heaven and prayed: 'Father, the time has come. Glorify your Son, that your Son may glorify you. For you granted him authority over all people that he might give eternal life to all those you have given him. Now this is eternal life: that they may know you, the only true God, and Jesus Christ, whom you have sent. I have brought you glory on earth by completing the work you gave me to do. And now, Father, glorify me in your presence with the glory I had with you before the world began.' "

Wonderful

In Isaiah 9:6, the prophecy was made, "For to us a child is born, to us a son is given, and the government will be on his shoulders. And he will be called Wonderful Counselor, Mighty God, Everlasting Father, Prince of Peace."

Seed

This could be a reference to the prophetic reference to a savior as "her seed" in Genesis 3:14-15 (NKJV): "So the LORD God said to the serpent: 'Because you have done this, you are cursed more than all cattle, and more than every beast of the field; on your belly you shall go, and you shall eat dust all the days of your life. And I will put enmity between you and the woman, and between your seed and her Seed; he shall bruise your head, and you shall bruise his heel.' "

It could also be a reference to the seed in Jesus' famous parable of the sower (see Matthew 13:3-38). Or, it may refer to His role as descendant of Abraham. (The Scripture does not say "and to seeds," meaning many people, but "and to your seed" in Galatians 3:16, referring to God's promises to Abraham.)

Gate and Gate/Entrance

In John 10:7, Jesus was quoted as saying, "I tell you the truth, I am the gate for the sheep."

Son of God (Elohim and Yahweh)

In several places in the Gospels, Jesus is referred to as "the Son of God." See, for example, Matthew 14:33; 26:63; and 27:40, 43, 54. Both Son of Elohim and Son of Yahweh are possible renderings of this.

Second Adam

"Second Adam" is a Christian term for Christ. The first man "was of the dust of the earth; the second man from heaven" (Romans 5:12-19; 1 Corinthians 15:45-49). "Adam" (אדם) is Hebrew for the word "man."

Treasure

Laying up treasure in heaven was often referred to by Jesus as that which characterized the acts of His followers (Matthew 6:21, Mark 10:21, Luke 12:33), or as a symbol for the kingdom of heaven (Matthew 13:44).

Thirty

This could be a reference to the 30 pieces of silver that Judas accepted as a bribe for betraying Christ, as described in Matthew 26:15-27:9. An ELS for "silver" with a skip of -40 and an ELS for "thirty" with a skip of +106 both cross the first word of Isaiah 52:14. The next word is crossed by an ELS for "money" with a skip of +13 and an ELS for "blood" with a skip of +6, perhaps referring to blood money. (See "Silver (Money)" above.)

Saul

Saul was the name of the apostle Paul before he converted to Christianity. Saul could very well have attended the crucifixion, although he never mentioned that in his epistles.

The Vine

In John 15:1, Jesus made the claim, "I am the vine; you are the branches."

The Blessed

Mark 14:61 reads, "But Jesus remained silent and gave no answer. Again the high priest asked him, 'Are you the Christ, the Son of the Blessed One?'"

Last (Terminal, Final)

Could be a reference to the Last Supper, or to the belief that Christ's death on the cross was the last guilt offering required by God to atone for sin.

Have Hemmed Me In

This one-word term ("hemmed") was borrowed from the literal text prophesying the crucifixion in Psalm 22:16, "Dogs have surrounded me, evil men have hemmed me in . . . ."

Prince

In Isaiah 9:6, the prophecy was made, "For to us a child is born, to us a son is given, and the government will be on his shoulders. And he will be called Wonderful Counselor, Mighty God, Everlasting Father, Prince of Peace." In Acts 5:31, Peter made reference to Isaiah 9:6 when he said, "God exalted him to his own right hand as Prince and Savior that he might give repentance and forgiveness of sins to Israel." (See "Wonderful" above.)

Subject: Jesus as the Creator

Codes such as "Jesus created to the father" and "It will be understood. Jesus created." beg the question, "Did Christ have a role in the creation?" Several passages in the New Testament refer to His participation in it. Probably the most notable is John 1:1-4: "In the beginning was the Word, and the Word was with God, and the Word was God. He was with God in the beginning. Through him all things were made; without him nothing was made that has been made. In him was life; and that life was the light of men."

According to one New Testament epistle, Jesus was the Creator: "For by him [Jesus] all things were created: things in heaven and on earth, visible and invisible, whether throne or powers or rulers or authorities; all things were created by him and for him. He is before all things, and in him all things hold together" (Colossians 1:16).

Subject: Jesus the Gift

Codes that speak of the gift, such as "Jesus the gift is master and my Lord," are echoed in the words of John 3:16: "For God so loved the world that he gave his one and only Son, that whoever believes in him shall not perish but have eternal life."

Appendix Four

One Word ELSs in the Isaiah 53 Cluster

This appendix provides a listing of the one-word ELSs discovered in the Isaiah 53 cluster. They are listed alphabetically in English with transliterations of Hebrew words where there is more than one word with a similar meaning. If there is more than one appearance of a word, the total is in parenthesis after it. (The Hebrew spellings of these codes and other information can be viewed on line at www.biblecodedigest.com/page.php/11.)

(A) Foundation
(A) Stone (8)
Abraham (2)
Accomplished *(referring to Jesus' ministry)*
Afflicted (3)
Alphaeus (4)
Andrew
Angel (9) *A-ral*
Angel (8) *M-lach*
Angel (2) *Ch-roob*
Angels
Angelic (4) *M-lach-ee*
Angelic (4) *T-heh-ver*
Annas (5)
Apostolic (3)
Archenemy
Armageddon (2)
Atonement (4)
Baptism *Hit-bil*
Baptism *T-veelah*
Baptism *Shi-mud*

Baptizer (Baptist)
Barrabas (2)
Bartholomew (5)
Bethlehem
Betrayal
Blasphemy (Insult)
Blood (3)
Branch (11) *Ca-pa*
Branch (25) *A-naff*
Bread (3)
Bribe
Bribe (3) *Sha-khad*
Bribe (5) *Sho-khad*
Buried
Caesar (2)
Caiaphas (2)
Carpenter (13)
Carpentry
Cast/Throw
Census
Census (6) *Mir-sham*
Chaggai
Christen
Controversial (3)

Conversion (6) *Ha-mara*
Conversion (2) *Hasa-va*
Counselor (5)
Crucified (3)
Crucifixion *Tseli-va*
Crucifixion *Hoka-a*
Cup (5) *S-fel*
Cup (3) *G-bay*
Cup (9) *Ah-gun*
Cup (10) *Zeet*
Curse
Damascus
Darkness *Ala-ta*
Darkness *Kha-she-kha*
Darkness (2) *Afe-la*
Darkness (2) *Afee-la*
Darkness (2) *Kha-shee-kha*
David (3)
Deceived
Deception (4) *Meru-me*

263

Deception (2) *Rama-ut*

Deception (2) *Tar-meet*

Denial *Hakhekhsa-sha*

Denial (2) *Kfi-ra*

Denial (3) *Sheli-la*

Descendant of David

Disciple

Dozen, Twelve

Earthquake

Elijah (5)

Enemy

Enemy (2) *Tsor-er*

Field (2)

Fiery Serpent/Angel (8) *Ser-aph*

First

Fisherman (3)

Fishing

Follower (5)

Following (6)

Forever (Eternally) (4) *Le'o-lam*

Forever (Eternally) (5) *Ta-mid*

Forever (Vanquish)

Forgot me (2)

Forsaken

Foundation (4) *Ye-sud*

Foundation (5) *Keren*

Founder *Meya-sid*

Founder (8) *Bo-ne*

Founder/Promoter (4)

Fountain

Fulfill (3) *L-keem*

Fulfill (3) *Lab-tseh-ah*

Fulfill (4) *Lema-leh*

Fulfillment *Bit-zoah*

Fulfillment (8) *Ki-yum*

Galilee

Gate/Entrance (16) *Pe-takh*

Gate (8) *Sha-ar*

Gatekeeper (9)

Glorification

Glorify (2) *L-halel*

Glorify (4) *L-par*

Glorious *M-fo-ar*

Glorious *Nehe-dar*

Glory (15) *Hod*

Glory (12) *Eder*

Glory/Magnificence (14) *Pe-er*

Glory/Splendor (10) *He-der*

God (2)

Guard (2) *Msh-mer*

Guard (2) *Sho-mer*

Guilt Offering (30)

He Rose (4)

He Was Oppressed (4)

He Will Rise (4)

Her Seed (3)

Healer/Physician (2)

Healing (8)

Heaven (3) *M-room*

Heaven (Empyrean) (3) *Ra-kiy-a*

Heaven (7) *Sh-mime*

High *Ga-voha*

High (7) *Ga-voha*

(His) Cross (5)

His Signature (Image) (2)

Humiliate (2) *Le-akh-leem*

Humiliate/Aggrieve

Humiliation *Hash-pallah*

Humiliation *El-bon*

I AM

Immaculate (3)

Immanuel

It is Finished

Jairus (6)

James (4)

Jesse

Jesus (8) *Yeshu*

Jesus (7) *Yeshua*

Jewish

John (2)

Jonah (2)

Joseph (2)

Judas (2)

Kidron (3)

Kill *La-harog*

Kill (Execute, Slay) (2) *L-hameet*

King (23)

Lamb

Last (4) *Akh-ron*

Lazarus

Let Him be Crucified *Yetz-lav*

Let Him Be Crucified (4) *Y-yetz-lav*
Levites (4)
Life (5)
Lifted Up (10)
Linen (3)
Lord (3)
Lots (2) *Go-ral*
Made Incarnate (7)
Majestic (10)
Manger *Ey-voos*
Manger (2) *E-voos*
Martha (4) *Mar-ta*
Martha (4) *Mar-tah*
Martyr *So-vel*
Martyr (v) (4) *La-ahnoot*
Mary (12 others)
Master (2) *Ah-dohn-eye*
Master/Lord (9) *Ah-dohn*
Master/Teacher (3) *Mo-re*
Matthew *Mat-tee-hoo*
Matthew (15) *Mah-tee*
Matthias (7) *Mattee-ah*
Meal (3) *Aru-kha*
Meal/Feast *Sa-oh-dah*
Messiah (4)
Messianic
Miracle *Mo-fet*
Miracle (5) *Pele*
Miracle (14) *Nes*

Miraculous *Muf-lah*
Miraculous (4) *Nif-la*
Mock (6)
Money (3)
Moriah (4) *Ha-Moriah*
Moriah (3) *Moriah*
Mourner (10)
Multitude (5) *Ha-mohn*
Murder
My Name (10)
My Servant
Naked (23)
Nazarene
Nazareth (4)
Nethaneel
Obed (4) *Oh-bed*
Obed (2) *Ah-oh-bed*
Offering (4)
Olives
On a Pole (4)
Only Way (2)
Overpowering (12)
Pariah (2) *M-noo-dah*
Passover
Paul *Polus*
Paul (6) *Powl*
Peter (3) *See-pha*
Pharisee (8)
Philip (4)
Pieces
Pierce *Da-kar*
Pierce (2) *L'nakev*
Pierced (5)
Piercers of My Feet

Pluckers (3) (of His beard)
Potter (8)
Precious (2)
Prince (13) *Na-si*
Prince/Ruler (3) *Na-gid*
Purple
Ransom (8)
Recompense (5)
Redeemer (2)
Remorse (9)
Resurrection (7)
Resuscitate
Revolution
Risen (2)
Robe, Cloak (6)
Rock *Even*
Rock (3) *Sela*
Rock (4) *Tsur*
Sacrifice (7) *O-la*
Sacrifice (5) *Kor-bahn*
Salome
Sanhedrin
Satan (3)
Saul (7)
Savior (3) *Go-el*
Savior (3) *Ma-tsil*
Savior (5) *Mo-shee-a*
Scar (2) *Tsal-ketz*
Scar *Letz-lek*
Scoff (4)
Scoffer *La-a-gan*
Scoffer *Lag-le-gan*
Scourge
Second Adam
Seed (3)

Servant (2) *Mesha-ret*
Servant (11) *She-ret*
Shall Be Cut Off (4)
Shame *Boosh-ah*
Shame *Khe-lee-mah*
Shame *Lehakh-leem*
Shamed *M-boish*
Shekels (5)
Shepherd (2)
Shiloh (2)
Silver/Money (5)
Simon (3)
Soldier
Soldiers (4)
Spikenard (9)
Spitting *Reki-ka*
Spitting (3) *Le-Rohk*
Spitting (4) *Yer-eekah*
Sponge
Strikers (2)
Stripped (8)
Sunday (2)
Teacher (2) *Mela-med*
Teacher (10) *Mor-eh*
Thaddeus (3)
(That He is)
  Hanged (2)
The Blessed
The Bread

The Gate *Ha-pe-takh*
The Gate (5) *Ha-sha-ar*
The Life (3)
The Nazarene
The Rock (3) *Ha-sela*
The Rock (6) *Ha-kef*
The Rock (7) *Ha-tsur*
The Rock (7) *Ha-even*
The Trinity (4)
The Truth (6)
The Veil
The Vine (2)
The Way (2) *Ha-Ofen*
The Way (3) *Ha-Derekh*
The Word (2) *Ha-deber*
The Word/ Circum-cision *Ha-Milah*
Thief (10)
Thirty
Thomas (4)
To Kill
Tortured (4)
Traitor (4)
Treasure (4)

Tried (2)
Truth (9)
Unleavened Matzoh
  (6)
Veil *Re-e-lah*
Veil/Curtain (2) *Pa-rokhet*
Veil/Curtain (4) *Pa-rokhet (no vav)*
Very (14)
Vine (8)
Vinegar (3)
Virgin (4) *B-toolah*
Virgin/Maiden (5)
  Al-mah
Water
Way (8)
Wine
Wonderful *Mak-sim*
Wonderful (2) *Nif-la*
Wonderful (3)
  Nehe-dar
Wonderful (4) *Mif-la*
Word (2) *Dy-bor*
Word (13) *De-ber*
Word/Circumcision
  (4) *Milah*
Zacchaeus (4)
Zealot
Zebedee

Appendix Five

Islamic Nations Study:
Bible Codes vs. *War and Peace* Codes

With the Islamic Nations Study, we undertook a research project designed to meet the need of a head-to-head comparison of Bible codes and ELSs discovered in a portion of a familiar but unencoded book, Leo Tolstoy's classic novel, *War and Peace*. A natural way to do this would be to conduct an experiment in which a Hebrew expert would be handed a sizeable collection of pre-defined initial ELSs, equally drawn from both the Hebrew Bible and from *War and Peace* (or some other control text). The Hebrew expert would then search for possible extensions of the ELSs. Then, the two collections of extended ELSs would be compared and analyzed. For six months in 2003, the BCD research team conducted such a study — the Islamic Nations ELS Extension Experiment. It is described in this appendix.

Using the Hebrew spellings of a group of Islamic nations, we located ELSs of them in a 78,064-letter portion of *War and Peace* that is provided with CodeFinder software. We also found them in the 78,083-letter book of Ezekiel using the same software. (Actually, in order to have enough letters to match the size of the *War and Peace* text used in the software, we had to use part of Jeremiah as well as the beginning of Hosea. So the text actually runs from Jeremiah 51:52 through Ezekiel to Hosea 1:9.)

The nations we searched for as ELSs appear in table App5A, along with their Hebrew spellings. We then conducted a blind experiment with the participation of our Hebrew expert, Dr. Nathan Jacobi. We sent him five occurrences from Ezekiel (and five occurrences from *War and Peace*) of the name of each of the nations as an ELS. We asked him to tell us whether letters before and after the terms created longer terms.

Conducted as a blind experiment, throughout it Dr. Jacobi did not know which of the initial ELSs and surrounding letter strings were from Ezekiel and which were from the Tolstoy classic. This experiment was conducted over a six-month period by slipping in sets of letter strings from both sources to our routine search ELS

Table App5A

Islamic Nations ELS Extension Experiment	
Nations	
English	**Hebrew**
Algeria	אלגיר
Abu Dhabi	אבו דאבי
Bahrain	בחרין
Dubai	דובאי
Kuwait	קוויט
Lebanon	לבנון
Libya	לוב
Qatar	קטאר
Somalia	סומליה

Sudan	סודן
Yemen	תימן

correspondence, without Nathan knowing when we started doing so and when we were finished.

(Curiously, at one point in this process, soon after we had sent him a sizeable group of Islamic nation ELSs, he commented that he was frustrated with how few long codes he had been finding lately and that he was thinking of quitting such searches altogether. He noted that he felt that he was "losing his touch.")

Perhaps the most surprising finding of the experiment was that two of the longest ELSs we discovered were from the text of *War and Peace* (we'll refer to it simply as *War and Peace*). These ELSs were each more than 30 letters long. They are the longest ELSs of which we are aware from any text other than the Bible. These long ELSs clearly underscore the fact that lengthy ELSs can be found in any Hebrew text, however religious or secular.

On the other hand, eight of the ten longest ELSs were from the Ezekiel text. Apart from the two long ELSs in *War and Peace*, there was a relative dearth of long ELSs that emerged from Tolstoy's novel.

We counted the total number of extensions found around 50 initial ELSs in Ezekiel and 50 initial ELSs in *War and Peace*. An extension is a phrase or brief sentence that appears entirely on one side of an existing ELS. The extension must represent a grammatically reasonable continuation of the existing ELS. As such, it could either incorporate part of the existing ELS or be a stand-alone phrase or sentence that could reasonably precede or follow the existing ELS. It is, of course, possible to find several extensions around an initial ELS to form one lengthy final ELS. The average extension found in this experiment consisted of two Hebrew words that totaled seven letters.

Table App5B summarizes the results of the experiment. In all, 23 ELS extensions were found around the initial ELSs in *War and*

Peace, while 37 extensions were located by Nathan in Ezekiel. This represents a 34.8% higher frequency of extensions in Ezekiel, a significant difference.

Table App5B

Islamic Nations ELS Extension Experiment			
	War & Peace	Ezekiel	Percentage Difference
Total Extensions Found	24	37	54.2%
Percentage of Opportunities Where Extension Was Found	19.4%	27.0%	39.2%
Total Hebrew Words in Extensions	48	62	29.2%
Total Hebrew Letters in Extensions	133	183	37.6%

As table App5B shows, there were 48 Hebrew words in the entire group of extensions from the control text, whereas there were 62 from Ezekiel, a 29.2% difference. And there were 133 letters in the control extensions, versus 183 in the Ezekiel extensions, a 37.6% difference.

Table App5C provides a listing of all of the extensions found in Ezekiel, in both Hebrew and English. It also displays the number of Hebrew words and number of Hebrew letters in each extension.

Table App5C

ELS Extensions Found In Ezekiel				
Initial ELS	No. of Words	No. of Letters	Translation of Extension	Extension in Hebrew
Abu Dhabi	3	11	You are in his debt in the gulf.	חובו אתה בפער
Abu Dhabi	4	6	Is (Abu Dhabi) Gentile for me?	הלי ערל....
Abu Dhabi	3	9	Raise wine in his throat	העל לחו יין
Abu Dhabi	2	6	My mouth is understood.	מובן פי
Abu Dhabi	1	3	Please	אנא
Abu Dhabi	1	6	and love her	ואהבוה
Abu Dhabi	2	7	and let your shadow praise . . .	וצלך הלל
Abu Dhabi	1	?	The heart of	לב
Abu Dhabi	2	5	is a wild analogy	משל בר
Dubai	3	9	Where did he wander	תעה אי ואנה
Dubai	1	6	from her dream of (Dubai)	מחלומה
Kuwait	2	6	Sing like the one	רון כמי
Kuwait	2	9	that the famine will silence	שהרעב ידום
Kuwait	1	4	and curse (Kuwait)	מנאץ
Libya	3	8	they hung a sheep	המ רחל תלו
Libya	1	3	What is it?	מהו
Libya	1	3	Go away.	לכו
Libya	2	9	My wrath is your salvation.	אפי ישועתך
Libya	3	10	My wrath sniffed with you.	רחחה אפי בכם
Somalia	3	8	Talk to us from the sea.	שחי לנ מים
Somalia	3	6	in which fire is coming	בו בא אש
Somalia	2	6	and to his pillows	ושחי לנ
Somalia	1	6	he talked about prison	מלל שבי
Sudan	3	5	Who (of Sudan) is alive?	מי חי מ...
Sudan	2	6	Are the poor there	מי חי מ
Sudan	3	7	not soft and honest?	לא רכ ישר
Sudan	2	9	He completed my truth.	השלים אמתי
Sudan	2	7	and was the farmer	והיה אכר
Sudan	1	4	that he created	בראו
Yemen	3	6	The house of a . . . Yemen(ite)	בית תפ...י

Yemen	2	6	(itc) drum is inherited in me.	מורש בי
Yemen	2	7	Started to empty	שי לפתוי
Yemen	2	7	the gift for temptation	החלה הרק
Yemen	2	5	There was a fast in the rebellion.	צם מרד
Yemen	1	4	They will wonder about (Yemen)	יתהו
Yemen	4	11	Where to without the gift of a brain?	אנ בלי מתת מוח
	76	239		

Table App5D provides a listing of all of the extensions found in Ezekiel, in both Hebrew and English. It also displays the number of Hebrew words and number of Hebrew letters in each extension.

Table App5D

ELS Extensions Found In *War and Peace*				
Initial ELS	No. of Words	No. of Letters	Translation of Extension	Extension in Hebrew
Algeria	2	4	A son is asleep.	נמ בנ
Algeria	1	4	in the (Algerian) audience	בקהל
Bahrain	2	9	The rest of your ports	שאר נמליכמ
Bahrain	3	13	Will be a lesson to all who smoke them.	דכל מעשננ שעור ל
Bahrain	2	7	Let us please answer them	נא נע נמה
Bahrain	3	9	or all of it, God.	או שכולו יה
Kuwait	5	15	From the anger a vessel came and arrived	אפ בא הכלי הגיע מעמ
Kuwait	2	7	Be a parent, . . .	היי הורה
Kuwait	4	12	God is our tooth and tiger	יי השנ לנו ונמר
Lebanon	2	7	I will ride its wave	ארכב גלו
Libya	2	7	Give his bread	את פתו תנ
Libya	3	5	Let it be in me	תהי בי
Libya	1	3	. . . is his mother	אמו
Libya	2	3	and he owes	וחב

Somalia	3	10	The liar will hate the monument.	עי ישנא בדאי
Sudan	2	5	Who is suitable for . . . Sudan	מי יאה
Sudan	1	3	Here is (Sudan)	כאן
Sudan	2	7	Her might is weakening.	שוכך לחה
Sudan	1	5	Will he let go?	הירפה
Sudan	3	7	The son of Japhet is pure.	בן יפת זך
Sudan	2	6	The devil is the money of (Sudan)	שד ממון
Yemen	2	4	Enough, God,	די יה
Yemen	1	3	his heart is in . . . Yemen	לבו
Yemen	2	6	Perhaps not.	אולי לא
	53	161		

A useful statistic that emerged from this experiment was an estimate of the percentage of opportunities for finding an extension in the control text. That rate of "discovery" was 19.4%. Having that rate, one can determine how many long ELSs of various lengths would be expected from a control text. We did exactly that for the Isaiah 53 cluster in chapter 4 and for the Ezekiel 37 cluster in chapter 6. We then compared the actual number of long ELSs found in Ezekiel 37 with those expected by chance for several length categories. By doing so, we can draw a reasonable estimate of the probability that a cluster as extensive as Ezekiel 37 could be the result of chance from standard testing procedures.

The rate of discovery in Ezekiel was 27.0%, which is 39.2% higher than the discovery rate of 19.4% from the control text. The discovery rate is defined as the ratio of the actual number of extensions found to the number of opportunities available for potentially finding an extension. At the beginning of each search of a new letter string, there are two opportunities to find an extension — one before the name of the given Islamic nation, and one after. If an extension is found, one new opportunity (not two new opportunities) to find yet another extension is created. That opportunity will consist of the new letters that are now next to the extension that had just been discovered. There is no new opportunity on the other side of the ELS where an extension wasn't found, since that opportunity has already been counted.

Why is it that the total number of extensions found in Ezekiel was 34.8% higher than in *War and Peace*, while the discovery rate was 39.2% higher? It is because the denominators are not the same. Each new extension opens up a new opportunity to find yet another extension. So there were more opportunities to find new extensions in Ezekiel because more extensions were initially found in Ezekiel.

We also noted that:

- The average number of Hebrew letters per word in the extensions found was 2.95 in Ezekiel and 2.77 in *War and Peace*.

- The average number of Hebrew words in the extensions found was 2.00 in Ezekiel and 2.09 in *War and Peace*.

- The average number of Hebrew letters in the extensions found was 5.90 in Ezekiel and 5.78 in *War and Peace*.

From the above summary observations derived from this experiment, we constructed a model to determine the expected number of lengthy ELSs that may be found in a non-encoded text, or a text not expected to yield codes, given the total number of original ELSs that have been searched for possible extensions. The model is based on the following two assumptions:

- The discovery rate is 19.4% of the opportunities for finding extensions.

- The average number of Hebrew letters to be found in extensions is assumed to be 7.0 (the actual average was 5.78 in *War and Peace*).

The key formula resulting from the model is that the total number of final ELSs consisting of k extensions expected to emerge from a search around n initial ELSs is

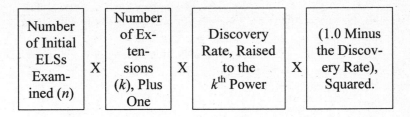

Number of Initial ELSs Examined (n)	X	Number of Extensions (k), Plus One	X	Discovery Rate, Raised to the kth Power	X	(1.0 Minus the Discovery Rate), Squared.

Derivation of this formula is detailed in appendix 7.

Appendix Six

Determining Benchmarks for the Number of Final ELSs That Would Be Relevant or Plausible in Content

In order to derive benchmarks for the number of final ELSs that would emerge from an examination of a given number of initial ELSs and that would be regarded as being relevant or plausible in content, it was necessary to categorize a sizeable group of final ELSs that emerged from the examination of a non-encoded text. Table App6A summarizes the results of an examination of extended codes found in a Hebrew translation of Tolstoy's *War and Peace* and in the book of Ezekiel from the Islamic Nations Experiment described in chapter 6. These results were previously presented in tables 3B and 3C.

Table App6A

ELSs Rated Relevant, Plausible, or Mysterious		
	Ezekiel	*War and Peace*
Relevant	3	1
Plausible	17	8
Mysterious	18	15
TOTAL	38	24

If we cumulate these results from the top down, we end up with the following compilation.

Table App6B

ELSs Rated Relevant, Plausible, or Mysterious		
	Ezekiel	War and Peace
Relevant	3	1
Relevant or Plausible	20	9
Relevant, Plausible, or Mysterious	38	24

Table App6C presents the results from table App 6B in terms of percentages.

Table App6C

ELSs Rated Relevant, Plausible, or Mysterious			
	Ezekiel	War and Peace	Selected
Relevant	7.8%	4.2%	10%
Relevant or Plausible	52.6%	37.5%	50%
Relevant, Plausible, or Mysterious	100.0%	100.0%	100%

The selected probabilities in the far right column are "conditional" probabilities. In other words, given that such and such is true, what is the probability that something else is also true. So, given that we have found an extension that consists of grammatically reasonable Hebrew, we estimate that there is a 10% chance that the extension will also appear to be relevant to the subject matter of the surface text. To get the probability that both conditions are satisfied (i.e., the extension is both grammatically reasonable Hebrew and is relevantly related to the subject matter of the literal text), the two probabilities are simply multiplied together.

So, given that there is a 20% chance of finding an extension that is a grammatically reasonable Hebrew phrase or sentence that connects to the previously existing ELS, we have only a 2% chance of finding an extension that is both clearly relevant to the topic of the literal text and is comprised of grammatically reasonable Hebrew. If we relax our standards to also include long ELSs that are either relevant or plausible (relative to the topic of the literal text), and are reasonable Hebrew, there is a 10% chance of finding such a long ELS by examining any one initial ELS. This is summarized in table App6D.

Table App6D

ELSs Rated Relevant, Plausible, or Mysterious			
Type of Extension	Selected	Probability of Any Extension	Probability of Given Type of Extension
Relevant	10%	20%	2%
Relevant or Plausible	50%	20%	10%
Grammatically Sound	100%	20%	20%

The probabilities in the last column of table App6D served as the basis for the expected number of final ELSs with different numbers of extensions that were presented in tables 4H and 4I.

R. Edwin Sherman

Appendix Seven

The Markov Chain ELS Extension Model:
Determining How Many Long ELSs Would
Be Expected to Be Found in a Non-Encoded Text

After a Hebrew expert examines the string of letters resulting from taking every j-th letter before and after the initial ELS with a skip of *j* letters, one of two results will occur in each instance that there is an opportunity to find an extension of the initial ELS. If no extension is found, this will be denoted by [nothing] and if one is found, by [extension].

So the Hebrew expert starts with:

[preceding letters] [initial ELS] [succeeding letters].

Four possible things can happen:

1. [nothing] [initial ELS] [nothing]
2. [nothing] [initial ELS] [extension]
3. [extension] [initial ELS] [nothing]
4. [extension] [initial ELS] [extension]

To shorten things these outcomes are denoted by:

1. NIN
2. NIE
3. EIN
4. EIE

Once an N occurs, the search process is over on that side of the initial ELS. But if an extension is found, there is an opportunity to find yet another extension. So if NIN happens, the search is over. But if NIE happens, two things could result from the additional search (NIEN and NIEE). If NIEN occurs, the process is over. But if NIEE occurs, two things could result from the additional search (NIEEN and NIEEE). And so forth. By calculating the probability that each of these events could occur by chance, and organizing the results in a certain way, it is possible to simplify all this down to a straightforward formula. This is done in the last section of this appendix. The formula for the expected number of ELSs with k extensions to emerge from an examination of an initial group of n ELSs found in a text is given in figure App7A.

Figure App7A

Number of Initial ELSs Examined (n)		Number of Extensions (k), Plus One		Discovery Rate, Raised to the kth Power		(1.0 Minus the Discovery Rate), Squared
	X		X		X	

As an example of usage of the formula in figure App7A, suppose we reviewed 100 initial ELSs for extensions and that the extension discovery rate was 20%. Then, we should expect that we would end up with 25.6 final ELSs consisting of exactly one extension:

$$100 \times [1 + 1] \times [20\%]^1 \times [80\%]^2, \text{ or } 100 \times 2 \times 20\% \times 64\% = 25.6.$$

And we should expect that we would end up with 7.68 final ELSs consisting of exactly two extensions:

$$100 \times [2 + 1] \times [20\%]^2 \times [80\%]^2, \text{ or } 100 \times 3 \times 4\% \times 64\% = 7.68.$$

And so forth. The purpose of all this is to define a benchmark of how many long ELSs you would expect to find if you searched a presumably non-encoded Hebrew text. Having that benchmark, a standard statistical procedure, called the chi-square test, can be applied to estimate the probability of chance occurrence of the actual results differing from the expected benchmark.

Technical Derivation of the Markov Chain ELS Extension Model

This section of the appendix provides a derivation of the formula shown in figure App7A. Figure App7B presents the complete range of outcomes from the examination process up through the location of three extensions to an initial ELS. From this chart, the formula for determining the expected number of ELSs with a given number of extensions is evident.

Each outcome is represented first by a combination of the letters I, E, and N, indicating the order in which these events appeared in that letter string. In the middle section of the table is a row of formulae for the expected number of ELSs for each type of outcome in that column. In each formula, n is the total number of initial ELSs, d is the probability of finding a grammatically correct Hebrew extension of the preceding ELS, and (1-d) is the probability of failing to find an extension. It was assumed that d is independent of the number of extensions that have already been discovered — even though consideration of the different factors affecting d as the number of extensions increases suggests that d most likely declines as the ELS becomes longer.

Figure App7B

Initial Codes	Total No. of Extensions Found in Final ELS			
	Zero	One	Two	Three
EVENTS				
I	NIN	NIEN	NIEEN	NIEEEN
		NEIN	NEIEN	NEIEEN
			NEEIN	NEEIEN
				NEEEIN
PROBABILITY OF EACH OF THE ABOVE EVENTS				
n	$n(1-d)^2$	$nd(1-d)^2$	$nd^2(1-d)^2$	$nd^3(1-d)^2$
TOTAL PROBABILITY OF ALL EVENTS IN COLUMN				
n	$n(1-d)^2$	$2nd(1-d)^2$	$3nd^2(1-d)^2$	$4nd^3(1-d)^2$

The beginning of the search process is represented by the leftmost column of the table, where there are n instances that I, an initial ELS, appears. Each column represents the range of outcomes that would result in the indicated number of final extensions.

The only way that zero extensions will be found is the situation where no extension is found either before or after the initial ELS (denoted by NIN). The probability of this occurring for any given initial ELS is $(1-d)^2$. So the expected number of final ELSs that have no extension is $n(1-d)^2$.

There are two ways that a final ELS can have one and only one extension: NIEN and NEIN. The expected number of final ELSs that are of the NIEN type is $nd(1-d)^2$, as is the case for the NEIN type. So the total expected number of final ELSs with exactly one extension is $2nd(1-d)^2$, as shown at the bottom of the "One" column.

There are three ways that a final ELS can have exactly two extensions: NIEEN, NEIEN, and NEEIN. For any given column (representing k extensions), I can appear in the 1st, 2nd, ... or $(k+1)^{st}$

position after the first n. Thus the total expected number of final ELSs with exactly k extensions will be

(1) $$(k+1)nd^k(1-d)^2.$$

The above model is an example of a Markov chain, since the outcome of any trial depends at most on the outcome of the immediately preceding trial and not upon any other previous outcome, and the probability of each state is clearly defined. When the state n occurs, it is an "absorbing state."

Formula (1) for the expected number of ELSs with k extensions to emerge from an examination of an initial group of n ELSs found in a text has already appeared at the end of appendix 5 and earlier in this appendix. It is repeated here, for ease of comparison with formula (1).

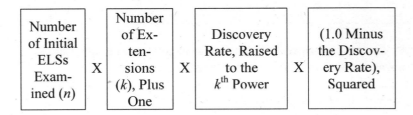

Number of Initial ELSs Examined (n)	X	Number of Extensions (k), Plus One	X	Discovery Rate, Raised to the kth Power	X	(1.0 Minus the Discovery Rate), Squared

Verifying the Formula

As a check on formula (1), it should be possible to show that the sum of (1) for k ranging from 0 to infinity is n, the total number of initial ELSs. That derivation is as follows:

Since n and $(1-d)^2$ appear in each term, we can factor them out of an expression for the total number of final ELSs, to get

$$n(1-d)^2 \left[\Sigma\, (k+1)d^k \right],$$

where k ranges from 0 to infinity.

If we multiply each term of this power series by d in both the numerator and denominator, we obtain

$$\{[n(1-d)^2]/d\} \left[\Sigma\, (k+1)(d^{\{k+1\}} \right].$$

If we shift the value of $(k+1)$ by one for each term, so that the series is summed from $k = 1$ to infinity, rather than from $k = 0$ to infinity, it becomes

$$(2) \qquad \{[n(1-d)^2]/d\} \left[\Sigma\, kd^k \right].$$

According to formula 40 on page 8 of *Summation of Series*, collected by L.B.W. Jolley:

$$\Sigma\, nx^n = x/(1-x)^2,\ \text{where } x < 1, \text{ and}$$

the series is summed from $n=1$ to infinity. If we substitute k for n and d for x in this formula, we have

$$\Sigma\, k(d^k) = d/(1-d)^2.$$

By substituting the expression on the right for the power series expression in (2) above, we get

$$\{[n(1-d)^2]/d\} \left[d/(1-d)^2 \right] = n.$$

Appendix Eight

Do Codes Only Express Viewpoints?

In topic A we claim that real Bible codes only express a viewpoint, and that if the viewpoint is that of an untruthful person, the content of the code is not reliable. This appendix presents tables of the top codes expressing specific viewpoints.

The first two tables present examples of the strongly conflicting viewpoints of terrorists and Americans. These tables thus provide substantive evidence that Bible codes only express a viewpoint, rather than always presenting true statements.

Table App8A

Terrorist Viewpoint			
ELS	Cluster(s)	Letters	Skip
Anthrax turns their blood thin. I am full of joy and abundant reward. Life is dimming.	Ezekiel 7	31	228
N. Korea, exalt, rejoice, see that my creed is the truth. Here, their congregation is in her.	Gen.-Exod. Deuteronomy Ezekiel 37	30	32,548
Woe, N. Korea, my protection has drowned and died.	Deuteronomy Ezekiel 37	20	34,089
Your total level of protection of N. Korea is that of a brother.	Gen.-Exod. Deuteronomy Ezekiel 37	19	62,873

I will wish that her hands form a line of madrases for us.	Ezekiel 7	21	2,485
An idol to reflect his lot, Taliban. I will thus rise eastward.	Ezekiel 37 Ezekiel 40	26	1,558
The beauty in me was quite destroyed by Binalshibh.	Ezekiel 37	17	309
My heart, Hussein, has elevated again.	Ezekiel 37 Ezekiel 40	13	1,735
Terror hot in me	Ezekiel 37	8	430
Place the gift of terror.	Ezekiel 37	10	369
Death wish and the imprisonment	Ezekiel 40	13	3,538
We have thus been destroyed by suicide.	Ezekiel 37 Ezekiel 40	9	5,114

Table App8B

American Viewpoint			
ELS	Cluster(s)	Letters	Skip
New York: They accompany the unfortunate who are stricken in it. The worshipers are gathering around God.	Ezekiel 7	28	15

He sang to the voice of the essence of God in your mother, United States.	Ezekiel 7	22	22
Ptooey! Bin Laden: Lofty mansion. Bel the father comes into them.	Ezekiel 7	21	1,386
He will wonder where the hiding bin Laden is sleeping (lodging).	Ezekiel 7 Ezekiel 37 Ezekiel 40	17	5,334
The island was restful, elevated, and it happened. Where is Libya? And you have disrupted the nation. She changed a word. He answered them with combat. Why the navy and the smell of the bottom of the sea?	Ezekiel 40	53	1,151
Let the oppressed be congratulated, saturated from him at 2001. And let them be guarded by the echo of the father's son, supported by the U.S. I will see but he has the knowledge.	Ezekiel 37 Ezekiel 40	48	1,804
Carry the mountain. Zubaydah will tell something of value as a gift as the monument of the sect is finished.	Ezekiel 37 Ezekiel 40	27	1,265
You will crush the guilty Saddam and the month of Iyar will be restful.	Ezekiel 37 Ezekiel 40 Micah 5	19	6,387
Provide a picture of terminal illness. The days of Saddam are over.	Ezekiel 37	20	139
She is as noble as my God, and I have suffered burns from the terrorism.	Ezekiel 37	24	10,763
Bin Laden, the innocent is moaning. He is gross with the blood of the poor.	Ezekiel 37	19	93
For the axis of evil is like the other one.	Ezekiel 40	12	2,250

The next three tables present examples of the top codes from three different religious viewpoints (Christian, Jewish and distinctively Catholic).

Table App8C

Christian Viewpoint			
ELS	**Cluster(s)**	**Letters**	**Skip**
Gushing from above, Jesus is my strong name, and the clouds rejoiced.	Isaiah 53	22	20
He offended. The resurrection of Jesus. He is risen indeed.	Isaiah 53	17	4,731
God is for them, and long live the exalted flame. God is Jesus.	Isaiah 53	19	14,676
The ascension of Jesus: for the sleeping one will shout. Listen!	Isaiah 53 Deuteronomy Psalm 22	20	39,731
And in his name, as he commanded, Jesus is the way.	Isaiah 53	17	7,468
Wonder! Jesus is the truth.	Isaiah 53	11	1,234
Only Jesus is the life, the memorial stone.	Gen.-Exod.	16	9,822
Go out to testify, and to God the I AM is Jesus.	Gen.-Exod.	17	1,466
Or come down, for the father of destiny will make you rejoice. Who is Yeshua? Our master over death. (Portion of 57-letter ELS)	Gen.-Exod.	32	465
Jesus the gift is master and my lord.	Isaiah 53 Jeremiah 17	12	9,140

Table App8D

Jewish Viewpoint			
ELS	Cluster(s)	Letters	Skip
Hussein is a vapor. Like a guarded lamb, God is keeping Jews and Levites whole. And the cell inside your dwelling will become a torture chamber.	Ezekiel 37 Ezekiel 40	41	1,620
Know who the chosen people are or God will be angry.	Isaiah 53	15	6,528
Make secret of the anger of the living. Terminate anti-Semitism.	Deuteronomy Ezekiel 37	22	40,054
The high official will answer the anti-Semite. My joy will be pure.	Deuteronomy Exodus 7 Ezekiel 37 Micah 6	20	49,552
Jehovah is my God. The perpetuity of Israel is the messiah's passion.	Ezekiel 40 Jeremiah 17	16	11,801
Behold his ark of the covenant and be still.	Gen.-Exod.	16	8,752
As the Old Testament, Mishnah is like an exaltation.	Gen.-Exod.	16	24,491
For the multitude there is the ark of the covenant and the sea.	Gen.-Exod.	14	3,102
Then he was elevated. Please recognize the chosen people.	Gen.-Exod. Deuteronomy	16	41,349
It is finished. And where is the resurrection of Jesus of blessed memory. For whom are the twelve? (Portion of 30-letter ELS)	Psalm 22	30	1,700

Table App8E

Distinctively Catholic Viewpoint			
ELS	**Cluster(s**	**Letters**	**Skip**
And thirst for all of him is the faith of Mary the mother.	Isaiah 53	18	1,169
He will illuminate. And they will come along the way. The I AM is Jesus. The mother is sad.	Gen.-Exod.	25	8,388
Flame of faith, be filled with the crucifixion of Jesus.	Ezekiel 40	16	62
Mary is the mother of God	Isaiah 53	9	23,615
Immaculate pregnancy	Micah 5	9	2,428
Jesus son of Mary	Gen.-Exod. Deuteronomy	9	69,904 & 116,228

I believe it would be difficult to carefully review the content of the codes in the five tables in this appendix and still maintain the position that codes only presented absolute truth. Rather, it certainly appears that codes typically represent a well-known viewpoint.

Endnotes

Chapter 1 — Much Ado About Nothing?

[1] "E" is actually only the 34th letter after the "L." This is not actually an equidistant letter sequence, but is only presented as an example of how it might appear.

Chapter 2 — An Irrepressible Urge

[1] The Kabbalah is a mystical tradition of Judaism that intertwines contemplative prayer with various numerological approaches to studying the Torah.

[2] Eliyahu Rips's Public Statement:
www.thei.aust.com/torah/coderips.html.

[3] Doron Witztum's Public Statement:
www.thei.aust.com/torah/codewitztum.html.

[4] Frontier Research Publications, Inc. of Toronto has published two books by Grant Jeffrey [*The Signature of God* (1996) and *The Handwriting of God* (1997)] and two books by Yacov Rambsel [*Yeshua* (1996) and *His Name is Jesus* (1997)]. Word Publishing has published one book by Grant Jeffrey [*The Mysterious Bible Codes* (1998)].

[5] Robert Kass's Editorial Comments:
www.thei.aust.com/torah/codekass.html

[6] Jeffrey Satinover, M.D., *Cracking the Bible Code*, (New York: William Morrow, 1997) xv-xvii.

[7] Dr. Reider Peterson, professor emeritus of statistics at Southern Oregon University, reviewed all of the formulae used in calculating the probabilities that any given code or cluster of codes could appear by chance. Dr. Peterson's review did not include checking whether or not each calculation was correctly performed, but only that the equations used were correct and appropriate.

[8] The expected number of occurrences of a given ELS in the Torah is simply the total number of possible ELSs divided by the number of different "words" that can be formed, giving us the following table.

(A)	(B)	(C)	(D)
Number of Letters	Number of Possible ELSs	Number of Different "Words" That Can Be Made With the Given Number of Letters	Expected Number of Occurrences of a Given ELS in the Torah (B)/(C)
2	92,905,783,220	484	191,954,098
3	46,452,739,208	10,648	4,362,579
4	30,968,391,204	234,256	132,199
5	23,226,217,202	5,153,632	4,507
6	18,580,912,800	113,379,904	164
7	15,484,043,200	2,494,357,888	6.208
8	13,271,993,486	54,875,873,536	0.242
9	11,612,956,200	1,207,269,217,792	0.00962
10	10,322,593,866	26,559,922,791,424	0.000389
11	9,290,304,000	584,318,301,411,328	0.0000159
12	8,445,703,200	12,855,002,631,049,200	0.000000657

For example, there are 15.5 billion ELSs that can be formed from the Torah that consist of exactly seven letters. And there are 2.5 billion possible "words" or letter sequences that can be formed using exactly seven letters. That means that, on average, you would be able to find any seven-letter sequence you pick about six times within the Torah.

[9] "Carbon-14 Tests Substantiate Scroll Dates," *Biblical Archaeology Review*, November/December 1991, and "New Carbon-14 Tests on the Dead Sea Scrolls," *Biblical Archaeology Review*, March/April 1993.

[10] *Cracking the Bible Code*, 11.

[11] Michael Drosnin, *The Bible Code* (New York, Simon & Schuster, 1997) 23.

[12] Ibid., 43-44.

[13] Op. cit., *Cracking the Bible Code*, jacket cover and www.satinover.com/main.htm, biography.

[14] From a letter quoted in the introduction to *The Added Dimension*, by Dr. Doron Witztum.

[15] Op. cit., *The Mysterious Bible Codes*, 54.

[16] Computronic Corporation offers a "Bible codes" search program and a "Super Milon" translation CD that you can purchase at www.biblecodedigest.com/store.

[17] Doron Witztum's Public Statement: www.thei.aust.com/torah/codewitztum.html.

[18] "Terror hot in me," discovered in the Ezekiel 37 cluster, is an example of a code spoken from the point of view of a terrorist.

[19] Genesis 3:1-5; Job 1:7, 8, 9; 2:2, 4; Matthew 4:3, 6, 8; Luke 4:3, and 4:9.

Chapter 3 — The Mega-Cluster of Jesus Codes in Isaiah 53

[1] www.aish.com/seminars/discovery/Codes/jcode1.htm

[2] Abegg, et. al., *The Dead Sea Scrolls Bible* (New York: Harper-Collins, 1999) xviii.

Chapter 4 — Using the Isaiah 53 Cluster to Answer Critics

[1] Table 4G differs from table 3D because two final ELSs were removed from the plausible category. This was done because these codes did not originate from the examination of an initial ELS that was found in the Isaiah 53 text. These two codes originated from the examination of initial ELSs from other clusters, but after extension these codes actually touched down in the Isaiah 53 text. Those codes are:

- He waited. He will emit my very light thunder in them proudly from Armageddon. And they will crush the echo.

- I will cool the priest from his faith. Since Babylon has fallen, his lamb is under the storm.

Chapter 5 — The Overwhelming Ezekiel 37 Cluster

[1] Op. cit., *Cracking the Bible Code*, 179

[2] www.crosswalk.com/news/1149315.html

INDEX

R. Edwin Sherman,

F.C.A.S., M.A.A.A.

R. Edwin Sherman is a Fellow of the Casualty Actuarial Society (F.C.A.S.) and a Member of the American Academy of Actuaries (M.A.A.A). [Actuaries use probability and statistical analysis to help manage self-insurance programs and insurance companies.] He has advised numerous large financial institutions, Fortune 500 companies and government agencies. Prior to heading his own consulting firm, for 7 years he was a Principal of PricewaterhouseCoopers, the world's largest accounting and consulting firm.

Mr. Sherman is the founder of the Isaac Newton Bible Code Research Society. The Society's web site (www.biblecodedigest.com) is the number one Bible code resource on the Internet. A Christian since 1972, Mr. Sherman is deeply committed to the impartial examination of the phenomenon of Bible codes. He works with a research team that includes two Hebrew experts, one an agnostic Jew, the other an orthodox Jew.

Mr. Sherman received a B.A. (with Highest Honors) and an M.A. (with High Honors) in Mathematics from the University of California at San Diego. He passed Ph.D. qualifying exams in probability, statistics and real and complex analysis before leaving graduate school to become an actuary. He has authored two prize-winning professional papers and over 70 articles in trade publications devoted to risk management and business insurance.

Mr. Sherman's articles have appeared in *Decision* (1998) and *Moody* (1997). In the late 1980s he played a major role in starting a Rick Warren style church in Marin County, California. He lives with his wife of 29 years in southern Oregon, where they attend a Calvary Chapel. Their two adult children live in the Seattle area.

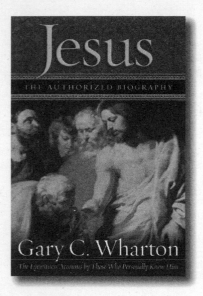

Jesus:
THE AUTHORIZED BIOGRAPHY

The eyewitness accounts by those
who personally knew Him

by Gary C. Wharton

The life of the most important and influential person in history
is presented here, recounted by the writers of the Gospels: Matthew,
Mark, Luke, and John; and the writings of Paul. Author Gary C.
Wharton has lifted the story directly from different versions of the
Bible, word for word, and blended it all into one truly inspiring
account of the life of Christ. Since the writers of the Scriptures
were inspired by the Holy Spirit, this book can truly be called an
"authorized" biography. The many features of this unique book
help make it a wonderful reference tool or a very readable narrative,
including contemporary language, relevant Old Testament prophecies,
words of Christ in bold, and several indexes and reference sections.

". . . super ideal for teaching Sunday School or adult Bible studies."
— Raymond Gaylord, pastor emeritus,
Cascade Christian Church, Grand Rapids, Michigan

ISBN: 0-89221-618-2 • $19.99
352 pages • hardcover

Available at Christian bookstores nationwide!

New Leaf Press

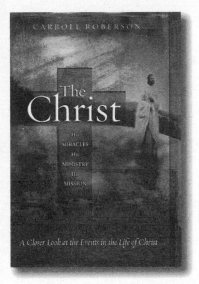